Stephen Kinzer is the bestselling author of *Overthrow* and *Star*, among others. An award-winning foreign *New York Times* bureau chief in Turkey. He teaches international relations at Boston University, contributes to *The New York Review of Books* and writes a world affairs column for the *Guardian*.

"[Kinzer] proposes a radical new course for the United States in the region. The United States, he argues, needs to partner with Iran and Turkey to create a 'powerful triangle' whose activities would promote a culture of democracy and combat extremism.... Kinzer's U.S.-Iranian-Turkish alliance is a long-term project, and the idea has ample grounding in the modern history of the region. Unlike other Muslim countries there, Kinzer shows, Iran and Turkey have at least a century's worth of experience struggling for political freedom... [and] share some fundamental values with the United States."

—*Foreign Affairs*

"Because we're so accustomed to bad news out of the Middle East, trouble seems inevitable. [Kinzer] suggests that needn't be so. But can anybody hear its lucid, historically grounded points above the shouting and the gunfire?"

—*Chicago Tribune*

"Kinzer provides a historical narrative and novel argument.... [His] style is lively and crisp. He renders a dramatic and engaging story—narrating events while alternating seamlessly between characters and countries.... One hopes that it is the missing wedge that initiates a serious discussion about America's friends and enemies."

—*The International Affairs Review*

"An original, unsettling critique... [and] an imaginative solution to the Middle East stalemate."

—*Kirkus Reviews*

"At once a stern critique of American foreign policy and a concise, colorful, and compelling modern history of Turkey, Iran, Saudi Arabia, and Israel. A former journalist for *The New York Times* and *The Boston Globe*, Kinzer is a masterful storyteller. His cast of characters leaps off the page... Kinzer makes a compelling case... that the road to peace in the Middle East runs through Ankara and Tehran, not Jerusalem."

—NPR.org

"Stephen Kinzer's deep knowledge of the Middle East is complemented by his lucid style and new ideas. He sees Turkey as a key state for the region and the world, suggests new and innovative ways to deal with Saudi Arabia and Iran, and calls for the United States to play a much more robust and determined role in the Arab-Israeli peace process. His historical perspective and trenchant analysis make this book an informative read for experts and newcomers alike."

—Thomas R. Pickering, former U.S. ambassador to the United Nations and Under Secretary of State for Political Affairs

"Stephen Kinzer argues that contradictory U.S. policies in the Middle East are producing serial disasters. He recounts with verve the dramatic historical events and the vivid personalities that brought us to these straits, and argues for a new realism about the rapid rise of Iran and Turkey as regional superpowers challenging the old, dysfunctional bargains struck in the twentieth century. This book is a must-read for anyone concerned with the future of the United States in the Middle East."

—Juan Cole, Professor of History, University of Michigan, and author of *Engaging the Muslim World*

"Does the United States have nothing but bad choices in the Middle East? Stephen Kinzer says we have attractive choices if our leaders will just abandon the premises of the Cold War and look instead at opportunities in front of their eyes. Kinzer elaborates grand ideas in the conversational voice of a story-teller and challenges conventional wisdom in the most reasonable tones. But let the reader beware: he will make you think, and you may never see the region in quite the same way again."

—Gary Sick, senior research scholar, Columbia University, and author of *All Fall Down: America's Tragic Encounter with Iran*

"A vivid account underscoring the persistent folly of Western, and especially U.S. policy in the Middle East. This is history with bite and immediacy. Yet Stephen Kinzer sees cause for hope: the possibility of change exists if we but seize it."

—Andrew J. Bacevich, author of *The Limits of Power: The End of American Exceptionalism*

"I read and relished it—kudos to him for approaching the enduring problem of the Middle East in a fresh way. Even old hands may learn something new in these fluent, timely, and provocative pages."

—Karl E. Meyer, coauthor of *Tournament of Shadows* and *Kingmakers: The Invention of the Modern Middle East*

"America in the Middle East: choose the right pals for a change. That is the central message of a new book by Stephen Kinzer…Intriguing."

—*The Economist*

RESET MIDDLE EAST

**OLD FRIENDS AND NEW ALLIANCES:
SAUDI ARABIA, ISRAEL, TURKEY, IRAN**

STEPHEN KINZER

I.B.TAURIS
LONDON · NEW YORK

Published in 2011 by I.B.Tauris & Co Ltd
6 Salem Road, London W2 4BU
175 Fifth Avenue, New York NY 10010
www.ibtauris.com

First published in 2010 by
Henry Holt and Company LLC
as *Reset: Iran, Turkey and America's Future*.

Copyright © Stephen Kinzer, 2011

Maps by Jason Joven
Designed by Kelly Too

The right of Stephen Kinzer to be identified as the author of this work has been asserted by the author in accordance with the Copyright, Designs and Patent Act 1988.

All rights reserved. Except for brief quotations in a review, this book, or any part thereof, may not be reproduced, stored in or introduced into a retrieval system, or transmitted, in any form or by any means, electronic, mechanical, photocopying, recording or otherwise, without the prior written permission of the publisher.

ISBN: 978 1 84885 765 0

A full CIP record for this book is available from the British Library

Printed and bound in Great Britain by CPI Mackays ME5 8TD

FOR MY GRANDPARENTS

Abraham Ricardo
1882 (Amsterdam)–1945 (Bergen-Belsen)

Jeannette Margaretha (De Jongh) Ricardo
1891 (Amsterdam)–1945 (Bergen-Belsen)

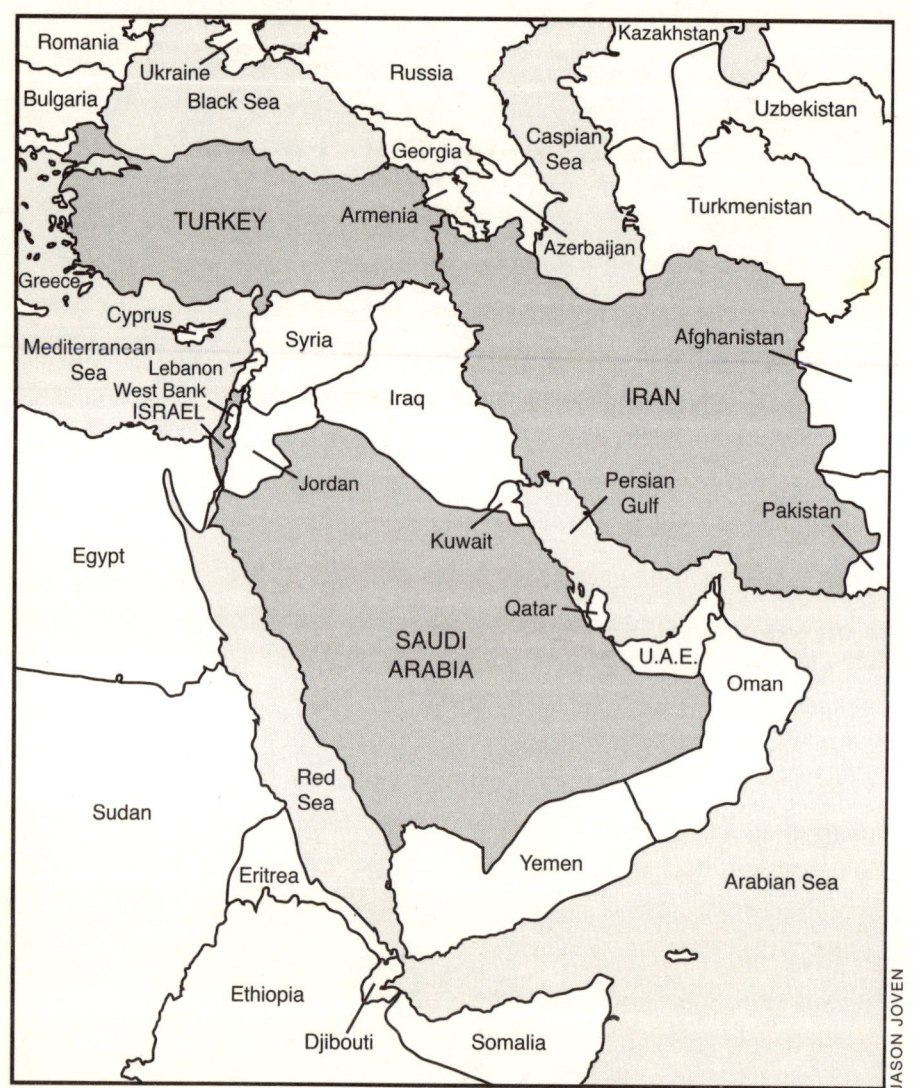

CONTENTS

Preface ix

Introduction 1

PART ONE: FOR THE PEOPLE, IN SPITE OF THE PEOPLE

1. The Real Life and Soul of the Show 19
2. Away with Dreams and Shadows! 31
3. We Have No Choice But to Catch Up 59

PART TWO: OUR NAME HAS NOT BEEN AN HONORED ONE

4. This Dizzy Old Wizard 87
5. Sowers of Corruption on Earth 116

PART THREE: VERY FAR AWAY

6. You Win, You Bald-Headed Son of a Bitch 145
7. So Deeply Entwined 176

PART FOUR: THE DOOR IS SO WIDE OPEN

8. Where They Come Together 195

Notes 219
Bibliography 239
Acknowledgments 261
Index 263

PREFACE

The world has become a far scarier place in recent years, largely because of threats and instability emerging from the Middle East and nearby regions. Outside powers are eager to promote their interests there, but their policies often intensify crises instead of easing them.

What these powers are doing in the world's most volatile region is not working. They are using old thinking to solve new problems. Only new and big ideas—a sweeping strategic re-imagining of the Middle East and the outside world's role in it—can produce any real change. Western governments, however, are trapped in a suffocating policy straitjacket. For a variety of reasons, ranging from the pull of history to the inertia of bureaucracies to the power of political lobbies, they have proven unable take the big steps that are essential for peace.

Yet this troubled region is not destined to be a pit of reactionary rule, oil-fueled corruption and religious hatred forever. Alternative approaches—a 'reset' of the West's approach—hold great promise. Policymakers may not yet be ready to embrace this idea, but in Washington and other Western capitals there is a growing recognition that the paradigm of the Cold War no longer fits the Middle East.

I discovered this after delivering a speech in Washington about the ideas at the center of this book. After I finished, a White House aide who works on national security issues approached me. "One thing you said, most of us would agree with," he told me. "We know that our Middle East policies aren't working, and that we need a totally new approach if anything is going to change there. But two things we haven't figured out: what that new approach should be, and how we would sell it to the electorate."

This book begins with the premise that the West needs a new approach to the Middle East; continues by suggesting that one aspect of that new approach would be finding partners in the region who share Western values and strategic goals; and concludes that the two most likely candidates for that partnership are Turkey and Iran.

Selling the idea of Turkey as a good long-term partner for the West is easy. Turkey has been a NATO ally for more than half a century, and is the world's most democratic Muslim country. Anything the West can do to help Turkey project its example of capitalist democracy to other Muslim countries is good for everyone except violent fundamentalists.

Proposing Iran as a partner is more difficult, because Westerners have been conditioned to think of Iran as a dangerous rogue state at the center of a global "axis of evil." This obscures the fact that Iranian society is far closer to the ideal of Western democracy than some of the West's so-called allies, like Pakistan or Saudi Arabia. In addition, the West's long-term strategic interests dovetail far more closely with Iran's than they do with those of Pakistan or Saudi Arabia. This only becomes clear when cool analysis replaces the emotion that clouds so much debate over the Middle East.

This book, however, is not really about policy. It is a sweeping story populated by grand characters who dared to take history into their own hands. Much of the story focuses on the last century of life in Turkey and Iran, showing how and why those countries evolved toward democracy while most of the rest of the Muslim world remained trapped in torpor and tyranny. This is a spectacularly eventful story—and one of the least known in modern history.

Besides setting out the narrative of two countries that could become the West's partners in a new regional security arrangement, *Reset Middle East* also tells how Israel and Saudi Arabia became the West's main allies there during the last century. These four countries—old friends Israel and Saudi Arabia, potential new alliances Turkey and Iran—will play crucial roles in determining not simply the future of this region, but of the world. Much depends on how effectively outside powers deal with them, balance them, work with them, and pressure them.

None of the West's main goals in the greater Middle East—destroying al-Qaeda, stabilizing Iraq, settling the Israel-Palestinian conflict, ending sectarian violence in Lebanon, pacifying Afghanistan, integrating militant groups into peaceful politics, reducing tensions over nuclear weapons—can be reached without Iran's cooperation. Just as clear, however, is that most can also not be reached without Israel's cooperation. These two countries are in comparable positions. They are mistrusted by many of their neighbors, and their governments are loathed by huge numbers of people around the world. Anti-Iran and anti-Israel emotions run high. Treating these countries as pariahs—punishing and sanctioning and isolating them—may redeem those emotions, but it does not advance the cause of peace. Only a new regional security architecture can calm the Middle East, and that cannot be achieved without active participation by Iran and Israel. Bringing both of these countries out of their isolation and back into the global mainstream—which means encouraging them to moderate policies that inflame hatred and violence—is an absolute pre-requisite for peace. Unconditional support for them is no more productive than unconditional opposition.

We are accustomed to seeing the greater Middle East as a rolling catastrophe.

Images and words scream out its pain: Hamas, Hezbollah, Mossad and al-Qaeda; oppressed women, religious zealots, revolutionary guards and millenarian settlers; targeted killings, drone attacks, suicide bombings and improvised explosive devices. Yet despite the tragedy and turmoil that afflicts the greater Middle East, there are good options as well as bad ones there. The world is not chained to a ticking Middle East time bomb that is destined to explode and wreak global havoc. Positive alternatives exist if we can open our minds to them.

This book is, at its core, a collection of stories—many of them as astonishing as they are unknown. It uses the dazzling momentum of history as a lens through which to view today's Middle East. It aims to entertain and to open minds at the same time. From readers, it asks no more or less than that they turn themselves inside out and see the world in a new way.

INTRODUCTION

A broken line of terrified schoolboys, laden with rifles and homemade grenades, crept through the streets of ancient Tabriz as dawn broke over the starving city. Weakened by hunger after months of siege, many of them sick, these young men nevertheless understood that they were the vanguard of Iran's struggle for democracy. Above all they were inspired by the man they followed. He was not, like other guerrilla leaders, a defiant officer, a bandit turned patriot, or the product of a long line of Persian fighters. Instead he was as unlikely a revolutionary as could possibly have emerged in this proud and ancient land: a twenty-four-year-old schoolteacher from Nebraska named Howard Baskerville.

Neither the inspiring figure of their leader nor the invigorating spring breeze blowing down from the nearby Sahand Mountains, however, was enough to persuade most of these boys and young men that this day, April 20, 1909, was their day to die. A hundred followed Baskerville as he set out at first light. By the time their column approached the city wall an hour later, fewer than a dozen remained. Nonetheless Baskerville pressed on.

Patriots in Tabriz were resisting a counterrevolution aimed at crushing Iran's new democracy and restoring the decadent Qajar monarchy. Royalist forces had surrounded the defiant city. Their siege was terrifyingly effective; hunger and disease killed people every day, and many of the living were reduced to eating grass. They could survive and continue to resist only if someone, somehow, could break through the siege line, reach a nearby village, and return with food and medicine. Baskerville volunteered to try.

"Be careful," one of his American friends begged him before he set out. "You know you are not your own."

"No," he replied. "I am Persia's."

Born in the Nebraska prairie town of North Platte and raised in South Dakota's Black Hills, the son and grandson of Presbyterian preachers, Baskerville was an improbable candidate for martyrdom. As a teenager he was pious, sober, and studious enough to win admission to Princeton University. There he studied religion, excelled in horsemanship, and became a modestly successful boxer. He also took two courses taught by Woodrow Wilson, one called "Jurisprudence" and the other "Constitutional Government." Wilson's lectures stirred the passion for democracy that shaped his short life.

After graduating in 1907, Baskerville decided to postpone his entry into Princeton's theological seminary and work for a time as a missionary. That autumn he arrived in Tabriz, a two-thousand-year-old city in northwest Iran that is the supposed birthplace of the prophet Zoroaster and was built, according to legend, on the site of the Garden of Eden. There he taught history, geometry, and English to mixed classes—he insisted on accepting girls as well as boys—at the American Memorial School. He also became the school's tennis coach and riding instructor, directed a student production of *The Merchant of Venice*, and closed his first Thanksgiving sermon with a stirring verse from Sir Walter Scott:

Breathes there a man with soul so dead
Who never to himself hath said,
"This is my home, my native land!"

Baskerville's students would have found those words excruciating. For decades their prostrate homeland, heir to a great empire led by heroic kings like Cyrus, Darius, and Xerxes, had been misruled by a dissolute dynasty and looted by rapacious outside powers. In 1907, Britain and Russia signed a convention dividing Persia—as Iran was then known—into "spheres of influence." Britain took the southern part of the country, Russia the north. No Iranian participated in or even knew about the negotiations that produced this agreement.

Yet the early twentieth century was an age of ferment and rebellion as well as imperial power. The Boers inflicted heavy casualties on British forces in South Africa. Russian insurgents forced Czar Nicholas II to establish a legislature. The Russo-Japanese war ended with victory for Japan, suggesting that Europeans were not fated to dominate Asians forever.

None of these shattering events went unnoticed in Iran. Anger at the docile Qajar dynasty, and at the foreign powers it served, sparked waves of protest. In 1906 these protests achieved their unimaginable goal: democratic revolution. The king, Muzaffer al-Din Shah, was forced to make concessions like those King John had made seven centuries earlier when he signed the Magna Carta. He agreed to permit the proclamation of a constitution, the holding of elections, and the establishment of a parliament. Under the new constitution, freedom of speech and press were guaranteed, monarchs were forbidden to sign treaties or borrow money without approval from Parliament, and all citizens were declared equal before the law.

Forty days after reluctantly accepting this constitution—the pain may have been too great for him—Muzaffer al-Din Shah died. His son and successor, Mohammad Ali Shah, described by one contemporary as "perhaps the most perverted, cowardly and vice-sodden monster that had disgraced the throne of Persia for many generations," loathed the new democracy. Determined to crush it, he dissolved Parliament and then, on June 3, 1908, sent Russian-led artillery units to bomb the building where it met. Scores of deputies were killed. Protests broke out across the country, but the shah ruthlessly crushed them. The only city he could not subdue was Tabriz, which, because of its location near the borders with Russia and Turkey, was the portal through which democratic ideas had been streaming into the country for years.

Howard Baskerville was in Tabriz when royalist soldiers imposed their siege at the beginning of 1909. He was instinctively drawn to the constitutional cause and spent many evenings with volunteer brigades bringing food to fighters defending the city. Slowly he came to conclude that this was not enough. News of the Anglo-Russian Convention outraged him, and he delivered withering tirades to his students aimed especially at Sir Edward Grey, the British foreign secretary, whom he scorned as a hypocrite for spouting the platitudes of democracy while supporting the slaughter of Iranians who were fighting for it. One of his closest Iranian friends, Hussein Sharifzadeh, became a leader of the Tabriz resistance, and when Sharifzadeh was assassinated, Baskerville's outrage reached new heights. In the spring of 1909 he decided to raise a volunteer force and join the defense of Iranian democracy.

"I cannot watch calmly from a classroom window as the starving people of this city fight for their rights," he told his students on his last day at school.

A few days later, Baskerville was asked to speak at a dinner honoring officers who were leading the defense of Tabriz. "I hate war," he told them, "but war can be justified in pursuit of a greater good—in this case, the protection of a city and the defense of constitutional liberty. I am ready to die for these causes!" The audience broke into applause and cries of "Long live Baskerville!" He responded by singing a chorus from his favorite song, "My Country 'Tis of Thee."

By this time, Baskerville was spending his days drilling schoolboys in the arts of war and his evenings poring over encyclopedia articles that explained how to manufacture grenades. This horrified the American consul in Tabriz, Edward Doty.

"I am compelled to remind you that as an American citizen, you have no right to interfere with the internal politics of this country," Doty told him one day in front of his young recruits. "You are here to act as a teacher, not as a revolutionary."

"I cannot remain and watch indifferently the sufferings of a people fighting for their rights," Baskerville replied. "I am an American citizen and proud of it, but I am also a human being."

On the night of April 19, 1909, Baskerville shared his last meal with Reverend Samuel Wilson, the principal of the American Memorial School, and his wife, Annie, who had been born in Iran and passionately loved its people. They drank milk, and joked about how odd it was for this to be the last drink a man would want before setting off to battle. A few hours later Baskerville met his hundred volunteers and began leading them toward the outskirts of Tabriz. Every few minutes, another handful of them lost their nerve and deserted.

Baskerville pressed on. Just after he passed through the city wall, a sniper's bullet whizzed by his head. He fired back, then paused until he felt satisfied the sniper had retreated. That was his fatal mistake. When he stood to wave his boys ahead, the sniper reappeared and fired twice. A bullet pierced his heart and killed him.

"The boys rushed to the gate to carry him in, all of us sobbing and lamenting," Annie Wilson wrote the next day in a tormented sixteen-page letter to Baskerville's parents. "We carried him to our room and laid him out on our own bed, and Mrs. Vannemen and I washed the dear body, with blood staining through his shirts and covering his breast and back.... We dressed him in his black suit, and when all the sad service was done, he looked beautiful and noble, his firm mouth set in a look of resolution and his whole face calm in repose. I printed a kiss on his forehead for his mother's sake. A white carnation is in his buttonhole, and wreaths of flowers are being made. Our children made a cross and crown of the beautiful almond blossoms now in bloom. The governor came at once, expressing great sorrow, saying, 'He has written his name in our hearts and in our history.'"

Thousands gathered silently to watch as Baskerville's coffin, covered with sixteen floral wreaths, was drawn through the streets of Tabriz to the Presbyterian church. A leader of the embattled Parliament that Baskerville had died to defend, Sayyed Hasan Taqizadeh, was among the eulogists.

"Young America, in the person of young Baskerville, gave this sacrifice to the young Constitution of Iran," he said solemnly.

Five days after Baskerville's death, Tabriz fell. Royalist troops and their Russian allies stormed into the city and disarmed every resistance fighter they could find. Their victory, however, was short-lived. As soon as citizens returned to health, they resumed their fight for democratic rule. So did others across Iran. Their defiance grew into a national movement, and finally Muhammad Ali Shah's counterrevolution collapsed. He abdicated on July 16, 1909, just three months after Baskerville's martyrdom. Parliament reconvened, constitutional government was reestablished, and Iran resumed its march toward democracy.

Today Howard Baskerville is an honored figure in Iran. Schools and streets have been named after him. His bust, cast in bronze, commands a salon at Constitution House in Tabriz. A plaque beneath it says, "Howard C. Baskerville—Patriot and Maker of History."

Baskerville is more than just an Iranian hero. He embodied the shared values that bind Iranians to Americans. Long before many other Middle Eastern nations had come into existence, the Constitutional Revolution brought modern ideas to Iran. These ideas have produced a nation that has more in common with the United States than almost any of its neighbors in the world's most troubled region.

Only one other country in this region shares Iran's long history of struggle for democracy: Turkey. The Iranians rebelled against and deposed their servile monarchy during the first decade of the twentieth century. So did the Turks.

The spread of egalitarian ideas among the Turks dates to the early nineteenth century. In 1839 the enlightened Ottoman Sultan Abdul Mecit proclaimed a series of reforms known as *Tanzimat*, including a list of civil rights to which all citizens were entitled, regardless of religion or group identity. The reform period culminated with the proclamation of a constitution in 1876 and the election of a parliament soon afterward. Within a year, however, the new sultan, Abdul Hamid, suspended the constitution. He closed Parliament and ruled by decree for the next three decades, suppressing dissent, directing an army of spies, and casting a paralyzing pall over society.

In Paris and other European cities, groups of Turkish radicals nurtured the democratic flame. They formed committees, published newsletters, and studied the history of past revolutions. Some of them tried to overthrow the sultan in 1896. They failed, but their radical ideas captivated many young patriots.

One of these idealists was an ambitious cadet named Mustafa Kemal. After entering the Ottoman military academy in 1902, Kemal began reading broadsides smuggled into the country from Europe. He and a handful of other cadets even started a clandestine newspaper of their own. They were quickly discovered, and escaped punishment only by the intercession of the academy's director, who was himself unhappy with the absolutist regime.

Soon after graduating, Kemal landed in trouble again; an informer named him as part of an illegal cell devoted to studying books by Voltaire and Tolstoy. He spent several weeks in military prison. Finally a sympathetic judge agreed to ascribe his crime to youthful indiscretion. He was released and posted to faraway Damascus.

Until this moment, Kemal had known only vibrant, cosmopolitan cities. He was born and grew up in the cultural cauldron of Salonika—modern-day Thessalonica, the second-largest city in Greece—surrounded by Turks but also by Greeks, Jews, and expatriates from across Europe and beyond. As a cadet he lived in Istanbul, one of the world's most dazzlingly diverse capitals. On his way to his new post he stopped for a time in Beirut, "the Paris of the Middle East," where energy and excitement crackled through the air. Damascus was a stark contrast to all of this, the somnolent heart of old Arabia. Most of its people lived as their ancestors had for a thousand years: illiterate, caught in a deadening web of orthodoxy, untouched by the outside world and largely unaware of it. Damascus repelled the twenty-four-year-old Kemal. Later he wrote that he found it "all bad."

"For the first time he came to know a city which still lived in the darkness of the Middle Ages," one biographer has written. "Damascus was a city of the dead. The narrow streets, which he paced after dark, were deserted and silent. Not a sound came from within the high shuttered walls of the houses. One night, to his surprise, he heard the sound of music floating from a café. He looked in, to find it filled with Italians, workers on the Hafez Railway, playing the mandolin, singing and dancing with their wives and girls. As an officer in uniform, he might not enter. But on an impulse he went home, changed into rough clothes, and returned to join them in their gay and uninhibited Western pleasures.... Here in Damascus, Kemal felt imprisoned. He longed to break his bars, to bring life to this moribund community. The remedy, of course, lay in political action."

One day while wandering through the back streets of Damascus, Kemal stumbled into a shop that sold books in French, which he had learned to read. Among them were novels and collections of social criticism.

"What are you," he asked the shopkeeper in surprise, "a tradesman or a philosopher?"

The shopkeeper turned out to be both. A couple of nights later, he invited Kemal to his home, and Kemal brought a couple of like-minded officers. They talked for hours. One of the officers blurted out that he was willing to "die for the revolution." Kemal had a different idea.

"Our aim is not to die," he said simply. "It is to carry out the revolution, to turn our ideas into reality."

In the autumn of 1905, Kemal and a small group of comrades formed a secret society called *Vatan* (Fatherland), dedicated to overthrowing absolutism and bringing self-rule to the Turks. Over the next few months, while ostensibly traveling for military duties, he established branches of *Vatan* in the Ottoman outposts of Jaffa, Beirut, and Jerusalem. Each initiate pledged to fight for the revolutionary cause until death, then kissed a pistol to symbolize his commitment.

Soon afterward, in a rotation of officers, Kemal was transferred to his home city of Salonika. Few places on earth have such conspiratorial traditions. Saint Paul created clandestine Christian cells in Salonika nearly two thousand years ago. Since then it has welcomed all manner of plotters, dreamers, and rebels. Kemal's revolutionary society and several others merged into a coalition called the Committee of Union and

Progress, known abroad as the Young Turks. In true Salonika tradition, CUP leaders initiated new members with elaborate rituals involving blindfolds, swords, and oaths. They even designed a coat of arms, dominated by the image of a book, representing the short-lived Constitution of 1876, and a crescent bearing the motto "Fraternity, Freedom, Equality, Justice."

The dying Ottoman Empire was ablaze with the fire of revolution. People in a dozen cities erupted in protest, sometimes over local matters like grain shortages but always with demands for a less distant, more responsive government. Anger rose over the loss of three key Ottoman territories—Bulgaria, Bosnia-Herzegovina, and Crete—in the space of just a few weeks in the spring of 1908.

That same spring, several hundred soldiers in Salonika rebelled against Ottoman authority, looted armories, and took to the hills. Sultan Abdul Hamid ordered his local commander to crush their insurrection, but the commander was assassinated. Then the sultan sent troops from the Turkish heartland. They not only failed to defeat the rebels, but joined them in a defiant march on Istanbul.

Young Turk leaders skillfully wove these protests into a unified movement with a single demand: the sultan must reopen the Parliament he had closed thirty years before. A group of them sent the monarch an ominous ultimatum warning that if he did not agree, "blood will be shed and the dynasty will be in danger."

Like their brethren across the border in Iran, the Turks were fed up with absolutism and intoxicated by the European ideas of liberty, self-rule, and the rights of man. Sultan Abdul Hamid had to face the reality that these ideas had infected much of his own officer corps. Rather than risk his throne, he agreed to allow elections for a new parliament. This was a shattering collapse of absolutism. Istanbul exploded with jubilation.

"The city's Muslim holy men, Christian priests and Jewish rabbis paraded arm in arm in a joyous mood," according to one account. "Calls from the minarets mingled with sounds of church bells, celebrating the dawn of the Young Turk millennium."

Turkish life changed almost overnight. Newspapers stopped submitting their articles for review by the royal censor. Forbidden books appeared for sale, and the subversive ideas that sprang from their pages became political rallying cries. Long-exploited laborers staged strikes. A young feminist writer, Halide Edib, founded the Society for the Elevation of Women, and in Istanbul and other cities, Muslim women not only walked on the streets unveiled but attended political meetings and established pressure groups. The power of the sultan, revered for centuries as "the shadow of God on earth," was crumbling.

The Turkish people had not been allowed to vote for more than a generation, and they poured out for the election of 1908. The new Parliament convened amid great pageantry. A few months later, troops loyal to the democratic regime, calling themselves the "Action Army," suppressed a royalist counterrevolution. That further inflamed the surging reform movement.

On April 28, 1909, after a series of impassioned nationalist speeches, Parliament gave four of its members—an Armenian, a Jew, and two Muslims—a historic mission. They rode to Yildiz Palace, demanded entry to its inner sanctum, and announced that "the people" had decided the sultan must abdicate. He had no choice but to obey.

For a few hours, Sultan Abdul Hamid believed he would simply be moved to the smaller but still luxurious Çirağan Palace, which had served for years as a golden prison for unwanted royals. That night, however, military officers told him he had to leave for exile immediately. Accompanied by two of his sons and a handful of concubines, he boarded a carriage, was driven to the train station and conveyed to exile in Salonika. He had been in power for thirty-three years, during which time the Ottoman Empire lost wars, suppressed democracy, and became "the sick man of Europe." His doddering brother replaced him, but never again would an Ottoman sultan be more than a figurehead.

The Young Turk revolution of 1908 and the overthrow of Sultan Abdul Hamid a year later set off a burst of reform unlike anything the Turks had ever known. Political parties emerged, new magazines and newspapers sprang up, the royal family's fortune was confiscated, laws restricting business were repealed, banks opened in many towns, roads and bridges were built, the education budget was increased sixfold, and girls were encouraged to attend school. The constitution was amended to give Parliament more power. Because the Young Turks were concerned above all with salvaging the state, they were wary of democracy and did not hesitate to restrict public freedoms when they wished. Nonetheless their revolution was profound. Perhaps its greatest achievement was inspiring a generation of visionary patriots who, over the coming years, would produce a radically new order.

These tumultuous events were the product of Turkish history, and not directly related to the upheaval in neighboring Iran. Yet it is more than coincidence that both nations won their democratic revolutions at the same time. On the day Howard Baskerville was killed in Tabriz, Turkish soldiers of the "Action Army" were fighting the sultan's power in Istanbul. Within a couple of months, almost unbelievably, the Turks and the Iranians had liberated themselves from dissolute monarchies. Their path to freedom was suddenly and brilliantly illuminated.

A century has passed since Iran and Turkey turned toward democracy. It has been a century of unsteady progress. The Iranians and the Turks have won epochal victories but also suffered bloody defeats. From their long struggles, both peoples have developed an understanding of democracy, and a longing for it, that makes them good soul mates for Americans.

The stories of modern Turkey and Iran suggest that democracy can take root anywhere, but only over the span of generations. It cannot be called to life simply by proclaiming a constitution or holding an election. Democracy is not an event but a way of facing the world, an all-encompassing approach to life. Only long years of experience can make it real. In the Muslim Middle East, just two countries have this experience: Turkey and Iran.

Turkey has become the world's most democratic Muslim country, vivid proof that Islam and freedom can thrive side by side. It has for decades been a member of the North Atlantic Treaty Organization and closely tied to the United States. Today it is embarking on the most ambitious diplomatic project in its history, seeking to project power by resolving regional conflicts through dialogue and compromise. This style fits well with America's new, more cooperative approach to global politics.

In only one other Muslim country in the Middle East does the democratic heart beat as passionately as in Turkey. It is also the only country that might suddenly emerge to rival or even surpass Turkey's level of political freedom: Iran. The explosion of protest after Iran's disputed 2009 presidential election brought down fierce repression, but it was also thrilling confirmation that the ideals of democracy have taken deep root in that country. Beneath the heavy veneer of theocratic rule, a vibrant civil society thrives there. No generation in the world understands democracy better or wishes for it more fervently than young Iranians. Their ardor is part of a bridge of values between Iran and the United States that provides the basis for a sound future partnership.

Although these countries have been enemies for more than a quarter century, they have vital interests in common. Both want a stable Iraq, a stable Afghanistan, and a stable Pakistan. Both detest radical Sunni movements like al-Qaeda and the Taliban. Both would like to limit Russian influence in the Middle East. Iran needs massive investment in its collapsing oil infrastructure; American companies are ideally placed to provide it.

Reaching an accord with Iran would not be easy, for cultural as well as political reasons. It might well require the emergence of a new regime in Tehran. But because the two countries' political cultures as well as their strategic interests overlap so fully, logic pushes them together.

A partnership that unites Turkey, Iran, and the United States makes sense for two reasons: they share strategic interests, and their people share values. This is the tantalizing "power triangle" of the twenty-first century.

The old triangle—actually two bilateral relationships, the United States with Israel and the United States with Saudi Arabia—served

Washington's interests well during the cold war. It has not, however, produced a stable Middle East. On the contrary, the region is torn by violence, hatred, terror, and war. Yet for economic as well as strategic reasons, the United States must remain engaged there. Its dilemma can be simply stated: America wants to stabilize the Middle East, but its policies are having the opposite effect. What new policies could America adopt to replace those that have failed?

Here is one answer: First, build an ever-closer partnership with Turkey and, in the future, with a democratic Iran. Second, reshape relations with Israel and Saudi Arabia in ways that will serve their long-term interests and those of the United States—even if they protest.

Israel deserves special treatment from the United States, both for historical reasons and because there can be no regional peace without a secure Israel. America, though, has at times treated Israel in ways that weaken Israel's own security. The bond between the two countries has become distorted. As a result, the United States has failed to promote policies that will assure Israel's long-term stability. Instead it lurches helplessly from crisis to crisis, hostage to the hothouse clamor of Israel's domestic politics. It is right for America to stand by Israel, but not the way it does now.

The long conflict between Israel and the Palestinians has, for better or worse, become the world's conflict. It permanently destabilizes the Middle East, blocks the settlement of urgent crises, and intensifies looming threats to the West. Yet it has become painfully clear that if the task of finding peace is left to the warring parties, there will be no peace. A settlement to this conflict cannot emerge from within. Neither Israeli nor Palestinian society has the cultural, political, psychological, or institutional resources to make the compromises that peace requires. The paradigm of conflict has become too deeply embedded in too many minds.

Allowing a friend to careen toward self-destruction is not friendship. That is a habit the United States needs to break as it pursues a richer and more deeply supportive relationship with Israel.

Saudi Arabia presents America with an entirely different challenge.

Washington's decision to embrace this religious kingdom was among its most bizarre twentieth-century gambles.

The family that has ruled Saudi Arabia since it was created in 1932 relies on support from two vital allies: the United States and the clergy of Wahhabi Islam. To America, it offers a steady supply of oil and a rich market for defense contractors. The fundamentalist Wahhabis get something quite different: a stifling religious order at home, and backing for a global network of mosques and religious schools where generations of lost boys learn to chant the Koran and hate America. Such deeply contradictory policies had to produce an explosion. It came on September 11, 2001. Fifteen of the nineteen hijackers who seized planes that day, as well as the terror leader who sent them off to kill, were Saudis.

During the cold war, Washington's partnership with Saudi Arabia seemed logical. The Saudis were both militantly anti-Communist and unfathomably rich. Wherever the United States wanted money to fight Marxism, from Angola to Nicaragua to Afghanistan, the Saudis paid. Their message to the United States was irresistible: We have huge amounts of money, and you can have as much of it as you want. Just don't look too closely at what is happening inside our kingdom.

The end of the cold war led inevitably to a gentle distancing between the United States and Saudi Arabia. The attacks of September 11 gave the relationship another, sharper shock. They made it difficult for Americans to continue to overlook Saudi Arabia's role in fomenting global terror.

Saudi Arabia and the United States share some approaches to global politics; both are suspicious of the outside world, both thrive on exaggerated views of their own power, and neither is known for gentle diplomacy. Almost nothing in the way of values, however, ties America to a desert kingdom where dating is illegal, women are forbidden to drive, and a royal family rules by decree. The United States and Saudi Arabia have been allies of convenience, partners in a loveless marriage. In the twenty-first century they will continue cooperating, but each will prosper by distancing itself from the other.

The ties that bind America to Israel and Saudi Arabia cannot be reshaped with the stroke of a pen. A new "power triangle"—the United States, Turkey, and Iran—cannot emerge overnight. In order to become a reliable American partner, Iran would have to change dramatically. Turkey would also have to change, although not nearly as much. So would the United States. Our world, however, advances only as a result of strategic vision. First must come a grand concept, a destination; once the destination is clear, all parties can concentrate on finding the way to reach it.

Nowhere in the world is an overarching strategy more glaringly absent or more desperately needed than in the Middle East. For years, outside powers—especially the United States—have staggered through the region's forbidding deserts, steppes, and oil fields with policies that are manifest failures. During this period, threats emerging from the Middle East have become steadily more urgent and terrifying. Remaining wedded to failed policies is not simply unwise, but deeply dangerous.

Albert Einstein famously defined insanity as doing the same thing over and over, but expecting different results. That is what the United States is doing in the Middle East. What would be the alternative? This book proposes one.

The pages that follow seek to explain the past and then propose a way to reset American policy in the world's most volatile region. First comes an account of the modern histories of Turkey and Iran, showing how long and passionately these two countries have worked toward democracy. Then comes an exploration of the two oldest relationships in the Middle East: the one binding the United States to Saudi Arabia and the one binding the United States to Israel. These lead to a logical conclusion, albeit one that may seem startling because it pushes beyond the narrow policy options that too often stifle America's global imagination. It summons the logic of history to address the future.

PART ONE

FOR THE PEOPLE, IN SPITE OF THE PEOPLE

1

THE REAL LIFE AND SOUL OF THE SHOW

The sunburned, dust-covered gentleman who stepped out of a rough carriage in Tehran at dusk on May 12, 1911, arrived like a lawman into a terrified town. He came to help a once-proud country that had fallen pitifully from past glories. Two foreign powers, Russia and Britain, had signed a "convention" dividing Iran between them. To consummate it, they needed to crush Iran's fledgling Parliament. Members of Parliament cast desperately about for a way to resist and save their country's democracy. They decided they had but one hope: hire an American.

The one they found, Morgan Shuster, agreed to serve for three years in a post Parliament created especially for him: Treasurer General of the Persian Empire. His assignment, with no tool other than law, was to force the Russians and the British to submit to Parliament's will.

Turning to an American was a logical step for Iranian democrats. The United States was their inspiration: a former British colony that had thrown off its chains and advanced to glorious self-rule, just as Iran hoped to do.

"The United States at this stage looked like the partner Iran had long hoped to find in the West—anti-feudal, anti-colonialist, modern but not imperialist—a truly benevolent foreign power that would, for once, treat Iran with respect," one historian has written. "If we think of the

Spheres of Influence in Iran: Anglo-Russian Convention, 1907

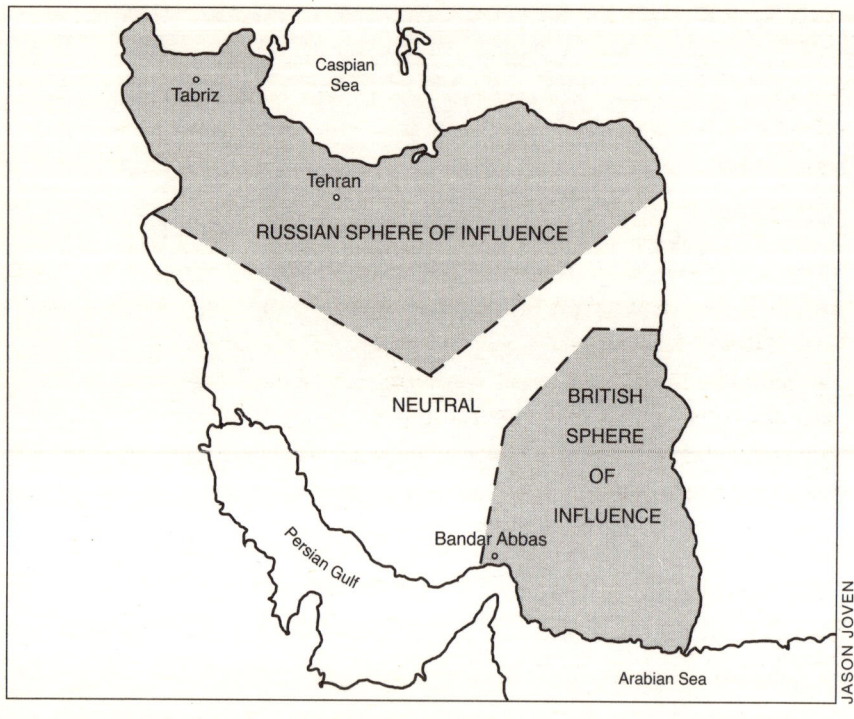

British and the Russians in the nineteenth century as the ugly sisters, then at this time Morgan Shuster and his United States looked like Prince Charming."

Though he was just thirty-four years old, Shuster had impressive experience in the esoteric art of organizing chaotic countries. He had designed a tax system for the Philippines, where he worked under governor-general William Howard Taft, and then became director of the Cuban customs service. In both posts he had won a reputation as hard-working and utterly incorruptible.

"I had never even dreamed of going to Persia before my appointment," he later wrote, "but the eloquence of the Persian *chargé d'affaires* at Washington, Mirza Ali Kuli Khan, removed my early doubts, and I finally decided to do what I could to help a people who had certainly given evidence of an abiding faith in our institutions and business methods."

Upon arriving in Tehran, Shuster made an instant and shocking impression, not by something he did but by something he failed to do. Foreigners normally called on diplomats from Russia and Britain—the countries that had divided Iran into "spheres of influence" four years earlier—to beg permission to begin work. Shuster ignored this custom. He let it be known that since he worked only for Parliament, he would pay fealty to no one else.

This was the beginning of his rise and fall.

Iran had made remarkable strides toward democracy in the five years since its Constitutional Revolution. There had been two elections. A royalist counterrevolution—the one in which Parliament was bombarded and Howard Baskerville killed—had been defeated. Universal male suffrage had been proclaimed. Religious minorities were guaranteed seats in Parliament. Two vigorous political parties had emerged, one favoring women's rights and public education, the other promoting conservative religious values.

This vibrant democracy, though, was only a shadow. Parliament had no authority over most of the country. British and Russian occupiers ignored its laws. Between these commanding imperial powers and an increasingly assertive Parliament, conflict was inevitable.

A few days after Shuster arrived in Tehran, parliamentary leaders visited him at Atabak Palace, the thirty-room stone villa they had given him as an office and residence. He told them he intended to follow the same principle that had guided his work in the Philippines and Cuba: taxation is the indispensable foundation of a stable state, and therefore taxes must be collected vigorously and impartially. In Iran, though, many wealthy landowners lived under British or Russian protection and paid no taxes to the central government. They would do so only if forced.

Shuster asked Parliament to raise a twelve-thousand-man gendarmerie dedicated exclusively to enforcing tax laws. Parliament agreed, and recruitment began. The first trained units were sent to confiscate property from tax delinquents in the Russian sphere of influence. That set off a fateful crisis.

The aroused Czar Nicholas II sent thousands of troops to Russian bases in northern Iran and threatened to occupy Tehran if Parliament did not stop its meddling. Britain joined the saber-rattling, reinforcing its garrisons in the south.

Shuster did not flinch. Parliament, he later wrote, "more truly represented the best aspirations of the Persians than any other body that has ever existed in that country. It was as representative as it could be under the difficult circumstances which surround the institution of the Constitutional government. It was loyally supported by the great mass of the Persians, and that alone was sufficient justification for its existence. The Russian and British governments, however, were constantly instructing their Ministers at Tehran to obtain this concession or block that one, failing utterly to recognize that the days had passed in which the affairs, lives and interests of twelve millions of people were entirely in the hands of an easily intimidated and willingly bribed despot."

The final confrontation began at midday on December 9, 1911, with an ultimatum from the Russian ambassador in Tehran. Parliament must dismiss Shuster within forty-eight hours—and also promise "not to engage in the service of Persia foreign subjects, without first obtaining the consent of the Russian and British legations."

Many Iranians were outraged by the directness of this demand. Shuster's insistent defense of democracy had captivated them, and he suddenly found himself the embodiment of a nation's dreams. Patriots clamored to defend him. One of the country's most beloved poets, Aref Qazvini, vented his passion in a *tasnif*, or popular song:

> *The thief is out for theft and the brigand for brigandage, my friend,*
> *Our history will become the laughingstock of the world if we allow*
>   *Shuster to go from Iran, from Iran Shuster to go.*
> *O life of the body, O soul of the world, O real treasure, O eternal*
>   *pleasure—O Shuster!*
> *May God keep thee here . . . Thou art a part of us, how can we live*
>   *apart from thee, O Shuster?*

By agreeing to dismiss Shuster, Parliament would be accepting the rule of foreign powers over Iran. Refusing would bring unknown but certainly terrible consequences. When Parliament convened on the morning of December 11, all of its members knew that Iran's infant democracy was facing its first decisive choice. Shuster was there, and described the scene in his poignant memoir, *The Strangling of Persia*:

> It was an hour before noon, and the Parliament grounds and buildings were filled with eager, excited throngs, while the galleries of the chamber were packed with Persian notables of all ranks and with the representatives of many of the foreign legations. At noon the fate of Persia as a nation was to be decided....
>
> The proposal was read amid deep silence. At its conclusion a hush fell upon the gathering. Seventy-six deputies, old men and young, priests, lawyers, doctors, merchants and princes, sat tense in their seats.
>
> A venerable priest of Islam arose. Time was slipping away, and at noon the question would be beyond their vote to decide. This servant of God spoke briefly and to the point: "It may be the will of Allah that our liberty and our sovereignty shall be taken away from us, but let us not sign them away with our own hands!" One gesture of his hands, and he resumed his seat.
>
> Simple words, these, yet winged ones. Easy to utter in academic discussions; hard, bitterly hard, to say under the eye of a cruel and overpowering tyrant whose emissaries watched the speaker from the galleries and mentally marked him down for future torture, imprisonment or worse.
>
> Other deputies followed. In dignified appeals, brief because the time was so short, they upheld their country's honor and proclaimed their hard-earned right to live and govern themselves.
>
> A few minutes before noon the vote was taken.... And when the roll call was ended, every man, priest or layman, youth or octogenarian, had cast his own die of fate, had staked the safety of himself and his family, and hurled back into the teeth of the great Bear from the North the unanimous answer of a desperate and down-trodden people who preferred a future of unknown terror to the voluntary sacrifice of their

national dignity and their recently earned right to work out their own salvation.

By its defiance, Parliament invited its own destruction. Russian troops marched on Tehran and occupied it. Their commander then ordered the submissive Ahmad Shah—actually his British-educated regent, since the shah was just fourteen years old—to dissolve Parliament and dismiss Shuster. The orders were quickly drawn up. Soon afterward, a despondent former Treasurer General of the Persian Empire stepped into an automobile to begin his long trip home.

"Our task in Persia, to which we had looked forward with both pleasure and pride, had come to a sudden and most unpleasant end," Shuster wrote. "As I stood in a circle of gloomy American and Persian friends, about to step into the automobile, I could not help recalling the evening of my arrival at the same spot just eight months before, and there swept over me the realization that the hopes of a patient, long-suffering Muhammadan people of reclaiming their position in the world had been ruthlessly stamped out by the armies of a so-called civilized and Christian nation."

Iran's first experiment with democracy was over, crushed by foreign power. It left a vivid imprint on the nation's collective psyche. During these early years of the twentieth century, Iranians discovered what democracy is. They wanted it—and might have had it if their country had not been found to be sitting atop an ocean of oil.

In photographs, William Knox D'Arcy looks like the eminent Victorian solicitor he was: portly, round-faced, and generously mustachioed, usually with a pipe in his mouth and a watch chain across his vest. In his youth he made a fortune backing gold miners in Australia, and then he did what many a man would do in such circumstances: he moved to Europe to enjoy his money. He married an actress, toured extravagantly, lived in palaces, and hired Enrico Caruso to sing at his Grosvenor

Square dinner parties. By the beginning of the twentieth century, his fortune was running out.

The petroleum age was just dawning, but geologists had already guessed that the Middle East would become a rich source of oil. British leaders wanted to know whether Iran had any; D'Arcy was looking for a speculative project that could make him rich again. They were ideal partners.

To drill in Iran, D'Arcy needed permission from the decadent and sickly Mozaffer al-Din Shah, who ruled with the aid of soothsayers and financed his regime by selling concessions to foreigners. British diplomats helped him secure the necessary royal order. Under their tutelage, he bribed everyone in the royal court from the prime minister to the servant who brought the shah his morning pipe and coffee. The concession agreement, signed in 1901, gave D'Arcy the exclusive right to seek oil in almost all of Iran's territory, and then, if he found any oil, the exclusive right to extract, refine, and sell it. For this concession, which was to run for sixty years, he paid £20,000 in cash, then equivalent to about $95,000; promised to pay an equal amount when he began production; and agreed to give Iran 16 percent of his future profits.

"Such was the contract that turned out to be one of the more significant documents of the twentieth century," one scholar has written. "Its subsequent fate, the vast industrial complex to which it gave rise, the passionate hatred it evoked, the conflicts it precipitated, could not have been guessed by its signers, who, in a city remote from the centers of world power, in almost total secrecy, acted out a drama the implications of which they were only half aware."

At four o'clock on the morning of May 26, 1908, after several years of frustration, geologists working for D'Arcy at a stony outpost called Masjid-i-Suleiman were awakened by a tremendous explosion. Oil was spurting high into the air. They had made the greatest find in the history of the young petroleum industry.

Winston Churchill, who became Great Britain's First Lord of the Admiralty soon after this spectacular strike, fully grasped its meaning.

He understood that in the coming era, navies and national economies would be powered by oil, meaning that countries with oil would rule. Britain had none, nor any colony that produced it. Upon learning of the gusher at Masjid-i-Suleiman, Churchill realized that controlling Iran would be a key to the survival of British power in the new century. On the eve of World War I he arranged for the D'Arcy concession to be transformed into a corporation, the Anglo-Persian Oil Company, and for the British government to buy 51 percent of its shares.

"Fortune brought us a prize from fairyland beyond our wildest dreams," Churchill later wrote. "Mastery itself was the prize of the venture."

This proved to be no exaggeration. In World War I, as the British statesman Lord Curzon observed, the Allies "floated to victory on a wave of oil." That made British leaders more determined than ever to control Iran. With the Russians gone—they renounced their claims in Iran after the 1917 Bolshevik Revolution—the British seemed to have a free hand. In mid-1918 they sent twenty-five hundred soldiers to fan out across Iran. Once they were in place, Curzon unveiled a staggeringly one-sided "Anglo-Persian Agreement" under which Britain would turn Iran into a protectorate by taking control of its army, treasury, communications system, and transport network. The three Iranian officials who signed this agreement were induced to do so by generous bribes. They were also promised asylum in the British Empire "should necessity arise."

Lord Curzon, a former viceroy of India who became foreign secretary in 1919, considered Iran one of "the pieces on a chessboard upon which is being played out a game for dominion of the world." Britain, he eloquently argued, must hold it at all costs:

> If it be asked why we should undertake the task at all, and why Persia should not be left to herself and allowed to rot into picturesque decay, the answer is that her geographical position, the magnitude of our interests in the country, and the future safety of our Eastern Empire render it impossible for us now—just as it would have been impossible for us any time in the last fifty years—to disinherit ourselves from what happens in Persia. Moreover, now that we are about to assume the

mandate for Mesopotamia, which will make us coterminous with the western frontiers of Asia, we cannot permit the existence between the frontiers of our Indian Empire and Baluchistan and those of our new protectorate, a hotbed of misrule, enemy intrigue, financial chaos and political disorder. Further, if Persia were to be alone, there is every reason to fear that she would be overrun by Bolshevik influence from the north. Lastly, we possess in the southwestern corner of Persia great assets in the shape of oil fields, which are worked for the British navy and which give us a commanding interest in that part of the world.

The Iranian people erupted in a paroxysm of outrage when the Anglo-Persian Agreement became public. Newspapers demanded that Parliament refuse to ratify it. Politicians venomously denounced it. Mullahs issued a *fatwa* declaring that any Iranian who endorsed it was an enemy of Islam. Warlords vowed to fight any regime that accepted it. Nationalists in Tehran formed a "Punishment Committee" dedicated to assassinating officials who supported it. They killed four of the prime minister's aides; the prime minister resigned.

"It does not appear to be realized at home how intensely unpopular Agreement was in Persia," the British military commander wrote in a dispatch to London. "Secrecy with which Agreement had been concluded, fact that [Parliament] was not summoned and attempt created to pack [Parliament] by resorting to most dishonest methods in carrying out elections, all added to conviction that Great Britain . . . was in reality no better than the hereditary foe, Russia."

Little is known about the childhood of the soldier called Reza. He was born in the Caspian province of Mazandaran, probably in the early spring of 1876. His father, a soldier, died when he was still an infant, and his mother took him from their mountain village to live with her family near Tehran. According to legend, a blizzard broke out during their trek. Reza froze, apparently to death, but revived after his mother was able to find shelter and place him beside a fire.

When he was about fifteen, at the urging of an uncle, Reza showed up at an outpost of the famed Cossack Brigade and asked for work. He was a strapping youth, and the soldiers took him in. By various accounts he was a stable boy or servant; a photo shows him on duty as a guard at the Belgian embassy.

The Persian Cossack Brigade had been established in 1885 after Russian Cossacks impressed the Persian king, Nasr al-Din Shah, during a visit to St. Petersburg. It had traditionally been commanded by Russian officers, though its soldiers and some of its officers were Iranian. By the time Reza joined, it was ten thousand strong, with powerful infantry, cavalry, and artillery units. Its fighters wore Cossack-style uniforms that set them starkly apart from the tattered regular army. This brigade was Iran's premier fighting force and also a center of political power. Its commander reported directly to the shah.

British officers, who took control of the Cossack Brigade in 1917, could not have overlooked Reza. He had grown into a giant of a man, possibly the tallest in Iran. His face was grim and pockmarked but nonetheless striking, dominated by bushy dark eyebrows, a full mustache, and a bold, stern jaw. Before long he was a soldier, and by the time he was in his early twenties, he was leading attacks against rebels, warlords, bandits, and a socialist-styled guerrilla army that had established a rump state in the northern province of Gilan. He was famous for mowing down enemies with his Maxim gun, which fired six hundred rounds per minute. His men called him "Reza Maxim." Above all he was admired for his fearlessness. He was always active, always on the offensive, always eager to attack. One British officer described him in a dispatch as "a first-rate soldier who grasped things quickly." Another called him "the real life and soul of the show." Soon after the legendary general Edmund Ironside arrived to take command of British forces in Iran, he heard that Reza's Cossack unit had crushed rebels in a battle near Tabriz, and asked to meet him.

"He was well over six feet tall, broad shoulders and a most distinguished face," Ironside wrote. "His hooked nose and sparkling eyes gave him a look of animation.... Shivering from a severe bout of malaria, he never went sick."

This meeting came at a propitious moment. In the face of bitter opposition, the British had given up trying to impose the Anglo-Persian Agreement, under which British officers and colonial administrators would have run Iran. Instead they decided to turn the job over to Iranians who were sympathetic to British interests. They set out to find what the British minister in Tehran called "a reactionary prime minister," and settled on Sayyed Zia Tabatabai, a submissive journalist who had been on their payroll for years. All they needed was someone with the military muscle to place him in power. Ironside had just the man.

On February 17, 1921, a day before leaving to meet Winston Churchill (now the colonial secretary) in Cairo, Ironside summoned Reza and told him that if he wished to stage a coup and depose the shah's government—though not the shah himself—Britain would not object.

"I have interviewed Reza and put him definitely in charge of the Cossack Brigade," he wrote in his diary. "I made two things clear to Reza when I agreed to let him go: 1) That he mustn't shoot me from behind as I go; that would lead to humiliation and good to nobody except the revolutionary party. 2) That the Shah on no account must be deposed. Reza promised glibly enough."

This, then, was the team Britain wished to leave behind in Iran: Sayyed Zia as prime minister and Reza as commander of the Cossack Brigade. That, at least, was the official plan. Ironside sensed what would actually happen.

"I have seen only one man who was capable of leading the nation," he wrote in one of his last diary entries before leaving Iran. "That is Reza."

The stage was set for action. On February 20, Sayyed Zia appeared at Reza's camp carrying bags of silver sent by the British for distribution to his men. Reza distributed the money, along with new shoes the British had also sent, and then ordered his men to assemble for dinner. When they had finished eating, he rose to speak.

"Dear comrades!" he told them. "You were eyewitnesses to our situation in Gilan. We were neck deep in mud and filth. They gave us no clothes and did not pay our salaries. We were forgotten. We must put an end to this state of affairs! I have been inspired by God to put an end to it!"

At midnight Reza began marching toward Tehran with six hundred Iranians of the Cossack Brigade. They were ready to fight, but when they entered the city at first light, no force emerged to challenge them. By midday they had arrested most of the cabinet ministers and demanded that Ahmad Shah recognize them as Iran's new government. He had no way to resist. Sayyed Zia became prime minister. Three months later Reza pushed him aside, forced him to leave Tehran, and took his job.

Historians still debate Britain's role in bringing Reza to power. Neither the British minister in Tehran nor the Foreign Office approved or even knew about Ironside's maneuvering, and the story about British silver being passed to Reza's men has been cast into doubt. In any case, as one scholar has written, "Iran was ripe for a strong and autocratic leader, and desperately yearned for a savior."

Ironside was in Cairo when Reza struck. "I fancy that all the people think I engineered the *coup d'état*," he wrote in his diary. "I suppose I did, strictly speaking."

2

AWAY WITH DREAMS AND SHADOWS!

Like many restive officers in the Ottoman army, or any other, the young Mustafa Kemal devoted much of his energy to drinking and carousing with women. Istanbul offered limitless opportunities for both. Kemal also, however, had another obsession. From the days of his early youth, when he rebelled against his mother's wish to send him to religious school, he had been repelled by Muslim, Ottoman, and Middle Eastern traditions. Yet he was still unsure what the alternative might be. So when he returned to Istanbul in 1912, his ideal companion would be someone who offered him not only a place to drink and the pleasures of the boudoir, but also a window into the modern world of ideas and action.

That was Corinne.

Born in Genoa, trained as a pianist at the Paris Conservatory, fluent in several languages, daughter of a physician and the young widow of a Turkish officer, Corinne Lütfü was a paragon of the sensual sophisticate. She lived in Pera, the European quarter of Istanbul, which was a kaleidoscope of Western pleasures. Instead of retreating into solitude after her husband's death, she did the opposite. She turned her home into a salon where the city's urbane cosmopolitans met for long evenings of song, chamber music, food, drink, and above all, intense, uninhibited conversation. Most of the guests were European, but enlightened Turks were also welcome. A friend brought Kemal to one of her parties, and he was immediately smitten—with both the vivaciously attractive Corinne and the intoxicating ideas that filled the smoky air of her salon.

She was just as attracted to him. He was, after all, a fine figure of a man—blond, fair-skinned, immensely charming although essentially shy with women, and overflowing with virility. Already he had developed the obsessive concern for his appearance and personal cleanliness that would mark his entire life; in later years he would take breaks during battle to bathe. His most extraordinary feature, by all accounts, was his stare. A foreigner who met him reported that his eyes were "penetrating ice-blue." Another said they were "the coldest, most penetrating" he had ever seen. A woman he seduced wrote that his pupils "were so light blue as to be almost colorless; it was like looking at a blind man and yet one whose eyes pierced you through."

Kemal lusted after what Corinne represented: a radical alternative to the dreary lassitude he had seen in Ottoman provinces. Under her tutelage he read novels, learned to love Western music, improved his French, and above all came to meet men and women whose ideas and experiences opened to him a dazzling new universe. Corinne introduced him to Istanbul's *beau monde*, a world of pleasure but also one that was intimately connected to Europe, where political explosions were blowing kingdoms apart.

For years Kemal had been fuming about what he saw as his people's ignorance and backwardness. Once while directing a training maneuver with a German officer, the officer commended him on his mastery of field tactics. He answered that his military skill would only be valuable if he could use it to free Turks from "fanaticism and intellectual slavery." Then he added a remark that distilled everything he believed into a few tart words.

"The Turkish nation has fallen far behind the West," he said. "The main aim should be to lead it toward modern civilization."

In the early years of the twentieth century, the Ottoman army suffered a series of devastating defeats. Kemal himself commanded units that fought in unsuccessful attempts to hold Libya and Albania. Then, in the Balkan War of 1912, the Greeks, Macedonians, Bulgarians, and Serbs overthrew Ottoman rule in a lightning uprising. These were stunning losses, cutting away almost all of the empire's territory in Europe, including regions that had been under Ottoman rule for five hundred years.

Floods of wretched Muslim refugees surged into Istanbul, and their plight set off violent protests. On January 23, 1913, an angry mob surrounded the government office complex, shouting curses at the well-meaning but impotent liberal regime that had taken power after the previous year's election. One group of rioters broke into the building, found and killed the minister of war, and forced the prime minister, then known as the Grand Vizier, to resign.

Into this void stepped the revolutionary Young Turks, whose agents had organized the uprising. They seized power and installed their leader, Enver Pasha, a charismatic and ruthless general, in place of the murdered war minister. Enver quickly emerged as the crumbling empire's dictator, ruling at the head of a triumvirate under a figurehead sultan but holding essential power in his own hands.

Mustafa Kemal, who never reached a high position in the Young Turk movement and considered Enver a narrow-minded brute, was distraught and adrift. When one of his friends, Fethi Bey, was named Ottoman ambassador to Bulgaria, Fethi invited him to come along as military attaché. He accepted. The next period in his life unfolded in Sofia, the Bulgarian capital, where a young nation was reveling in its new freedom. Sofia was pulsating with a sense of enthusiasm and possibility that thrilled Kemal and his friend.

These two dashing young diplomats aroused great curiosity, and were welcomed into society by an emerging elite that had until then seen Turks only as oppressors. Soon after their arrival, Kemal saw the opera *Carmen*. He was so overwhelmed that when, during the intermission, he was introduced to King Ferdinand and the king asked him what he thought of the performance, he could only blurt out one word: "Wonderful!"

The social whirl was not all that occupied Kemal during his fifteen months in Sofia. He marveled at the number of Bulgarian Turks who owned businesses and whose wives walked unveiled and mixed freely with their Christian neighbors. Here he also had his first experience with politics, spending many days in the gallery of Parliament, watching debates, studying factional tactics, and paying special attention to the skill with which ethnic Turkish deputies pressed their points. Every day he became more convinced not only that the Turks must reinvent themselves as a nation, but that he himself had been chosen by fate to make them do it.

"I have ambitions, and even very great ones," he wrote in one of his many letters to Corinne. "I seek realization of these ambitions in the success of a great idea."

Unshakable self-confidence, sometimes so extreme as to border on the pathological, shaped Kemal's psyche from his earliest years. Biographers describe a truculent, outspoken, and boastful child who talked back to teachers and fiercely resisted discipline. His father, a penniless clerk, died when he was seven, and when his mother remarried he became, according to one historian, "jealous as a lover of another man in his mother's life." He moved out of the family home, took up lodging with a relative, and for several years immersed himself in an inner world, enveloped by extravagant fantasies. It was during this period, according to two scholars who have written his "psycho-biography," that Kemal developed the "inflated and grandiose self-concept" that propelled his wild ride into history.

"He believed he was a unique man, above all others, and endowed with the right to assert his will," they wrote. "He saw others in two categories—those who were his admirers and followers and those who were not, and who therefore had no existence at all as far as he was concerned."

Kemal was in Sofia when the heir to the Austro-Hungarian throne, Archduke Franz Ferdinand, was assassinated in another former Ottoman city, Sarajevo, on June 28, 1914. He had no way to influence his government's reaction; that was up to Enver Pasha. From his enormous office at the Sublime Porte, Enver made a historic miscalculation. For years he had relied on German officers for military advice, and when World War I broke out, his boundless confidence in German military power led him to presume the kaiser would win a quick victory.

On August 2, in a secret ceremony at a mansion beside the Bosphorus, Enver signed a pact allying the Ottoman Empire with Germany. In the days that followed he summoned scores of officers home from abroad and ordered them to prepare to fight. Among them was Mustafa Kemal. The mission Enver gave him would change his life and Turkish history.

Capture Istanbul: this was one of the central goals British commanders set for themselves as the Great War unfolded.

First Lord of the Admiralty Winston Churchill easily persuaded his comrades on the British War Council that the Ottoman army, which was on a long losing streak, would crumble before a British-led assault. His plan was for Allied ships to seize the strategic Dardanelles strait and then sail north to subdue Istanbul. That would open new supply lines to Russia and perhaps shift the dynamic of the war.

Allied warships made their first efforts to force the Dardanelles in early 1915, but retreated after coming under fire from Turkish guns. In order to pass safely, the British would have to suppress those guns. That meant a land assault on the Gallipoli Peninsula overlooking the narrow strait. Enver named a German general to direct the peninsula's defense, supported by six Turkish division commanders. The key "mobile division" was to be commanded by Lieutenant Colonel Mustafa Kemal.

In one of the bloodiest marine landings of World War I, waves of soldiers from Britain, Australia, and New Zealand stormed the beaches at Gallipoli as the sun rose on April 25, 1915. Under heavy Turkish fire and at horrific cost—only twenty-one of the first fifteen hundred soldiers in the landing force made it to cover, and over the next three days ten thousand were killed or wounded—they secured two beachheads and began pushing northward toward the main Turkish force. As they advanced, Turkish squad leaders called urgently for help. Kemal, who was stationed nearby, ordered his men to charge toward the contested hills. He ran ahead of them, and as he drew near, he met a platoon of retreating Turks. They were out of ammunition and terrified, but he ordered them to turn back and face the enemy, with bayonets if necessary. When they hesitated, he gave what became his most famous command.

"I am not ordering you to attack, I am ordering you to die!" he shouted. "By the time we are dead, other units and commanders will be here to take our place."

Turkish defenders blunted the Allied assault, and in the months that followed, what Churchill had imagined as a walkover turned into a grotesque fellowship of death. Hundreds of thousands of shells were fired. Men spent months in fetid trenches just a few dozen yards from the enemy. Thousands were cut down while attempting over-the-top bayonet charges. As the fighting dragged on, Kemal's reputation grew.

"Mustafa Kemal fought like a man possessed," according to one account of the Gallipoli campaign. "He was everywhere, indefatigable despite flare-ups of the malaria he had suffered.... Masterful in his diagnoses, rapid in making decisions and energetic in carrying them out, Mustafa Kemal's performance in this campaign claimed for him the status of military genius. Experts agree that here he was even more brilliant than in his later achievements in the Turkish struggle for independence, holding that at Gallipoli he was alone, and obliged to improvise rather than to execute carefully conceived maneuvers."

On December 19, nearly eight months after Allied troops stormed the beaches at Gallipoli expecting a quick victory, they began an ignominious retreat. Behind they left a narrow peninsula drenched in blood. Forty-four thousand Allied soldiers died in the failed attempt to take Gallipoli. Twice that number of Turks died defending it.

Victory at Gallipoli was the turning point in Kemal's life. He was the only Turkish officer to emerge from World War I as a hero: the savior of Istanbul. Reality had finally come to match his outlandish fantasies.

"Prior to being swept into military exploits at the age of thirty-four, he had consistently beaten on any door in the hope that its opening would provide the adulation he so desperately needed and sought," according to one biography. "Gallipoli had made Mustafa Kemal a hero at last, but he was mistaken if he thought he had arrived at the center of the stage.... Others still remained to be convinced of the superiority that was so evident to him."

In the spring of 1915, while Kemal was frantically occupied at Gallipoli, Enver's triumvirate faced another crisis at the opposite end of their war-torn empire. Armenians had lived under Ottoman rule for centuries in what is now eastern Turkey, and with the empire collapsing, some decided to seize their historic chance. Militants formed armed bands and, with Russian support, launched an uprising aimed at turning five Ottoman provinces into a Russian-backed Armenian state. They seized one important town, Van, and attacked several others. The ruling triumvirate decided that the only way to crush them was to force all Armenians, whether or not they were involved in the rebellion, out of Anatolia. Families were torn from their homes and forced to flee. Hundreds of thousands died or were murdered. In what Mustafa Kemal later called a "shameful act," Young Turk leaders committed one of the twentieth century's most heinous crimes.

By the time World War I ended in 1918, Kemal had risen to the rank of general, entitling him to be called Mustafa Kemal Pasha. That was scant consolation in a ruined landscape. The Turks were among the war's losers. Days after it ended, the three Young Turk leaders responsible for this disaster fled across the Black Sea in a German submarine. Enver was killed a few years later in Central Asia, pursuing his mad dream of a Turkic empire. Armenian gunmen, guided by British and Soviet secret services, tracked the other two into exile and assassinated them.

With the Young Turks gone, the overwhelmed sultan Mehmet VI Vahdeddin, who had replaced his brother just four months earlier, named a new Grand Vizier and sent him to negotiate terms of surrender with the British. The two sides met aboard the British ship HMS *Agamemnon*, anchored off the Greek town of Mudros. Britain dictated harsh terms, and the sultan's envoys, believing they had no alternative, accepted. The armistice required most of the Ottoman army to demobilize. It also gave the Allies control of Istanbul, sovereignty over all Ottoman territories in Arabia, and the right to occupy any Turkish town or region where "security problems" emerged.

"News of the Mudros armistice terms shocked Kemal," according to one account. "Eight days after the armistice was signed, he was told that his army group had ceased to exist.... Not until November 13 did he step down once more at Haydarpasha Station. It was a black day for the homecoming of a proud military commander."

Towering like a Teutonic castle over the Asian shore of the majestic Bosphorus, surrounded on three sides by water and resting on eleven hundred wooden pilings, the new German-built Haydarpasha train station was among the most imposing edifices in all Istanbul. On the day Mustafa Kemal Pasha arrived there from the Anatolian hinterland, a stunned crowd was gaping in awe as an astonishing spectacle unfolded outside. A parade of warships sixteen miles long, the grandest ever seen on the Bosphorus, was arriving to begin an Allied occupation of Istanbul. Fifty-five ships of the line carrying thirty-five hundred soldiers and marines, most of them British, maneuvered their way past stunned crowds lining both shores. When they anchored, the ships were so closely packed that no water could be seen between them.

Ferry traffic on the Bosphorus was suspended as these warships made their triumphant passage through the defeated city. Among those who had to wait and watch were passengers who had arrived at Haydarpasha and wished to cross to the European side. Mustafa Kemal was one of them. As he waited, though, he felt none of the anguish, dread, or helplessness that coursed through the crowd. History was playing into his hands. For a long time he watched silently as British warships steamed past. Then he turned to his aide-de-camp.

"As they come," he said, "so shall they go."

Impatient as always and unwilling to wait for ferry service to resume,

Kemal ordered his aide to find a rowboat that could carry them across the Bosphorus. Once on the European side, he made his way to Istanbul's finest hotel, the Pera Palas, and checked in. The hotel was packed with Allied officers, all in a triumphant mood. Not only had their armies won the Great War, but by their arrival in Istanbul they seemed to have sealed forever the fate of "the Turk," a prostrate nation that had once threatened to overrun Christendom and, in Christopher Marlowe's words, "mangle all thy provinces."

Istanbul was everything one might expect from the occupied capital of an empire in its death throes. Public order had broken down and thieves roamed freely. Streets were dark. Food was hard to find. The currency was worthless. Refugee families slept on streets and in parks. The Turks had for several years been gripped by the fear that doom was approaching; now it was at hand. How could they turn this tide?

Mustafa Kemal had an answer: follow me.

"If I obtain great authority and power, I think I will bring about by a coup—suddenly in one moment—the revolution we need in our national life," he wrote in his diary. "Because unlike others, I don't believe that this deed can be achieved by raising the intelligence of others slowly to the level of my own. My soul rebels against such a course. Why, after my years of education, after studying civilization and society, after spending my life pursuing freedom, should I descend to the level of common people? I will make them rise to my level. Let me not resemble them; they should resemble me."

For a time Kemal hoped Sultan Vahdeddin would name him minister of war so he could organize resistance to the occupation, but the sultan, who believed resistance was futile, refused to appoint him. This proved fortunate, because soon afterward the British arrested many senior government officials and sent them to detention in Malta. That would likely have been Kemal's fate, with incalculable consequences for history.

After it became clear that there was no place for him in the sultan's cabinet, Kemal began to imagine alternatives. At the beginning of 1919, he and a handful of like-minded officers informally agreed on a revolutionary plan. Somehow, they decided, they would escape from Istanbul and make their way to the Anatolian heartland. There they would raise an army of their own and lead it in rebellion against their new masters.

Why did they choose such a radical course? Not simply because their country was occupied. Most Turks were ready to accept an orderly occupation, make indemnity payments, and submit to other penalties that winners in war traditionally impose on losers. But their army had not been defeated in the field, and they did not believe their leaders had accepted an unconditional surrender—certainly not one in which their traditional homeland, the great landmass of Anatolia, which the poet Nazim Hikmet described as "jutting out into the Mediterranean like a mare's head," would be dismembered.

Dismemberment, though, was precisely what the Allies had in mind.

During the winter of 1918–19, British prime minister David Lloyd George, who considered the Turks "a human cancer," persuaded other Allied leaders to endorse a sweeping partition of Anatolia. This vast region, the size of Britain and France combined, had been the Turkish homeland for a thousand years. From it Lloyd George wished to carve a Greek state or two, an Armenian state, perhaps a Kurdish state, and large colonies for France and Italy.

"It was not European military occupation," one historian has written, "but the prospect of losing the country to local Christian minorities, which, after the first shock had worn off, called forth Turkish popular resistance."

Unable to afford long-term rent for his suite at the Pera Palas, Kemal moved to a three-story house a couple of miles away. There he spent his crucial, conspiratorial winter. The military police kept a desultory watch outside, and he did what he could to disguise his plotting. He brought his mother and sister to live with him, installing them on the third floor like a dutiful son and brother. Never did he convene a large meeting. But one by one, usually dressed in civilian clothes, nationalist officers came by to drink, muse, and plot.

The Allies were tightening their noose around Anatolia. French troops occupied the Mediterranean port of Adana. The Italians landed at Antalya, a few hundred miles west. The Russians held Kars and other eastern provinces. In several regions, tension between triumphant Christians and humiliated Muslims exploded into violence.

Each step the Allies took toward partitioning Anatolia sparked more anger. Slowly the Turks turned toward the idea of revolt.

If there was a moment when this outlandish idea began to seem realistic, it might have been the evening of April 11, 1919. One of the most senior Ottoman officers, General Kazim Karabekir, was leaving Istanbul the next morning to take command of the last intact Ottoman army, a force of 12,500 men and twenty-two artillery pieces based in the eastern town of Erzurum. After paying his farewell calls at the war ministry, Karabekir slipped away and came to Kemal's house. The two generals had fought together at Gallipoli and trusted each other implicitly. Karabekir confided what he could tell no one else: he was going to Erzurum not to serve the sultan and his Allied masters, but to break with them. Kemal, he said, should find a way to join him.

"It's an idea," Kemal replied.

A couple of days later an undersecretary at the war ministry, Ismet Pasha, visited Kemal with his own version of the same idea. He reported that many officers were eager to resist their country's dismemberment, and that some seemed ready to follow a revolutionary leader if one were to emerge. The two men pored over a map of Anatolia, marking the location of military bases and armories.

"What's the best way to get there?" Kemal finally asked Ismet.

"Then you've made up your mind?"

"We won't talk about that yet."

"There are as many roads as measures we can take. The problem is to decide what we want to do. When are you going to tell me what you have decided?"

"When the time comes."

For years Mustafa Kemal had tried in vain to break into the power elite in Istanbul. Now he was in the opposite position, trapped in Istanbul and eager to find a way out. Courtesy of the British, he found one.

Among places where the Turks had risen up against the Allies' dictates was the Black Sea port of Samsun. Allied commanders could not spare a force to go there and restore order, so they ordered the sultan to send some of his own men. The Grand Vizier, who had grown uncomfortable with Mustafa Kemal's presence in Istanbul, persuaded the sultan to appoint him "inspector" of Samsun, with power to command Ottoman forces there.

"What a wonderful feeling!" Kemal later wrote of the moment he was ordered to make for Samsun. "Fortune smiled on me, and when I found myself basking in her smile, it is hard to describe how happy I was. I recall biting my lips with excitement as I left the office. The cage had been opened. The whole universe lay before me. I was like a bird about to soar."

At a farewell dinner with officers and cabinet ministers, there was some grumbling about the scope of Kemal's mandate. He brushed it aside with assurances that he intended to operate only in a "small area." One of those present, Cavad Pasha, incoming chief of the general staff, not only sensed that to be untrue but hoped it was. After dinner he pulled Kemal aside.

"Are you going to do something?" he asked quietly.

"Yes," came the reply. "I am going to do something."

The next afternoon, as Kemal was making final preparations to depart, stunning news arrived from Izmir, the main city on the Aegean coast of Anatolia, known to Greeks as Smyrna. Greek warships had landed and disgorged an occupation force of twenty thousand soldiers. British and French vessels hovered offshore to support them. The Turks were first thunderstruck, then outraged.

"The Greek civilian population swept along the streets, crying curse on the Muslims," the British historian Lord Kinross wrote in his account of this landing. "Turkish troops hoisted the white flag and, with their officers, were marched down to the waterfront to a troop ship with their hands above their heads, while a mob of civilians jeered at them, struck at them with clubs and tore at their fezzes. A Turkish colonel who refused to take off his fez and stamp on it was shot and killed. The governor was similarly marched off to the quay, at the point of the bayonet, together with other notables dragged from their houses. The Greek troops then got out of hand, and some hundreds of Turks were killed. Their bodies were thrown over the sea wall into the harbor."

On his last night in Istanbul, Kemal told his mother and sister that he was leaving on an "important mission." They pressed him for details, but he would say only that he had deposited some money for them in a nearby bank. The next morning he met his staff officers at the teeming harbor and boarded the *Bandirma*, a lumbering old freighter that had been built in Britain and sold to the Ottomans after her active life seemed over.

The *Bandirma* weighed anchor on the evening of May 16, 1919, headed for Samsun. Fearing that the British might sink her, Kemal ordered the captain to keep close to shore so he and his comrades might row or swim to safety if they were attacked. There was no attack, but in Istanbul, British commanders belatedly learned of Kemal's appointment and became suspicious. They sent an emissary to warn the Grand Vizier against entrusting the Hero of Gallipoli with such a delicate mission.

"You are too late, Excellency," the Grand Vizier replied, leaning back in his chair and pressing the fingers of both hands together. "The bird has flown."

Rough seas battered the *Bandirma* as she approached Samsun on the cloudy afternoon of May 19. Rather than risk a landing, her captain anchored in the choppy harbor. Rowboats were dispatched to bring Kemal and his men—fifty-four in all—to a welcoming reception.

In later years, when Kemal was asked the date of his birth, he would reply, "May 19, 1919." His nation agrees; May 19 is now a national holiday in Turkey.

The government sent Kemal to Samsun with orders to suppress unrest, but he planned to do the opposite: shape inchoate Turkish anger into a revolutionary movement strong enough to expel occupying European armies.

"The Mustafa Kemal who now embarked on the crucial phase of his own and his country's career was a seasoned and self-confident campaigner, two years short of forty, who had proven himself as a soldier in fourteen years of hard service," Lord Kinross wrote. "He now had to prove himself as a politician and statesman. The challenge which he had sought through those smoldering years of frustration at last confronted him, bold and exciting and clear."

Samsun would have been an isolated place were it not for the fact that twenty years before, the paranoid sultan Abdul Hamid, eager to stay in touch with his legion of spies, had built a telegraph network connecting every Turkish town. Kemal recognized this network as a great prize. He spent hours each day in the Samsun telegraph office, dictating patriotic messages, scornful letters to the sultan's ministers, and tirades against the Allied occupation. Copies went to newspapers, foreign embassies, governors, mayors, and military commanders.

The British were appalled at Kemal's insolence and insisted that the Grand Vizier recall him. By the time the order was issued, Kemal had moved inland. In the verdant orchard town of Amasya, where Julius Caesar made his famous proclamation, *Veni, vidi, vici,* he conceived the next stage of his rebellion. He would summon resistance leaders from across Anatolia and secure from them a declaration, in the name of the Turkish people, that the Istanbul government had fallen under foreign control and was therefore illegitimate.

In Amasya, Kemal met secretly with his three closest comrades—Rauf Orbay, a former commander of the Ottoman navy; Ali Fuat, scion of an old military family and a hero of the Balkan War; and Refet Bele, who had commanded Ottoman forces in Palestine—and told them of his plan. All agreed to support him; so did the last member of their inner circle, Kazim Karabekir, who was commanding troops farther east but assented by telegram. The five of them issued a public declaration, later known as the Amasya Circular, that proclaimed for the first time in writing what would be this revolution's central demand: the Turks must rule all of Anatolia. They would accept no partition, no mandate, no foreign occupation, no rule by Christians.

This declaration also had a secret annex, which the signers communicated orally to trusted comrades. It ordered that no resistance group allow itself to be disbanded, that no officer surrender his command to a foreigner, and that no arms or ammunition be handed over. Ahead lay war.

The government reacted sternly to the Amasya Circular, ordering mayors and governors not to cooperate with "insubordinate, disrespectful and illegal organizations." Two weeks later it tried a different tack, offering to pardon Kemal's offenses if he would return to Istanbul.

"When we have independence," Kemal replied by telegram, "I will return from Anatolia."

This made Kemal's separation from the army inevitable. The telegram dismissing him arrived moments after he sent one with his resignation. In a speech at Erzurum—capital of the Hittites and Urartians in the days before written history and a prize for conquerors from Xerxes to Tamerlane—he bid farewell to the army and pledged himself to "the achievement of our sacred national purpose."

On the morning of July 23, 1919, delegates to the grandly named Erzurum Congress convened at a one-story building that had once been an Armenian school. Most were leaders of resistance groups from Black Sea towns and eastern Anatolia. As they assembled, Kemal called for Muslim prayers and the sacrifice of a sheep. He also proposed that a warm telegram be sent to the sultan. This was part of his ruse. In order to raise an army, he had to be seen as defending the two institutions for which the Turks were ready to die: Islam and the sultanate. In fact he scorned them both.

Kemal, despite some opposition, managed to have himself elected chairman of the Erzurum Congress. In speeches over the next few days, he denounced the Allies and the pliant Istanbul government that did their bidding. So did other delegates.

"It is essential that our central government submit to the will of the nation," they asserted in their final declaration. "Decisions not based on the will of the nation have no validity."

Six weeks later, Kemal called a second "congress," this one to be held in Sivas, 350 miles to the west. The Grand Vizier decided this would be a good time to arrest Kemal, and ordered the local governor to storm the town with a force of Kurdish tribesmen. A force was assembled, but at the last moment the governor could not bring himself to attack.

"Wretches, murderers, traitors!" Kemal railed in a telegram to cabinet ministers after he learned of the aborted plot. "You are conspiring with foreigners against the nation."

Following the example of Erzurum, the thirty-eight delegates to the Sivas Congress adopted resolutions declaring that Anatolia must not be divided. A few days later, armed nationalists walked into the governor's office in the Black Sea town of Trabzon and arrested him. Istanbul's authority was collapsing. The Grand Vizier was forced to resign.

Four months after stepping off the *Bandirma* to launch his rebellion, Kemal had brought down a government. Power began flowing from the Ottoman regime into his hands. It never flowed back.

"The first phase is at an end," Kemal said after learning of the Grand Vizier's resignation.

While Kemal was in Sivas, an American delegation studying conditions in Anatolia passed through. Its leader, General J. G. Harbord, became one of the first Americans to have an extended conversation with Kemal. He found "a young man of force and keen intelligence" whose fair complexion suggested "Circassian or other blond blood in his ancestry." They spoke for two hours. When General Harbord asked what Kemal hoped to do with the army he was assembling, Kemal mused for a moment and then ripped open the string of worry beads he had been fingering. Beads scattered across the floor. Kemal bent down, gathered them up, then held them together in his palm and showed them to his guest. This, he said, was what he would do for his dismembered homeland.

General Harbord told him frankly that hoping to defeat Allied power so soon after the Allies had won the Great War was "against logic, against military facts."

"What you say, General, is true," Kemal replied. "What we want to do, in our situation, is explainable neither in military or any other terms. But in spite of everything, we are going to do it."

The new regime in Istanbul was sympathetic to the nationalist cause. It sent an emissary to ask Kemal what he thought about calling an election for a new Parliament. Guessing that many nationalists would be elected, Kemal gave his full support. The election turned out just as he had expected. Barely a week after the new Parliament was seated, it passed a resolution rejecting any partition of Anatolia and insisting on "full independence." More resolutions followed. Finally the British lost patience. They sent soldiers to arrest the leaders of Parliament and seize government offices, and announced that execution would be the punishment for further defiance.

"Today the Turkish nation is called to defend its capacity for civilization, its right to life and independence—its entire future!" Kemal declared in a passionate public telegram.

A few days later, on March 18, 1920, Parliament met in secret and voted to begin an indefinite recess in order to avoid collaborating with foreign occupation. Mustafa Kemal leaped to turn this vote to his favor. He urged members of Parliament to reconvene, not in Istanbul but in the Anatolian town of Ankara, where he had built a headquarters.

This was a stroke of brilliance. More than eighty members of what was to be the last Ottoman Parliament made the rugged trek to Ankara. There they joined a roughly equal number of delegates from resistance groups to form a new body, the Grand National Assembly, that had a powerful moral claim—though no legal one—to speak for the Turkish nation.

The British, of course, were hardly prepared to surrender a commanding imperial prize to a clique of guerrillas and cashiered officers. They directed the spineless sultan to reinstall his former Grand Vizier, and then arranged for the chief Ottoman cleric, the *Sheyhulislam*, to issue a *fatwa* condemning nationalist leaders as infidels and encouraging true believers to kill them. Kemal responded by recruiting 250 clerics from across Anatolia to sign a counter-*fatwa* declaring that foreigners had imprisoned the sultan, that good Muslims must rescue him by rebelling against foreign rule, and that in the meantime any *fatwa* from Istanbul should be ignored.

Ankara was a remote, muddy little town when the Grand National Assembly convened there for its first session. Despite some unhappiness over Mustafa Kemal's well-known fondness for loose women and alcohol, he was elected chairman with 110 of the 120 votes. In his inaugural speech, invoking the Muslim principle that power should rest with the greatest mass of believers, he urged the assembly to claim executive as well as legislative authority over the nation. Delegates agreed, and named a ten-member committee to function as a shadow government. Kemal, to no one's surprise, quickly emerged as its leader.

Until this moment, it might have been possible to consider Kemal and his comrades something less than rebels—a dissident force certainly, but one that aimed only to bring the government to its senses. Once the Grand National Assembly convened in Ankara and claimed state power, there could be no doubt. The cabinet in Istanbul reacted by announcing that Kemal and five other nationalists had been tried in absentia and sentenced to death.

Turkey's revolution took shape in ways comparable to America's revolution 150 years earlier. Rebels banded together to overthrow British power. They formed illegal bodies to guide their struggle and produced a leader who combined military prowess with great personal charisma. Among their principles were self-determination and a broadened— though not complete—recognition of each citizen's rights. When they launched their rebellion, the prospect of victory seemed dim. Patriotic fervor drove them to fight despite daunting odds.

Allied leaders, who considered the Turks incapable of resistance, utterly failed to grasp the power of this gathering rebellion. On August 10, 1920, eminent diplomats gathered at the Paris suburb of Sèvres to sign a treaty that dictated in excruciating detail the partition of Anatolia. The magnificent Aegean coast around Izmir would become part of Greece in five years, subject to a referendum. Eastern provinces would become a new Armenian state. The Kurds would also have a region of their own. Istanbul and the straits would come under "international control." For the Turks there would remain a rocky expanse in central

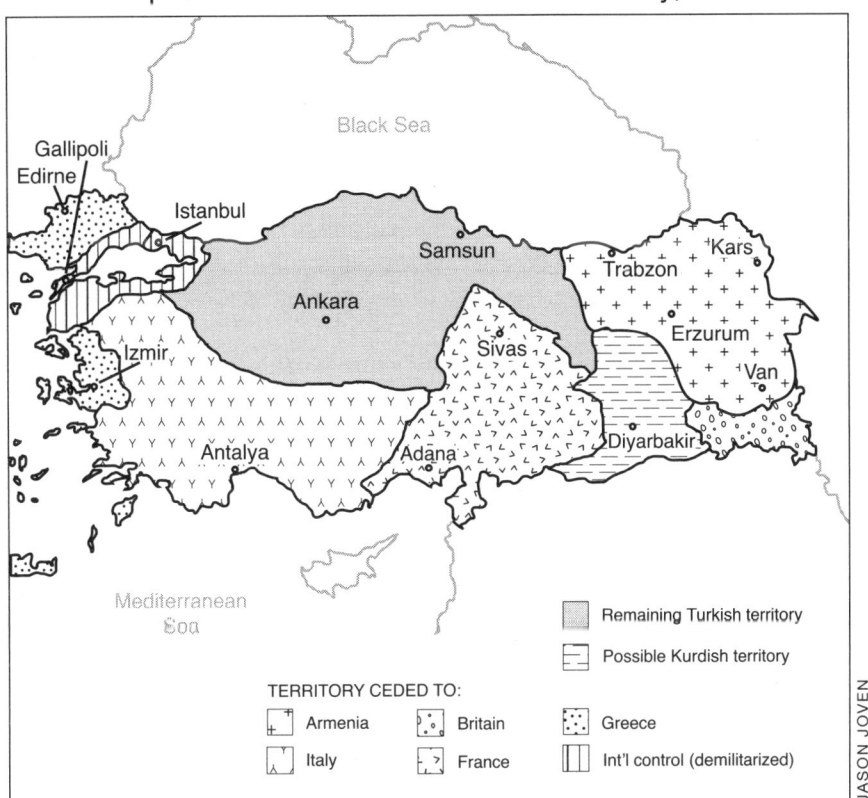

Proposed Partition of Anatolia: Sèvres Treaty, 1920

Anatolia, with access to the Black Sea but not to the Aegean or the Mediterranean. Their army would be limited to fifty thousand men. British, French, and Italian bankers would oversee their treasury.

"A sinister death sentence" was Kemal's pithy description of the Sèvres Treaty. Like many Turks, he understood it as an edict from colonial Europe by which the homeland was to be carved up and divided among enemies. But such proud people—heirs to mounted fighters who ravaged Asia under the command of fearsome khans, and to Ottoman conquerors who built one of history's most powerful empires—would not meekly accept their fate.

"Loaded with follies, stained with crimes, rotted with misgovernment, shattered by battle, worn down by long disastrous wars, his Empire falling to pieces around him, the Turk was still alive," Winston Churchill later wrote. "In his breast was beating the heart of a race that had challenged the world, and for centuries had contended victoriously against all comers. In his hands was once again the equipment of a modern army, and at his head a Captain who, with all that is learned of him, ranks among the four or five outstanding figures of the cataclysm. In the tapestried and gilded chambers of Paris were assembled the lawgivers of the world. In Constantinople under the guns of the Allied fleet, there functioned a puppet government of Turkey. But among the stern hills and valleys of 'the Turkish homelands' in Anatolia, there dwelt that company of poor men ... who would not see it settled so. And at their bivouac fires at this moment sat, in the rags of a refugee, the august Spirit of Fair Play."

The "captain" to whom Churchill referred, Mustafa Kemal, used the Sèvres Treaty as a rallying point. He steadily consolidated his political base and, by edging other generals aside, solidified his command over the growing rebel army. As war approached, his power was secure.

"He was by turns cynical, suspicious, unscrupulous and satanically shrewd," wrote Halide Edib, the only woman in Kemal's inner circle. "He bullied. He indulged in cheap street-corner heroics.... One moment he seemed to be the perfect demagogue, a second George Washington, and the next moment behaved like a Napoleon. Sometimes he would appear weak and an abject coward; sometimes he showed supreme strength and daring.... One knew all the time that there were men around him who were far superior to him in intellect, culture and education. But although he matched them in neither refinement nor originality, not one of them could match his vitality. Whatever their qualities, they were made on a more or less normal scale. In terms of vitality, he was not. And it was this alone that made him the dominant figure."

As Kemal prepared for war, he sensed a decisive advantage. His men were desperate patriots who believed their nation was on the brink of death. They were ready to give their lives to defend it. The occupying armies were exhausted after a long war and were not eager to fight.

This was Kemal's insight: We're prepared to die, you aren't. We want to win more fervently than you do, so we will.

What the Turks call their Independence War unfolded on three fronts, beginning in the middle of 1920. In the east, the resourceful Kazim Karabekir led forces that took the garrison at Kars and then methodically pushed the Russians and Armenians out of eastern Anatolia. Other forces relentlessly harassed French and Italian garrisons along the Mediterranean, finally leading both countries to sue for peace.

That left only the Greeks and their British patrons.

Greek commanders knew their occupation would not be secure as long as Kemal's rebels roamed freely. At the beginning of 1921 they decided to go on the offensive, attack Ankara, and smash the rebel force. King Constantine came from Athens to guide this assault personally. He fielded an army of 126,000 men, slightly larger than the Turkish force it would have to defeat. In equipment it enjoyed a decisive edge: 610 artillery pieces against the Turks' 400, four thousand machine guns against seven hundred, twenty airplanes against four. As this potent force approached Ankara, nationalist leaders made plans to flee if necessary.

Kemal and his comrades decided to make their stand sixty miles west of Ankara, at a bend in the broad Sakarya River. As they deployed their forces, they demanded help from all who lived nearby. Every able-bodied male was to present himself for duty, everyone with a means of transport was to turn it over to the army, and every family was to give the army all its firearms as well as one pair of boots and 40 percent of its cloth, leather, flour, candles, and soap. Weapons from the newly established Soviet Union, which saw Kemal's rebellion as a way to weaken Britain, arrived providentially; shipments were secretly unloaded at Black Sea coves and then, in episodes still celebrated in legend, hauled across Anatolia in carts, often by women, to Turkish camps along the Sakarya.

Greek soldiers spent a month on the west side of the river, preparing their assault. They were so confident of victory that their commanders invited British officers to a victory banquet in Ankara. As they planned their celebration, Kemal's men were feverishly digging bunkers and trenches.

"The Greek army was a long black dragon, coiling toward Ankara to devour it," Halide Edib wrote. "The Turkish army was another long coil, stretching out in a parallel line east of the Sakarya in order to reach Ankara first and prevent the black dragon from swallowing it."

Greek troops launched their attack on August 23, 1921. In their first surge they seized a strategic mountaintop. Halide Edib reports that Turkish commanders were stunned, that they contemplated "the ugliest sort of fate," and that as she watched Mustafa Kemal absorb the shock, she felt "as if the iron curtain of doom, something like the fire curtain in a theater, was coming down, ever so slowly but inevitably." Over the days that followed, however, the Turkish field commander, Ismet Pasha, sensed a flaw in the tactical approach of his Greek counterpart, General Anastasios Papoulas; he found Papoulas cautious, not persistent, reluctant to advance on victory. Shaping his own tactics around this insight, Ismet turned the tide of battle. After twenty-one days of intense fighting along a sixty-mile front, the Greek army broke and fled.

Losses at Sakarya were modest by the standards of World War I but terrible nonetheless: about four thousand dead and twenty thousand wounded on each side. It was not simply a Turkish victory but the war's decisive turning point. All real hope that the occupying armies could maintain a foothold in Anatolia drowned in the Sakarya River that autumn of 1921.

After this triumph, two Turkish officers asked the Grand National Assembly to bestow on Mustafa Kemal the historic title of Gazi, reserved for Muslims who are great warriors and defenders of the faith. There was no objection. For the rest of his life, Kemal was often called "Gazi Pasha" or simply "the Gazi."

Although the Turks had successfully defended Ankara, they were as exhausted as their Greek enemies and unable to chase them. The Sakarya front remained static for nearly a year. Finally, on August 26, 1922, the

Turks launched a coordinated wave of attacks on Greek positions across the entire zone of occupation. Greek officers were taken by surprise. They had not realized either the size of the Turkish force or the passion that still drove it.

"As at Gallipoli, Mustafa Kemal's narcissistic personality organization was an immense asset to him as he personally led the great offensive," according to his psychobiographers. "His grandiosity allowed him to disregard discouraging 'realities' and to envision successes others could not conceive of. It also permitted him to see himself as embodying the honor of all Turks, wrapped in a protective mantle bestowed upon him by the motherland. Projecting this air of invincibility, Mustafa Kemal was capable of imbuing himself and his troops with an inordinate sense of hope and purpose."

Kemal's offensive reached a peak on August 30, when Turkish artillery devastated Greek positions around a town called Dumlupinar. Thousands of infantrymen followed with bayonet charges, setting the Greek army into panicked flight. The Turks today observe August 30 as Victory Day.

"Armies!" Kemal shouted to his commanders as they overran Dumlupinar that day. "The Mediterranean is your objective! Forward!"

Over the next week, surging Turkish troops drove the Greek defenders from town after town. Two Greek generals fell into Turkish traps and were forced to surrender their entire armies, a total of five thousand soldiers, five hundred officers, and several hundred machine guns. In a period of days the Greek army, riven by factional disputes and worn thin by long deployment in hostile territory, collapsed.

Suddenly, incredibly, Greece's good fortune had turned to disaster. The government in Athens fell. Soon afterward, the first victorious Turkish cavalrymen staggered into Izmir. They had been riding without a break for nine days, mostly without food because the fleeing Greeks had burned villages and food supplies as they retreated.

"Men and horses looked spectral," Halide Edib wrote. "Not one ounce of flesh was visible on either."

The next day, wearing civilian clothes and riding in an open car, the

Gazi himself arrived in Izmir, where the town's Turkish population welcomed him with jubilant, delirious cheers. Much of the city, though, was in bloody chaos. Communal hatred had risen to a fever pitch. Muslims who had watched their brethren killed by Greek and Armenian thugs surged out of their homes and began killing Greeks and Armenians in revenge. The Greek Orthodox archbishop, who was closely identified with the occupation, was mutilated and lynched. Tens of thousands of Christians raced frantically toward the harbor, where Allied ships lay at anchor. As if to complete the hellish scene, fire broke out and swept across the city.

"The surface of the sea shone like burning copper," wrote a newspaper correspondent who watched from a British warship. "Twenty distinct volcanoes of raging flame were throwing up jagged, writhing tongues to a height of a hundred feet. The towers of the Greek churches, the domes of the mosques, the flat roofs of the houses, were silhouetted against a curtain of flame."

Over the hours that followed, more than two hundred thousand men, women, and children—the majority of Izmir's population—were evacuated to Greece. The Greeks were stunned. So were the British. No one had believed the Turks capable of such a victory.

British diplomats were under orders to avoid any contact with Mustafa Kemal, but the British consul in Izmir ran into him on a street soon after his victory. The consul told him that since Britain and Turkey were still technically at war, he had power to arrest any Turk in the city. Kemal was unimpressed.

"Aren't you the people who landed the Greek army in Anatolia?" he asked drily. "We are the people who defeated the Greek army and expelled it from our territory."

The Gazi had been in Izmir only a few days when he learned that a young woman named Latife Uşşaki wished to see him. At first he put her off, but when he saw that she was young and dressed in modern clothes, he invited her in. She turned out to be the vivaciously intelligent daughter of a local businessman, fluent in French and English, who was on a break from law school in France. Besides that, she was a zealous Turkish patriot who wore Kemal's picture in a locket. They talked at length. Later he accepted her invitation to move his headquarters to her family's home outside the city. She became his secretary and companion.

"In her forceful style she looked after his health and domestic comfort," wrote Lord Kinross. "She stimulated his mind with her fluent talk, her arguments, her advice, her ideas born of a wide European culture. Here was a woman to whom he could talk as to few of the men around him. It was a relationship he had tasted before . . . with such European women as Corinne Lütfü. . . . But Latife was of his own race, and she stirred his blood as the others had done only perfunctorily. . . . Used to women who were 'available,' who yielded easily, he made vigorous advances. But she firmly resisted him. She might become his wife, but would not become his mistress. She was an emancipated woman. Such were her principles."

Negotiating with the British would be easier. Lloyd George responded to the disaster at Izmir by vowing that Britain would never "run away from Mustafa Kemal." Many of his countrymen, however, wanted to do just that. A *Daily Mail* headline captured the public mood: "Stop This New War!" Lloyd George pressed ahead anyway. The political backlash brought down his government.

Five years after Allied warships sailed triumphantly into Istanbul, the British realized that they were not going to rule over the Turks after all.

The Gazi sent one of his confidants, Refet Bele, who held the post of prime minister in the revolutionary regime, to Istanbul with a message for Sultan Vahdeddin. They met at the sultan's Swiss-style pavilion on the grounds of Yildiz Palace, perched on a hill above the Bosphorus. Refet found the old man pale and frightened.

"Sir, the present situation cannot continue," Refet told him. "We cannot have two governments in Turkey, one in Istanbul and the other in Ankara. I come to beg you to bow before the force of events and put an end to this dualism, which is contrary to the interests of the nation, by requiring your government to resign."

The sultan demurred; he was "far from our way of thinking," Refet reported in a telegram to Ankara. That was all Kemal needed to hear.

He convened the Grand National Assembly and demanded that it take an unfathomably radical step: separate the sultanate from the Islamic caliphate, which had for centuries been vested in the same sovereign; abolish the sultanate; and give the position of caliph to "that member of the Ottoman family who is most qualified by learning and character." Some deputies protested. The idea of a Turkish state without a sultan was more than they could grasp.

Kemal replied with a tart summary of Turkish history and the lesson it had taught him.

"Gentlemen, sovereignty and the Sultanate are not given to anyone because scholarship proves that they should be," he told his fellow deputies. "Sovereignty and the Sultanate are taken by strength, by power and by force. It was by force that the sons of Osman seized the sovereignty and Sultanate of the Turkish nation. They have maintained this usurpation for six centuries. Now the Turkish nation has rebelled and has put a stop to these usurpers, and has effectively taken sovereignty and the Sultanate into its own hands. This is an accomplished fact. . . . The only remaining question is how to give expression to it."

Not all deputies agreed. A nation familiar only with the Ottoman monarchy, some argued, should not be forced to abolish it so suddenly without knowing what would replace it. Debate became heated. Sensing the current against him, Kemal huddled with his supporters at one side of the chamber. Then he took the floor and called for an immediate vote—by acclamation. That set off howls of protest.

"Several deputies demanded a vote by name," according to one account. "Mustafa Kemal refused to agree. His followers were armed; some of them were capable of any action; they would shoot if he ordered it. 'I am sure the House will be unanimous in accepting,' he said with a threat in his voice, and his followers shifted their revolvers in their cases. The [assembly] president, with one eye on Mustafa Kemal, put the motion. A few hands went up. 'Carried unanimously!' said the president. A dozen deputies leaped onto benches to protest. 'It is untrue! I am against it!' Others shouted and catcalled 'Sit down! Shut up! Pigs! Swine!'; spat filth and abuse at each other. There was pandemonium. At a nod from Mustafa Kemal, the president repeated his decision, shouting above the uproar ... and closed the Assembly. Surrounded by his followers, Mustafa Kemal left the chamber."

Upon learning that revolutionaries in Ankara had abolished his job, the disoriented sultan summoned Sir Horace Rumbold, the British high commissioner, and asked for advice. Sir Horace told him as delicately as possible that the British had no choice but to begin dealing with the victorious Ankara regime.

This was the end.

On November 10, 1922, the sultan sent a message to Sir Horace saying he wished to flee. At six o'clock the next morning, under a driving rain, a British ambulance arrived at Yildiz Palace and the sultan—described in different accounts as "the mere ghost of a monarch" and "dull and lifeless as an automaton"—stepped in. He was brought downhill to the shore of the Bosphorus and ferried by motor launch to a British battleship, the HMS *Malaya*. Her captain set a course for Malta. As Istanbul faded in the distance, the Ottoman sultanate came to an end after 634 years.

"Away with dreams and shadows!" the Gazi cried out after hearing this news. "I have banished the sultan and the rottenness of the Ottoman Empire."

Revolutionary leaders had considered arresting the sultan, but his departure was a better solution. After learning of it, Refet set off on his next piece of business. He called on one of the sultan's cousins, Prince Abdul Mecit, a painter, musician, and landscape gardener who had been excluded from politics because his family feared his liberal instincts, and asked him to become Caliph of All Islam. He agreed, and took office the following Friday. Instead of a traditional robe and sword, he wore a Western-style coat. The only music played at the ceremony was the newly composed Independence Anthem. A mullah chanted prayers, but in Turkish rather than the traditional Arabic.

Not content with shaking the Muslim world this way, Kemal also made a dramatic personal choice. On a January day in 1923, four months after meeting Latife, he announced to her that they must marry immediately—that afternoon. She managed to win a two-day extension.

The ceremony was simple, with Kazim Karabekir and a handful of the Gazi's other close comrades as witnesses. Both partners shared a fervent passion for the epochal project of modernizing Turkey, so they seemed well matched. But there was a large age gap between them—she was twenty-four, he was forty-two—and years as a hard-living bachelor and brusque military commander made him a less than ideal husband.

"Mustafa Kemal seems at no point to have seen Latife as an individual but to have viewed her as a token of his success," according to one biography. "She surely took great pleasure in marriage to her idealized hero, but had little or no desire to know him as a human being."

The two were married as Kemal was preparing to send a delegation to secure a final peace with Britain. Turkish triumphs on the battlefield had killed the hated Sèvres Treaty, and the Turks proposed that the former belligerents meet at Izmir to negotiate a new one. Lord Curzon, however, refused to hold talks on Turkish soil. Negotiators finally agreed to meet in the Swiss town of Lausanne. Ismet Pasha, leader of the Turkish delegation, was in a strong position. Turks had won their Independence War, and with it the right to dictate peace terms.

On July 24, 1923, reluctantly recognizing this reality, Britain agreed to accept the Lausanne Treaty, which gave Turks their prize: absolute control over all of Anatolia. They relinquished sovereignty over most Aegean islands near their coast and did not press Turkey's claim to the region around Mosul, which later became part of Iraq. Instead Turkey took a chunk of eastern Thrace, and with it a foothold in Europe.

The last Allied soldiers sailed from Istanbul on October 2, 1923. Behind them they left a nation devastated and torn from its roots, but free of foreign power and ready to remake itself. The world had tried to wrest the Turks' homeland away from them. To the world's shock, the Turks rebelled and triumphed.

"They think that this is the end, that I have reached my goal," the Gazi told a friend after the Independence War was won. "But it is only now that our real work is beginning."

3

WE HAVE NO CHOICE BUT TO CATCH UP

Cannon fire awoke millions of Turks before dawn on October 30, 1923. The volleys that shattered that darkness heralded the rising of a sun that had never before shone over Muslims. From the ruins of the Ottoman Empire, a nation unlike any in Islamic history had just been born.

A few hours earlier in Ankara, Gazi Mustafa Kemal, hero of the Independence War, had stunned the Grand National Assembly by announcing a decision he had made years earlier but kept secret until that moment. If Turks were to join the modern world, he said, they must have a modern political system. That required amending the constitution. He suggested how.

"The form of government of the state of Turkey is a Republic," Kemal's proposed amendment said. "The President of the Republic of Turkey is elected by the Grand National Assembly."

There had been rumors that the Gazi would take this radical step, but nonetheless it was profoundly shocking. Turks had been conditioned by centuries of fealty to the sultan. After the Ottoman dynasty was deposed, most assumed that a new one would take its place. They had fought the Independence War to expel foreigners, not to establish a republic. Few wanted it. Some considered the idea anti-Islamic. Mustafa

Kemal ignored them all. With a deft series of maneuvers, he pushed his amendment through the confused assembly.

This brought to life the first republic ever established in a Muslim country.

As soon as it was decided that Turkey would have a president, everyone understood who the first one would be. Mustafa Kemal was the only candidate. The tally was 158 votes for Kemal, none for anyone else, and, remarkably, over 100 abstentions. Many deputies feared what lay ahead. But Kemal was the preeminent Turkish hero, and his compatriots were ready to follow wherever he led.

As for the people's will, it mattered not a bit to Kemal. Only a tiny percentage of the Turkish population supported the radical project he envisioned. He didn't care; he knew what the Turks had to do and was determined to make them do it. The slogan of his Republican People's Party was "For the People, in Spite of the People."

In a brief speech after being elected president, Kemal promised that the Republic of Turkey would be "fortunate, successful and victorious." Then he ordered that news of these great events be flashed across the country by telegraph and that the people be awoken by hundred-gun salutes welcoming the new age.

Few Turks could grasp what this sudden change meant. A traveler who passed through Anatolia soon after the republic was proclaimed wrote that he was approached after dinner one night by a group of villagers who wished to ask him "a few questions."

> One of them said: "We have heard that the victorious Turkish Army has entered Istanbul. What has happened to our Sultan?"
>
> "He abdicated," I said, "and left Istanbul on a British warship."
>
> A deep silence followed, the villagers pondering over what I had said. "Who will be the Sultan, then?"
>
> "There will be no Sultan, only a Caliph, and he is the Sultan's Cousin, Abdul Mecit."
>
> "But how is it possible for the country to be without a sultan?"
>
> "There will be a Republic."

"What is that!" I tried to explain it to them, but they did not or did not want to understand, and kept on saying: "But without a Sultan, there could not be a State!"

As Kemal took power in Turkey, Reza was consolidating his hold over Iran. Becoming prime minister had not satisfied him. He set his sights on the ruling Qajar dynasty, which he despised as intensely as Kemal had despised the Ottomans. At the end of 1923 he forced Ahmad Shah, an obese simpleton, to leave on a trip to Europe. All understood that he would never return.

By a remarkable quirk of history—though not by accident—both Turkey and Iran produced in the early 1920s leaders obsessed with the idea of secular modernity. They were part of the same nation-building wave that in the previous century had produced Bismarck's Germany, Cavour's Italy, and Meiji Japan. The sweeping transformations they directed, utterly unlike anything ever seen in the Islamic world, ripped the Turks and the Iranians from their Middle Eastern roots and pulled them into the twentieth century while the people of other nations in the region remained trapped in tradition and obedience.

"The civilized world is far ahead of us," Kemal told one of the many audiences he addressed in Turkish towns during his first years in power. "We have no choice but to catch up."

Kemal's decision to turn Turkey into a republic inspired Reza to try the same in Iran. He bribed and cajoled members of Parliament to win their support, and even commissioned writers and cartoonists to publish works sympathetic to the republican ideal. One poem included this couplet:

The beloved face of Freedom encompassed by black hair,
What force can lure her from seclusion but that of the Republic?

Before the new Republic of Iran could be called into being, however, shocking news came from Turkey: President Mustafa Kemal had abolished the Islamic caliphate and sent the caliph into exile. He had done it almost nonchalantly, by slipping the necessary laws through his compliant Grand National Assembly. Afterward he said the new laws represented "the will of the nation," and that therefore there was "no need to look at them as something extraordinary." From Iran, though, they seemed an unimaginable use of political power—as if a president of Italy had taken it upon himself to abolish the papacy and expel the pope. Iranian mullahs were horrified, and decided they must at all costs prevent the establishment of a republic in their country. They drew twenty thousand angry believers to a protest rally in Tehran, and when Reza appeared and tried to calm them, they pelted him with rocks and sticks. Soon afterward, Reza announced that "it would be better for the welfare of the country if all efforts to promote a republican form of government were halted."

If there would be no Republic of Iran, how would the country be governed? Reza had an answer: make me king. Parliament hesitated, but saw no alternative. Iran was collapsing and Reza seemed its only hope. With only four dissenting votes—one of them cast by the Swiss-educated lawyer Mohammad Mossadegh, who warned that giving so much power to one man would make Iran "more backward than Zanzibar"—Parliament agreed to abolish the 132-year-old Qajar dynasty and place Reza on the Peacock Throne.

This vote brought the new monarch, in a carriage pulled by six white horses, to his coronation at Gulistan Palace in Tehran late on the afternoon of April 25, 1926.

Shahs had for centuries been girded in a ceremony suffused with Islamic tradition, but Reza scorned that tradition and wanted a Western-style coronation. No Iranian knew how to stage one, so Reza assigned his closest adviser, the worldly sophisticate Abdol-Hussein Teymurtash, to find out. Teymurtash, in turn, consulted two doyennes of the expatriate community, Lady Loraine, the wife of the British ambassador, and Vita Sackville-West, the wife of another British diplomat, the brilliant Sir Harold Nicolson. They were brought to view the crown jewels of the deposed Qajars and could not restrain themselves from plunging their arms into heaps of them.

"Linen bags vomited emeralds and pearls," Sackville-West wrote. "The table became a sea of precious stones."

Guided by these two accomplished women, and by accounts of European coronations that he solicited from the British, Spanish, Belgian, and Swedish embassies, Teymurtash choreographed an elaborate ceremony. Reza rode through streets decorated with his portrait, waving to cheering crowds. When he arrived at the palace, trumpets sounded. Tribal leaders, generals, and foreign envoys bowed to greet him. They brought gifts ranging from a jewel-studded polo mallet to a photo of President Calvin Coolidge framed in gold.

Reza cut a commanding figure as he walked slowly into the ornate Audience Hall. A sash laden with glittering medals crossed his chest, and a pearl-encrusted cape covered his broad shoulders. The world's largest unflawed diamond glistened from his plumed cap.

He stopped briefly before the throne—inlaid with gold, studded with gems, and hung with strings of emeralds—and then sat down. Teymurtash approached. In his hands he held a red plush cushion on which rested a new crown, made in Russia and modeled after one that Persian emperors had worn in pre-Islamic times. Reza removed his cap, took the crown in his hands, placed it on his head, and proclaimed himself Shah of Shahs and Light of the Aryans—though not, as past kings had, Shadow of the Almighty, Vice-Regent of God, and Center of the Universe.

"I must make known my wish for fundamental reform in our country," he said in a brief speech after crowning himself. "No allowance of any kind will be made for inaction or hesitation."

Like most people in the Middle East at that time, Reza had no surname. Now that he was founding a dynasty, he needed one. He chose Pahlavi, the name of an ancient Persian dialect and also a word that connotes heroic strength.

"We now have as king of Persia a man who, notwithstanding his humble origin, his total lack of Western education, and his inexperience of conditions in any country but his own, has some elements of real greatness," wrote Sir Percy Loraine, the British ambassador, after the coronation. "I am not blind to his shortcomings nor dazzled by his personal success, but I do feel convinced that he is the one man able to put the affairs of this country in order."

President Mustafa Kemal and Reza Shah took over wretched, miserably poor countries. World War I and the attendant shocks of famine, disease, and communal violence had devastated their social fabrics and killed one-fourth of their people. Nearly everyone in both countries was an illiterate peasant. Religious orthodoxy permeated both societies. Automobiles and streetlights had begun appearing in Istanbul and Tehran, but most Turks and Iranians knew nothing of the outside world.

This was an era of political as well as social upheaval. Empires were collapsing, and new orders were emerging from their ruins. Democracy had proved unable to tame turbulent societies, and the idea of dictatorship was ascendant. It was the age of Hitler and Mussolini, Franco and Salazar, Lenin and Stalin.

Two realities—their countries' backwardness and their belief in strongman rule—shaped the regimes of Mustafa Kemal and Reza Shah. From early youth, both had been gripped by the belief that fate had marked them for greatness. In power they were driven almost mad by the intensity of their desire to transform their countries.

"History has proven incontrovertibly that success in great enterprises requires the presence of a leader of unshakable capacity and power," Kemal said in a speech after taking power.

Reza put it somewhat differently. "I am not an ordinary man who is satisfied with eating and drinking," he told a friend. "Whenever I thought I was not accomplishing something, I felt ill."

In their personal habits, the two men could not have been more different. Kemal was an alcoholic and compulsive womanizer; Zsa Zsa Gabor, who claimed to have had a liaison with him while visiting Istanbul as a teenager, wrote that she never saw him without a drink nearby. Although tending to melancholy in private, he was ebullient. He smiled often and gave long, folksy speeches. He wanted Turks to love him, and they did.

Kemal was also a dandy who had delicate hands and wore *crêpe de Chine* underwear from France. He had taken the waters at Carlsbad and stayed at the Adlon Hotel in Berlin. He may not have been a true European sophisticate, but he imagined himself so.

A normal night for Kemal involved carousing until dawn; for Reza it meant going to bed early and rising before the sun. Kemal was so predatory that some men sought to keep their wives and daughters away from him. Reza had a sober family life and never entertained. He was a man of few words—stern, prudish, and austere. He wanted only to be feared, and was.

As these two men set off on their life work, Kemal had four advantages:

- He was widely read, thoughtful, worldly, statesmanlike, and a master strategist; Reza was rough, uneducated, and tempestuous.
- The Turks had been on the path toward modernity far longer than the Iranians, and had advanced further.
- Turkey had thrown off foreign domination and was fully independent; Iran remained a quasi-colony of Britain.
- What Reza called "the dark forces of religious fanaticism" were stronger in Iran.

No leader in modern history attacked religious power as mercilessly as Mustafa Kemal did after becoming president of Turkey in 1923. By abolishing the caliphate he showed how little he esteemed Islam's most sacred institutions. Then he ordered all Koran schools and religious academies closed, and placed the entire education system under state control. Pilgrimages to the tombs of Muslim saints were forbidden. Religious courts were shut down and the Swiss codes of civil, criminal, and penal law were enacted to replace the Muslim code of *sharia*. Dervish sects, some of them the embodiment of rich Sufi traditions, were outlawed. Sunday replaced Friday as the official day of rest. The twelve-month Christian calendar replaced the Muslim lunar calendar, and the twenty-four-hour clock replaced prayer-oriented timekeeping. Muezzins were ordered to chant their call to prayer in Turkish instead of Arabic. Alcohol was fully legalized.

"Islam, this absurd theology of an immoral Bedouin, is a rotting corpse that poisons our lives!" Kemal railed in one speech as his campaign reached a peak.

He was able to get away with such outrageous attacks on religion—and to bring the clergy under state control—because of the nature of Sunni Islam, especially as it had evolved in Turkey. Conditioned by centuries of fealty to the sultan, who held ultimate religious as well as political power, Sunnis in Turkey were in the habit of bowing before the state. Shiite Muslims, who comprise the majority of Iranians, are taught something quite different: that fidelity to religion comes before loyalty to the state, that justice is a higher virtue than obedience, and that the clergy must never bow to temporal power. This allowed Kemal to domesticate the religious establishment in Turkey and prevented Reza from doing so in Iran.

Provocative as Kemal's speeches sometimes were, it was the way he looked that most amazed his people. He dressed completely differently from any Turk they had ever seen: in a suit and tie. In appearance, he was a paragon of the infidel. Turks were just as shocked as Americans would be if their president began showing up for work in a turban and mullah's robe.

One day in the summer of 1925, while visiting the Black Sea town of Kastamonu, the Gazi appeared wearing another novel garment: a bowler hat. In Ottoman society headgear was full of meaning. Men of substance wore the fez, but the fez was associated with the East. Kemal scorned it as "an emblem of ignorance, negligence, fanaticism, and hatred of progress and civilization." He decided that since he was building a society modeled on the West, men should wear hats like those worn in Paris and New York. Wearing a hat with a brim, he also understood, makes it more difficult for a man to pray in the Muslim fashion.

"A civilized, international dress is worthy and appropriate for our nation, and we will wear it," he told the puzzled people of Kastamonu.

"Boots or shoes on our feet, trousers on our legs, shirt and tie, jacket and waistcoat—and of course, to complete these, a cover with a brim on our heads. This head covering is called 'hat.'"

Two days later the Grand National Assembly approved the Hat Reform, under which the fez was banned and civil servants were required to wear bowler hats. Then came a law imposing Western numerals and the metric system. Next was one requiring every Turk to take a surname. Kemal became Atatürk—"father of the Turks." From then on he signed his name "K. Atatürk."

As he looked for Middle Eastern influences to purge from Turkish life, Atatürk quickly focused on Arabic script, which he called "incomprehensible signs." In 1928 he invited a group of writers and linguists to Ankara and gave them an extraordinary task: transliterate the Turkish language into Roman letters. He asked them how long it would take. Their estimates ranged from five to fifteen years.

"It will be done in three months or not at all!" he commanded.

Working on this frantic schedule, scholars designed a new written language. Schoolbooks were rushed into print and children began learning the new letters. The old script was banned, creating a nation of illiterates almost overnight. Academies were opened to teach the new language to adults; one million learned it within a year after the Alphabet Reform.

Reza Shah did not seek to impose a new written language as Atatürk had done, but he fought religious power just as vigorously. Iran's clergy, though, was more powerful than Turkey's and fought back. Clerics blocked or delayed some of Reza's cherished projects. When he ordered that all Iranians be inoculated against smallpox, clerics ruled that good Muslims must refuse inoculation because vaccines made from human cells are *haram*—forbidden by Islamic law. When he tried to close public bath houses, which were rife with disease, and encouraged people to install home showers instead, the clerics also resisted; they asserted that Muslims could be ritually clean only after being fully immersed in water, so showers were also *haram*.

These antagonists—mosque and state—circled around each other until Reza finally exploded. One day in 1928, a mullah in the holy city of Qom reprimanded one of his wives for not covering herself appropriately in a shrine. News of this insult sent Reza into a volcanic rage. He assembled an armored column, rode at its head to Qom, stormed into the mosque without removing his shoes, pummeled the mullah, and then had him arrested.

It was the shock of radical social change, imposed by decree from above, that set off civic rebellions like this in Iran. Comparable rebellions broke out in Turkey. Atatürk crushed them just as ruthlessly.

Most of the close comrades with whom Atatürk waged the Independence War turned against him during his first year in power. In 1924 Kazim Karabekir, who resented being pushed aside as the Gazi centralized power in his own hands, formed an opposition party that demanded "respect for religious opinions and beliefs." Among its other leaders were Ali Fuat, Rauf Orbay, and Refet Bele—meaning that all four of the men with whom Mustafa Kemal signed the Amasya Circular in 1919 had broken with him. The feminist writer Halide Edib, arguably the most brilliant woman of her generation, who had been close to Kemal for years and knew him as well as anyone, also joined the new party.

It survived for just eight months, until a Kurdish revolt broke out in southeastern Turkey. Atatürk, concluding that the country was not ready for competitive politics, ordered the opposition party shut. Karabekir and other party leaders were imprisoned. Halide Edib left the country. All were later rehabilitated—Karabekir and Edib would become members of Parliament—but only after Atatürk's death.

Kurds were already well established in eastern Anatolia when Turkic tribes from Central Asia began arriving in the eleventh century. As a people, they are famous for resisting authority. Many fought in the Independence War after Kemal promised that his new state would respect their traditions.

"Every one of the Muslim elements living within this fatherland has its own specific environment, customs and race," Kemal told Kurdish leaders when he wanted their help. "Privileges related to them have been accepted."

Once in power, though, Atatürk saw the Kurds as a threat to his nation-building project. He cracked down on Kurdish militias and curbed the power of traditional chiefs. At the beginning of 1925, led by a warrior cleric named Sheik Said, the Kurds rebelled. Among their demands were the restoration of the caliphate and the *sharia* legal system.

Rebels briefly held a few towns, but Atatürk flooded the area with troops and soon turned the tide. Sheik Said and his comrades were captured and publicly hanged at Diyarbakir, the main Kurdish town. Soon afterward the government issued an order closing Kurdish newspapers, outlawing the terms "Kurd" and "Kurdistan," banning Kurdish names, and restricting the use of Kurdish languages. The Kurds responded with a string of rebellions.

For all their passionate attachment to the ideals of freedom, Turkish nationalists were uncomfortable with ethnic diversity. In 1915 they saw Armenian rebels as a mortal threat and responded by wiping out a huge and deeply rooted community. In 1923, soon after taking power, they agreed to a "population exchange" under which 1.1 million Ottoman citizens of Greek descent were forced to leave their homes in Anatolia and make their way to Greece, while four hundred thousand Muslims living in Greece trekked in the opposite direction, to Turkey. These campaigns of what would today be called "ethnic cleansing" destroyed a foundation of Anatolian society and immeasurably impoverished the Turkish nation.

The Kurds believed they were simply defending their way of life, but Atatürk saw them the way many people in the United States saw Native Americans: as primitives who needed to be civilized. In Iran, Reza Shah saw his country's nomadic tribes the same way.

"It is not becoming that you, the sons of an ancient nation like Iran with its illustrious history of civilization, should wander over desert and mountain like predatory animals," Reza told the tribesmen in an open letter. "You must give up that nomadic and tent-dwelling life."

Nomads, of course, had no desire to give up the only way of life they had ever known. To Reza this was defiance, and defiance always evoked his most terrible response. He ordered the nomads rounded up and placed in settlement camps where conditions were miserable. Thousands died, including many in mass executions. Clans that resisted were hunted by the army and in some cases bombed from the air. Like the Kurds in Turkey, these nomads were victims of a relentless modernizing campaign in which there was no more room for tribes than there was for dervishes.

These campaigns, waged in the name of "universal civilization," pushed the Turkish and Iranian people in a direction no Muslims had ever gone. Beginning in the 1920s they were forced to add Western ideas to their rich but stagnant traditions. They developed national identities shaped by the Enlightenment as well as Islam. This was a new synthesis. It invigorated Turkey and Iran, and set them starkly apart from the countries around them.

Atatürk was hardly the first reformer in Turkish history. He was heir to a rich tradition that stretched back more than a century. Nonetheless, some found his radicalism unbearable. They could not challenge him politically because he would not tolerate opposition parties. But they might kill him.

Three members of the Grand National Assembly resolved to make an attempt on Atatürk's life on June 15, 1926, when he was to be in Izmir; they would bomb and shoot his car, then flee in a motorboat. By chance Atatürk's visit was postponed by a day, and during that time the hired boatman had a change of heart and told police what was afoot.

During the previous year's Kurdish revolt, the Grand National Assembly had given Atatürk a two-year grant of martial power. In the hours after the assassination plot was discovered he used that power to order a wave of arrests. Some of those detained were conspirators, but dozens of others were simply critics or opposition figures. Many were tried by summary courts called independence tribunals. Eighteen were hanged. Between 1925 and 1927, when he abruptly ordered them dissolved, independence tribunals sent more than five hundred supposed subversives to the gallows. By all accounts the Gazi signed death warrants easily.

"One should not wait before crushing a reactionary movement," he reasoned. "One should act at once."

As he wiped away what he considered the evils of the old order, Atatürk worked eagerly to shape a new one. The number of children in school increased tenfold during his presidency, and schoolteachers were exalted as patriots. For years, though, he could make no progress toward his greatest educational goal: building a European-style university. Turkey did not have nearly enough scholars to comprise a faculty, and few qualified foreigners would come to such a backwater.

That changed dramatically in 1933, after Adolf Hitler took power in Germany and ordered Jews purged from university faculties. Hundreds of the world's most brilliant scholars suddenly found themselves out of work and desperate for refuge. They could not find shelter in other European countries or in the United States, because universities there were also averse to hiring Jews. Atatürk saw his chance. He offered asylum and a teaching position in Turkey to any qualified professor who had been expelled from a research faculty in Germany. Nearly two hundred accepted. Among them were eminent specialists in fields ranging from engineering, medicine, and industrial chemistry to architecture, musicology, and Roman law. They included the city planner and future West Berlin mayor Ernst Reuter, the visionary theater director Carl Ebert, and the psychoanalyst Edith Weigert, who introduced Freudian theory to Turkey. This galaxy of stars became the core of Istanbul University.

"At a stroke, one of the world's most prestigious Teutonic universities was established in Turkey," one historian has written.

Atatürk never showed any antipathy toward Jews; on the contrary, his enemies, pointing to his background in heavily Jewish Salonika, at times spread rumors that he was himself a Jew. He read Hitler's *Mein Kampf* and was repelled by "the meanness of his language and the madness of his thoughts." Yet Turkey's welcome for German Jews in 1933 was the product of a long history, not just one man's instinct.

"I proclaim to you that Turkey is a land wherein nothing is lacking," Rabbi Isaac Sarafatti of Adrianople—now Edirne—wrote to oppressed German Jews five centuries earlier, in 1454. "Here every man may dwell at peace under his own vine and fig tree."

Sixteen years later, by Ottoman edict, Jews exiled by King Ludwig X of Bavaria were welcomed in Turkish cities. When Ferdinand and Isabella expelled Jews from Spain in 1492, more than 150,000 settled in the Ottoman Empire. By the seventeenth century, more Jews lived in Ottoman territory than in the rest of the world combined. Many physicians at the Ottoman court and many leading Ottoman diplomats were Jews. In 1840 Sultan Abdul Mecid, in his capacity as caliph, issued a *firman* officially rejecting the anti-Jewish "blood libel" and ordering that no Jew "be worried and tormented as a consequence of accusations which have not the least foundation in truth."

Only one other Middle Eastern culture can claim as long and friendly a relationship with Jews: Persians. It was Cyrus, the founder of the Persian Empire, who freed the Jews from their Babylonian captivity in 537 BC, allowed them to rebuild the Temple in Jerusalem, and gave them a chance to regroup as a nation. In the Old Testament, Cyrus is praised more highly than any other non-Jewish leader; the prophet Isaiah calls him "my shepherd." During most of the time since then, Iranians have welcomed Jews. Many feel a kinship because both peoples prize learning and draw sustenance from ancient tradition.

Reza Shah, however, shared neither Atatürk's warm feeling for Jews nor his contempt for Hitler. Like many Iranians, he deeply resented Britain and Russia for their pitiless looting of his country. When a force emerged in Germany that opposed both these powers, he was instinctively sympathetic. He admired the order Hitler had brought out of Germany's chaos, and also was attracted by Hitler's belief in the inherent superiority of Aryans, who are said to be ancestors of modern Iranians. The two dictators exchanged friendly notes. Nazi functionaries were welcomed in Tehran. By 1940 half of Iran's foreign trade was with Germany.

Reza would not hire Jewish professors, as Atatürk did, but he was nonetheless deeply impressed by the opening of Istanbul University in 1933. Two years later, in what one account calls "the most significant academic event of the century" in Iran, he laid the cornerstone for Tehran University. The speech he gave that day was one of his concise classics. This is the full text:

"A university should have been established a long time ago. Now that it has begun, all efforts must be made to complete it quickly."

The sprawling university campus was only part of Reza's master plan for Tehran. Whole neighborhoods that he considered unsightly were razed to make way for broad avenues and European-style buildings. Many Qajar monuments fell to his wrecking ball, including the city's intricately tiled ceremonial gates. Dervishes and fortune-tellers were swept away. Ritual slaughter in public was forbidden. Five cinemas were licensed; among the first films they showed were *Tarzan, Ali Baba and the Forty Thieves, The Thief of Baghdad,* and *The Gold Rush*. Restaurants, cafés, boutiques, and bookshops sprouted near these cinemas. Tehran more than doubled in population during Reza's rule, to more than half a million. A thriving university fed a burgeoning middle class. Gramophones were all the rage.

For boys who came from the countryside, Atatürk and Reza had another plan: use compulsory military service as a tool for social transformation. Many recruits arrived not only illiterate but unfamiliar with such refinements as toothbrushes and plumbing. By the time they were released from service, most had become comfortable with modern life. They returned home as missionaries for the new secular culture.

Atatürk and Reza were among the first leaders in Middle Eastern history who believed that girls deserved as much access to education as boys. Restricting women was an ancient part of Muslim and Middle Eastern traditions; Atatürk and Reza hated those traditions, and both became passionate advocates of women's rights.

In the years before World War I, the Young Turks had legalized civil marriage and divorce; Atatürk went further, giving women equal inheritance rights and opening the civil service to them. All schools became coeducational. Beaches were opened to mixed bathing. Female police officers appeared on the streets. In 1930 women were given the right to vote, and in the next election, eighteen women—all handpicked by Atatürk—were elected to the Grand National Assembly.

Although Atatürk exalted women in the abstract, he had trouble with the one he had chosen to share his life. Crowds welcomed Latife warmly when she traveled with the president, and she inspired more than a few Turkish women. Their relationship, however, never took root. Atatürk continued his rough nightlife as if he were still single; Latife would not play the dutiful wife. In 1925, after two and a half years of marriage, he abruptly announced that he was divorcing her. He was able to do it by simply putting her aside, in traditional Muslim fashion, because his law giving women divorce rights would not take effect until several months later.

"I was married," he told a visitor near the end of his life, "but it seems marriage was not made for me."

Reza Shah was, if anything, even more frustrated than Atatürk with the exclusion of women from public life. During his rule, as in Turkey, it became normal for unaccompanied women to walk on streets, ride buses, sit in restaurants, and even pursue university degrees. Under pressure from the clergy he did not grant women the vote, but he legalized civil marriage and divorce, and raised the minimum marriage age for girls from nine, as prescribed in the Koran, to fifteen. There were ten girls' schools in Iran when he came to power; a decade later there were more than eight hundred.

"The women of this country have been isolated from society and prevented from demonstrating their intrinsic abilities," Reza said at the opening of one of his girls' schools. "Now, however, they are going to enjoy social advantages beyond the exalted privilege of motherhood."

Changes in religious and social life, sweeping as they were, could not alone have transformed Turkey and Iran. They also needed something no country in the modern Middle East had ever developed: national economies. Turkey had to start from less than zero, because nearly all of the Armenians and Greeks who had dominated commerce during the Ottoman period were gone. Iran had developed a thriving bazaar culture but not a business class, largely because Britain and Russia dominated its economy so fully that there was little left for the Iranians to do. In both countries, people had to learn modern skills for the first time. Slowly they did. State-owned banks spread credit through the countryside. Power plants, roads, bridges, ports, and railway networks were built. City streets were paved and lit. Yet although the pace of change was dizzying, it was never fast enough for Atatürk or Reza.

"I am always dissatisfied," Reza once lamented. "There is so much to be done, and I cannot do it quickly enough."

In trying to develop Iran, Reza confronted a great obstacle that Atatürk never had to face: foreign intervention. Britain insisted on retaining decisive influence in Iran, for powerful strategic reasons. Iran was a vital part of Britain's land route to India. It shared a long border with the Soviet Union and was vulnerable to Soviet influence. Most important, it produced the oil that fueled the Royal Navy and powered Britain's economy. To keep the oil flowing, Britain needed to control Iran.

Reza's relationship with the British was prickly and difficult. A British officer helped place him in power, but he was above all a nationalist, famous for consulting only Iranian doctors and banning foreign words from street signs. British diplomats treated him as an odd combination of partner and adversary.

"He gets straight to what he has to say, and does not waste time in exchanging the delicately phrased but ultimately futile compliments so dear to the Persian heart," Sir Percy Loraine wrote in a dispatch to London. "An ignorant and uneducated man, nevertheless he betrays no awkwardness of manner, nor self-consciousness. He has considerable natural dignity, and neither his speech nor his features reveal any absence of self-control."

Reza won several concessions from the British, including a slightly improved oil contract. Over strong British protests, he established a National Bank of Iran to replace the British-owned Imperial Bank of Persia. Then he took back control of the post office and telegraph service, which Britain had traditionally run.

"The real cause of the setback to the British position in Persia is due to that spirit of exaggerated—I do not necessarily say unworthy—nationalism which is spreading everywhere," Lord Curzon wrote. "The ferment of these new ideas is at work particularly in the veins of a singularly sensitive and proud people like the Persians, just as it is in other Eastern countries, and you cannot expect in the future—you certainly do not get it now—any of that sort of natural, instinctive, automatic deference to Western ideals and Western opinion to which we were accustomed in olden days."

Reza Shah and Atatürk saw themselves as partners. For years they worked side by side, in countries that share a three-hundred-mile border. But it was not until June 16, 1934, when Reza stepped off a ceremonial train in Ankara, that they met for the first time. Also present, according to one account, was "the entire population of the city."

This was more than a simple state visit. Turkey and Iran sought to establish themselves as modern nation-states—a new phenomenon in the Middle East. The meeting of their leaders was a chance for each country's new order to confer legitimacy on the other. Turkish and Iranian flags were everywhere. National anthems were sung at every stop.

The two leaders watched gymnastics and equestrian competitions, drove through Ankara in an open car, and marched in a military parade with female scouts—an episode that drew fascinated coverage in the Iranian press. Atatürk's biggest surprise for his guest was the world premiere of an opera he had commissioned for the occasion. The opera, called *Özsoy* (*Pure Lineage*), is an ode to the friendship between ancient Persia and ancient Turan, the semi-mythic homeland of the Turks. It was intended not simply to celebrate the long friendship between these peoples—sometimes to the point of exaggeration—but also, as one scholar has written, "to demonstrate to Reza Shah the extent to which Turkey had made the transition to a secular democratic nation."

That night at the opera was supposed to be the last of Reza's visit, but the two men had found much to admire in each other and wanted to spend more time together. Atatürk suggested that they visit western Anatolia, and they set out by train for what became a nine-day tour. At every stop they were warmly welcomed—in the town of Uşak, too warmly for Atatürk's taste. One member of the party later reported what happened:

> The platform was full of people waiting to greet Atatürk and Reza Shah, although it was midnight. Atatürk opened the window, and scores of people tried to seize his hand, the Gazi looking quite pleased by this mark of his popularity. Then suddenly his face became flushed with anger, and snatching back his hand, he shouted in a terrible voice, "How dare this so-and-so damned fellow try to touch my hand? He is, like all his kin, the enemy of the people! Take him and destroy him!"
>
> Looking out of the window, I saw a mullah who had had the misfortune of trying to shake Atatürk's hand throwing his turban in the air, and then, plunging into the crowd, he disappeared with a dexterity engendered by fear. People rushed toward the turban, but the man was gone. Atatürk continued to shout: "Tomorrow this town must be razed to the ground! Let the Governor come." The governor, in morning coat with his top hat in hand, was ushered into the carriage, pale and trembling.
>
> "Dismiss him at once!"
>
> "I obey, Pasha, on my head," promptly said Ismet Inönü, writing something in his notebook. Of course the next day nothing happened, but Atatürk had not forgotten the incident, as he ordered that from that day mullahs should be forbidden to wear their clerical clothes outside the mosques, this measure being applied to representatives of other religions as well.

Atatürk took Reza back to Istanbul by sea, so he could point out the Gallipoli Peninsula where he had won his first great battle. Their yacht's arrival at Istanbul was a spectacular affair, complete with huge crowds, fireworks, and a twenty-one-gun salute. Atatürk's final treat for his guest was a gala "Eastern Night" of entertainment featuring nude belly dancers. It was a fitting end for the encounter of two leaders who upset every notion of how Muslim potentates were supposed to behave.

"I admire your sovereign so much that if I had not been President of Turkey, I would go to Iran to serve him as you do," Atatürk told one of Reza's aides before the two men parted. A few hours later, after the farewell, Reza turned to the same aide and said, "We have been privileged to see a very great man."

Reza realized during his visit that despite all he had done to modernize Iran, his country remained far behind Turkey. He returned home more passionately devoted to reform than ever. His first step was to issue a new dress code requiring schoolteachers and the wives of government officials to uncover themselves. Men were required to wear a hat with a brim, not exactly a bowler but a slightly different design that became known as the Pahlavi cap. Reza also issued decrees banning the use of religious titles, opening sacred shrines to non-Muslim visitors, and requiring mourners in mosques to sit on chairs instead of kneeling on carpets.

This campaign mightily upset the faithful. In the summer of 1935, several thousand protesters set up camp inside the shrine at Mashad. For days they listened to speeches in which mullahs denounced "the evil shah." They were testing a violently impatient man. Reza sent soldiers to surround the shrine and, when they were in place, ordered them to open fire. Hundreds inside were killed in what became Reza's best-known atrocity.

Soon afterward, as if to show his redoubled determination, Reza decreed a reform so radical that no leader of a Muslim country, not even Atatürk, had dared to propose it: a total ban on the veil for women. The day it took effect, January 7, 1936, marked a social earthquake of rare intensity. Police officers tore veils off women who appeared in public wearing them. Men on streets were thunderstruck. Some women felt liberated and eagerly adopted Western dress, but others, having never shown their faces to strangers, cloistered themselves at home. The most desperate committed suicide.

. . .

The incandescent energy that propelled Atatürk and Reza through life was too all-consuming to last long. By the time they met in 1934, both men were entering their second decades in unfathomably draining jobs. Lions in winter, their powers were fading. They responded by changing in opposite ways.

Reza spiraled down into murderous paranoia. He terrorized the political class so fully—sometimes knocking his generals and cabinet ministers to the floor with the flat side of his sword before ordering them imprisoned—that no one dared speak plainly to him. He even turned on Abdol-Hussein Teymurtash, his faithful adviser and one of the most brilliant men in Iran. The British, who mistrusted Teymurtash because of his increasing militancy on oil issues, fed Reza rumors that he was plotting a coup, and Reza, his judgment perhaps clouded by increasing opium use, had him arrested. In short order Teymurtash was tried for embezzlement, found guilty, and sentenced to five years in jail. Several months later he died in his cell, evidently killed on the orders of a disturbed tyrant.

As Reza raged, Atatürk gently faded from political life. He allowed his discreet and efficient prime minister, Ismet Inönü—the former Ismet Pasha, his Independence War comrade—to edge him gently toward the status of national icon. Many nights he drank away with a clique of male friends described in newspapers as "the usual group." During daylight hours he pursued private interests. Some were quirky, like his search for proof that Turkish was the "sun language" from which all others emerged. Other were eminently practical, like a model farm he supervised near Ankara. One of the best-known pictures of him from this period shows him on a tractor, wearing a Panama hat. It encapsulates his revolutionary message, but hides the melancholy that enveloped him.

Atatürk's earthshaking years were over. Life no longer offered him the crackling intensity that had set him afire at Gallipoli, at Sakarya, and in the first years of his revolutionary regime. He became tired, introspective, and unhappy.

"I'm bored to tears," he told his private secretary after the Grand

National Assembly elected him president for the fourth time in 1935. "I am usually alone during the day. Everybody is at work, but my work hardly occupies an hour. Then I have the choice of sleeping, if I can, reading or writing something or other. If I want to take the air for a break, I must go by car. And then, it's back to prison, where I play billiards by myself as I wait for dinner. Dinner doesn't bring variety. No matter where it is, it's roughly the same people, the same faces, the same talk. I've had enough."

In 1936 Atatürk's doctors diagnosed the first symptoms of cirrhosis. He took ill, the price for years of excess during which his daily routine included fifteen cups of coffee, three packs of cigarettes, and at least a liter of raki, the anise-flavored liquor he called "lion's milk." In his sickbed he wrote poignant diary entries lamenting his loneliness and wondering whether all he had achieved would prove ephemeral and meaningless. Finally, on November 10, 1938, his overburdened body gave out. He was fifty-seven years old.

The Turks were stunned. Photos and newsreels show them wailing, weeping, and tearing their hair in a veritable orgy of public grief. Hundreds of thousands filed past the Gazi's bier, many collapsing with anguished cries of *Ata! Ata!*—Father! Father! Throngs filled the streets to watch as his body, accompanied by the strains of Chopin's Funeral March, was drawn on a carriage to the Istanbul waterfront. There it was placed on a yacht and brought to the coastal town of Izmit, from which it was borne by slow train across the Anatolian plain to Ankara. Today it lies in a lugubrious mausoleum that is the closest Turkey has to a national temple.

Reza's career ended where it began: with the British. They could not tolerate his evident sympathy for Germany after World War II began, and in the summer of 1941 they and the Soviets invaded Iran, crushing its army in just two days. The British made clear to Reza that he could keep his throne only if he would do their bidding. All understood he would refuse.

"I have devoted all of my energies over the past years to directing the affairs of the nation, and today my strength is exhausted," he wrote

Parliament on September 16. "I therefore abdicate and transmit my powers to my heir and successor."

Later that day, Reza stepped into one of his Rolls-Royce touring cars and set out for the port of Bandar Abbas. On the morning of September 28, after putting on civilian clothes for the first time in his adult life, he boarded a British liner bound for Bombay. He planned to sail from there to Argentina, but the British had other plans. They consigned him to exile in South Africa. There he was unhappy and, before long, sick.

"I would be afraid of death if I had carried out the wishes of foreigners," he said upon learning that British radio stations were speculating on his health. "Since I have not done so, I am not afraid."

Reza died of a heart attack in Johannesburg on July 26, 1944. His body was embalmed and shipped to Egypt. Six years later it was brought to Tehran and buried in an imposing tomb.

The first full-length biography of Atatürk in English appeared in 1932, while he was still at the peak of his power. Its author, H. C. Armstrong, a British officer who had been imprisoned by the Turks during World War I and was later posted to Ankara, concluded that "his dictatorship—a benevolent, educating, guiding dictatorship—was the only form of government possible at the moment." In letters large enough to cover the book's entire back cover, Armstrong described his subject in one long and only slightly hyperbolic sentence: "The study of a MAN, cruel, bitter, iron-willed, who overthrew the Sultan in 1908; battered the British Empire off Gallipoli in 1915; chased the Greeks into the sea at Smyrna in 1922; harried the victorious Allies out of Constantinople in 1923; destroyed the power of the Caliph in 1924; hanged the entire opposition in 1926; and by 1932 had made out of a crumbling empire A NATION."

The Gazi destroyed at least as much as he built. Islam had been a central part of Turkish consciousness for centuries. Arabic script had been the vessel of Turkish intellectual life for just as long. Relations between the sexes had developed over many generations. So had people's loyalty to the sultanate and caliphate. None of this gave Atatürk the slightest pause as he set out to build the nation of his outlandish dreams.

Nonetheless, he was in some ways a conservative. He believed in order, structure, and institutions. Ideas like class warfare and permanent revolution were anathema to him.

Many Turks believe that without Atatürk, the Turkey of today would not exist. History lends weight to this view. Atatürk's extreme goal in the Independence War—to expel the occupiers from all of Anatolia—was not realistic. He imposed it on the nationalist movement by force of will, and then, against all odds, achieved it.

Greatness often settles on figures whose private character matches the needs of their era. The life stories of Christopher Columbus, Martin Luther, and Elizabeth I—as well as those of George Washington, Abraham Lincoln, and Franklin Roosevelt—argue for this thesis. So does Atatürk's.

"Atatürk emerged from his childhood an unusually creative and charismatic, yet seriously disturbed person," according to an article published in *Psychoanalytic Quarterly* half a century after his death. "Turkey's political, sociological and historical position after the First World War provided an ideal fit between Atatürk's grandiosity and capabilities and the nation's need for a God-like father-redeemer."

Yet the year Atatürk took power, 1923, is not year zero in Turkish history. It does not mark the moment when everything changed. Radical as Atatürk's reforms were, he built the Republic of Turkey on a foundation laid by generations of Ottoman reformers. Educated Turks had believed for a century in constitutions, republican government, women's rights, and secularism. Atatürk was the first to turn these ideas into principles of government, but he was hardly the first to embrace them.

In power, Atatürk understood that absolutism leads ultimately to instability, and that even dictatorship should have limits. Reza Shah did not. Atatürk knew that the Turks would one day have to be given political democracy. Reza was obsessed with preserving the Pahlavi dynasty so that his eldest son, Mohammad Reza, could succeed to the throne.

The balance of Reza's achievement is elusive. He took over a disintegrating nation and on its ruins built the foundations of a modern state. His social project, like Atatürk's, was revolutionary. Without him, Iran might never have pursued it—and might not even have survived as a country.

Reza set Iran on the path toward modernity, but he also reinforced a pattern of absolutism that shackled it to the past. He tolerated no dissent or critical thought. Fanatically devoted to the creation of a new state, he failed to do what was necessary to sustain it. He gave lip service to the Constitutional Revolution but rejected its democratic essence.

Both leaders were autocrats and radical reformers. These are the two legacies they left Turkey and Iran. Atatürk, however, built institutions, faded gracefully from power, and set his country on the path to liberation. Reza did not.

In 1938 the American writer John Gunther visited Iran—he called it "the magnificent and impregnable inner fastness of the Moslem world"—and published a vivid essay about Reza Shah in *Harper's*. He reported that Reza "has courage, he has vitality, he has vision.... He wiped out brigandage, which had defaced whole provinces for generations; he gave the land the lifeblood of new roads, new ports and harbors; he reorganized the army, which had been a rabble, on the basis of conscription. He got rid of foreign officers, foreign advisors, and made the army a kind of school.... [He] struck at the power of the church.... Women in the old Persia had about as many rights as cattle, and early in his reign Reza set about emancipating them.... He brought the breath of life into a decaying country."

What inspired Reza to do all of this? Gunther had a simple answer: "Beyond doubt the greatest personal and political influence on the life of the Shah is Mustafa Kemal Atatürk, the dictator of Turkey, whose career he has closely followed. Both have brought new life, new dignity to their peoples. And the careers of both are dominated by a tremendous zest to westernize, to modernize, to break the power of the old corrupt regime."

Both of these leaders restored to disoriented nations a sense of pride, identity, and purpose. Atatürk captured their new self-confidence at a state dinner he gave in 1936 for the visiting British king, Edward VIII. As the two men were chatting, a waiter stumbled and a serving plate crashed to the floor. Atatürk looked up, then turned back to his guest with an apology.

"I have been able to teach the people of this country many things," he said, "but I have not been able to teach them to be good servants."

PART TWO

OUR NAME HAS NOT BEEN AN HONORED ONE

· 4 ·

THIS DIZZY OLD WIZARD

Never were so many Turks so happy to see a war machine as they were when the USS *Missouri*, the world's most famous battleship, dropped anchor at Istanbul on April 5, 1946. Her mighty cannon had rained slaughter on Japanese soldiers across the Pacific, and on her deck, which stretched the length of three football fields, World War II had ended when General Douglas MacArthur accepted Japan's surrender. There were few more potent symbols of American power.

Sending a giant warship to a foreign port is not always the best way to win friends. President Harry Truman, however, had deftly combined the *Missouri*'s political mission with a humanitarian one. It carried the remains of a beloved Turkish diplomat, Munir Ertegun, who had died in Washington while serving as ambassador to the United States. Ertegun was a larger-than-life figure, famous for throwing jazz parties at the Turkish embassy that enraged Southern senators because they featured racially mixed bands; his sons stayed in the United States after his death and went on to found Atlantic Records. Truman's decision to send Ambassador Ertegun's body home on the *Missouri* deeply impressed the Turks. It signaled that the United States not only esteemed them, but would protect them.

"Russia knocks threateningly at the land gates of Turkey," wrote one journalist who covered the *Missouri*'s arrival. "America knocks at the sea gates . . . in a friendly way, and pays a visit, saying, 'Don't be afraid, I'm here.' The Russian shadow is cast over the Balkans. So America comes and tells us, 'Sit tight and don't worry. I'm with you.' The arrival of the *Missouri* is a gesture of good will . . . a symbol of freedom and justice for the whole world."

Less than a year after the war's end, the world was already dividing into new power blocs. Both superpowers, the United States and the Soviet Union, sought influence over smaller countries. Stalin had set out to crush the new democracies in Central Europe, and he decided to try intimidating Turkey as well. He sent President Ismet Inönü, who had assumed the post after Atatürk's death, two demands: Turkey must allow the Soviets to build bases along its strategically priceless straits, and it must also surrender two of its eastern provinces, Kars and Ardahan, which "had been ceded to Turkey at a time of weakness." To emphasize his seriousness, he moved Red Army units in Bulgaria and the Caucasus toward Turkey's borders.

These demands, coming as the Soviets were supporting communist guerrillas in Greece, led Western leaders to conclude that a vital region of the world was in danger of falling into Moscow's orbit. Speaking at Westminster College in Fulton, Missouri, on March 6, 1946, with Truman at his side, former British prime minister Winston Churchill warned that an "iron curtain" was falling across Europe. Truman heard what Churchill did not say: Britain was a declining imperial power and could no longer shape world events. Someone else had to.

Four weeks later, the *Missouri* arrived in Istanbul. Nineteen of its big guns boomed as the casket containing Ambassador Ertegun's body was lowered onto a Turkish patrol boat. From there it was brought ashore, placed on a ceremonial carriage, and slowly drawn by two horses past hushed crowds. Officers of the United States Navy marched with Turkish soldiers in the honor guard.

During the Atatürk era, Turkey had remained studiously neutral in regional and global politics. President Inönü kept Turkey neutral for most of World War II and hoped to keep it so indefinitely. The harsh reality of the cold war made that impossible.

Russia had been Turkey's chief enemy for generations; by one count, the two countries fought thirteen wars between 1600 and 1900. Czars recognized that control of the Turkish straits would give Russian ships free passage to the Mediterranean, that the Turkish coasts offered magnificent warm-water ports, and that dominating Turkey would allow them to turn the Black Sea into a Russian lake. Stalin too grasped all of this. It was logical that as the postwar world was taking shape, he would try to make Turkey a vassal state.

As Stalin pressured Turkey, he also tried to bend Iran to his will. Iran too has warm-water ports, and although its geography does not allow access to the Mediterranean, as Turkey's does, it has a strategic asset of equal magnitude: oil. That made it another logical target for Stalin.

Allied leaders had agreed during the war to withdraw all their troops from Iran six months after hostilities ended. When the deadline came, Stalin hesitated. His agents had taken control of Iran's northernmost region, Azerbaijan, and installed a Communist government there. Soon it became clear that Stalin wished to hold Azerbaijan and use it as a base from which to subvert the rest of Iran.

In his famous "long telegram" from Moscow, written at the beginning of 1946, the American diplomat George Kennan warned President Truman that the Soviets were casting covetous eyes on Iran and Turkey. Days after reading it, Truman sent the *Missouri* to Istanbul. Then he dispatched a new ambassador to Iran, with instructions to support its government against Soviet claims. Britain, which considered Iran a quasi-colony, also urged Iranian leaders to resist. That allowed Prime Minister Ahmad Qavam, a highly skilled diplomat, to negotiate a deal with Stalin under which the Red Army withdrew from Iran. Qavam accomplished this by a deft combination of threat—he warned that he would send Iranian soldiers to fight the Soviets—and the promise of reward in the form of an oil concession.

This was the only time Stalin pulled troops out of a neighboring country as a result of diplomacy. His decision to do so, according to a dispatch from the American ambassador in Tehran, stemmed "from internal considerations in USSR, from broader questions of foreign policy connected with Europe, from fear of [United Nations] and world opinion censure, or a combination of all of them." After the withdrawal, Qavam dutifully asked Parliament to approve the oil concession he had promised the Soviets. By a vote of 102 to 2, Parliament refused. Stalin was angry but did not strike back.

After this success in Iran, the Americans concentrated on Turkey. During the late 1940s Turkey received nearly $200 million in American military and economic aid. Stalin, who was intently focused on subverting Central Europe, finally concluded that Turkey, like Iran, was not worth fighting for, and he dropped his overreaching demands.

Stalin tried to rob Turkey and Iran of their independence and pull them into the Soviet bloc. Decisive action by the United States helped foil him. For this, the Turks and Iranians were immensely grateful. Many felt an admiration bordering on awe for Americans and their country.

Turkey and Iran became America's partners. Here lie the roots of this "power triangle."

Simply embracing the United States as a strategic partner was not enough for the Turks and Iranians. They also admired American democracy and wanted some version of it for themselves. Atatürk and Reza Shah had given them social and cultural freedoms that few Muslims in history had enjoyed. Now they wanted political freedom as well. Many had accepted the need for autocracy during the nation-building period, but by mid-century that time was past.

Help Wanted: New King of Iran to Replace Abdicated Reza Shah. No political power, but full access to palaces and crown jewels. Royal ancestry helpful. Must be willing to do the bidding of occupying armies. Potential for advancement if well behaved.

If there were a journal for exiled royalty, the British might have placed that advertisement in the classified section after forcing Reza from power in 1941. Iran needed a symbolic leader; the British took it upon themselves to find one. First they considered a Qajar prince who lived in London, but ruled him out after discovering that he could not speak Persian. In the end they settled on Reza's twenty-one-year-old son and chosen heir, Mohammad Reza, whom they found living a playboy's life in Europe.

"He is not credited with much strength of character, which if true may suit the present circumstance," wrote the British military attaché in Tehran after Mohammad Reza was installed in a low-key ceremony. "If unsuitable, [he] can be gotten rid of later. In the meantime it should be possible to prevent him from doing much harm."

Once the war ended, the Iranians were once again free to practice politics. Mohammad Reza Shah felt the pull of ambition. He dreamed of reestablishing a royal dictatorship like his father's. Many Iranians, however, wanted the opposite: the democracy for which they had been waiting since the Constitutional Revolution. None wanted it more fervently than Mohammad Mossadegh.

This elderly aristocrat would become the shah's nemesis. Then he would go on to shake the world as no Iranian had for centuries.

Mossadegh's father had served as Iran's finance minister for thirty years. His mother was a princess from the deposed Qajar dynasty. Although full of eccentricities, he had an exceedingly sharp mind. He was the first Iranian to win a doctorate of law from a European university. After returning to Iran, he held a series of government posts and won a reputation for brilliance and integrity. In 1925 he was one of four members of Parliament to vote against Reza's proposal that he be made king. Reza tolerated him for a while, but they could not reconcile. In the 1928 election Reza arranged for him to lose his seat.

For the next twenty years Mossadegh lived quietly in his home village, Ahmadabad, fifty miles west of Tehran. He read law books and served as a benign overlord for several hundred peasants. A once-promising political career seemed over.

With Reza Shah gone and World War II over, a new sense of possibility surged through Iran. People clamored for democracy. Many remembered Mossadegh as its champion in the face of Reza's dictatorship, and they turned to him. In 1946, 1948, and 1950, they elected him to Parliament with more votes than any other candidate.

The young firebrand had become an old one, but "Old Mossy," as the American press called him, was as erudite and passionate as ever. Tall and gaunt—he was said to subsist mainly on tea and pistachio nuts—he had long arms, shoulders that slumped as if weighed down with his country's burdens, deep-set eyes, a bald head, and an enormous nose that enemies compared to a vulture's beak. He had a weak constitution and was often ill. Sometimes he received visitors while in bed.

Tears would roll down Mossadegh's cheeks when he made emotional speeches in Parliament lamenting his people's backwardness. A few times he even swooned and collapsed; *Newsweek* called him a "fainting fanatic." He was highly theatrical, and at least some of his illnesses and attacks may have had nonmedical causes. The Iranians felt that he not only understood but shared their suffering. By the early 1950s he was the country's most popular figure—a passionate speaker, an uncompromising democrat, a fierce advocate of national independence, Iran's most highly educated citizen, and one of its most scrupulously honest.

In his speeches, Mossadegh always returned to his two central beliefs. First, the shah must be only a symbol of the nation, like the Queen of England, and not hold political power. Second, Iran must take back its oil.

Iran had become one of the world's largest oil producers, but nearly all the profit went to the Anglo-Iranian Oil Company—formerly Anglo-Persian, renamed at Reza Shah's insistence—and its principal owner, the British government. At mid-century, finally free of foreign occupation, the Iranians focused on this injustice as the essential fact of their national life.

Mossadegh was chairman of the Oil Committee in Parliament, and he gave speech after tempestuous speech denouncing Anglo-Iranian. When an American oil company, Aramco, made a fifty-fifty deal with nearby Saudi Arabia—half the profits from Saudi oil would go to the government and half to the company—Iranians demanded the same. The British refused to raise Iran's 16 percent share.

On April 28, 1951, as Iran's pomegranate trees were bursting into splendid bloom, Parliament met to elect a new prime minister; the previous incumbent had been assassinated by nationalists who considered him a British stooge. By a vote of 79 to 12, the deputies chose Mossadegh. He was the chamber's tallest, best educated, and most respected member—and also the embodiment of Iran's determination to take back its oil.

Immediately after his election, Mossadegh asked Parliament to approve a resolution supporting nationalization of the Anglo-Iranian Oil Company. Approval was unanimous. That set the stage for a confrontation whose effects would reverberate through the rest of the twentieth century and beyond.

The British had controlled events in Iran for generations, and at first they did not grasp what Parliament had done. Only slowly did they begin to sense that this time, the Iranians were serious. Mossadegh could not be bribed or otherwise intimidated. Britain had just been forced to withdraw from India, the erstwhile jewel in its imperial crown, and now faced the prospect of losing its most lucrative asset anywhere in the world. British leaders—especially the lifelong imperialist Winston Churchill, who returned to power in 1951—could not accept such a loss.

To prevent Iran from reclaiming its oil, the British took an escalating series of steps:

- They ordered all British technicians at the sprawling Abadan refinery to return home.
- They mounted a global campaign to assure that oil technicians from other countries could not travel to Iran.
- They persuaded oil companies in other countries, including the United States, to refuse to buy any oil Iran might produce.
- They imposed a naval blockade around Abadan to prevent tankers from entering to pick up oil.

- They froze Iran's hard-currency accounts in London and stopped exporting sugar, steel, and other key commodities to Iran.
- They asked the United Nations and the World Court to order Iran to hand back the oil company.

These measures brought hard times to Iran. The giant pumps at Abadan fell silent. Prices rose, jobs evaporated, and food became hard to find. Nonetheless Mossadegh did not budge. Neither did the Iranian people. Many, responding in part to the Shiite Muslim belief that nothing is more blissful than to suffer in a just cause, reacted to British pressure by supporting nationalization more fervently than ever.

For a time the British toyed with the idea of invading Iran and seizing its oil fields by force. When they asked President Truman for his support, however, he refused and warned the British not to try.

Truman attempted several times to mediate between Mossadegh and what he called "the block headed British." He failed because this dispute was in its essence not political but emotional, cultural, psychological, even spiritual. History had not prepared either side to compromise. The British, conditioned by centuries of colonial mastery, could not fathom the idea of giving natives something valuable that they wished to keep for themselves. The Iranians, for their part, were taking revenge for centuries of humiliation. Many believed that any concession to foreign power was treason.

"The oil resource of Iran, like its soil, its rivers and mountains, is the property of the people of Iran," Mossadegh told the United Nations Security Council in his historic defense on October 15, 1951. "They alone have authority to decide what shall be done with it."

Swayed by Mossadegh's appeal, the Security Council refused to censure, pressure, or sanction Iran. This was an unprecedented defeat for Britain. It made Mossadegh a world figure of the first rank. *Time* chose him as its Man of the Year for 1951, "not that he was the best or the worst or the strongest, but because his rapid advance from obscurity was attended by the greatest stir."

The stir was not only on the surface of events: in his strange way, this strange old man represented one of the most profound problems of his time. Around this dizzy old wizard swirled a crisis of human destiny. There were millions inside and outside of Iran whom Mossadegh symbolized and spoke for, and whose fanatical state of mind he had helped to create. They would rather see their own nation fall apart than continue their present relations with the West.... Mossadegh does not promise his country a way out of this nearly hopeless situation. He would rather see the ruin of Iran than give in to the British.

Unable to bludgeon Mossadegh into submission, the British decided to overthrow him. Their strategy was simple: bribe members of Iran's Parliament into supporting a no-confidence vote. Their agents began discreetly passing money around, but not discreetly enough. Mossadegh learned of their plot. He responded by closing the British embassy and sending all British diplomats home. Among these "diplomats" were the secret agents who had been assigned to overthrow him.

In desperation, Churchill turned to Truman. Could the Central Intelligence Agency, he asked, overthrow Mossadegh as a favor to an old ally?

The CIA was just five years old and had never overthrown a government. Truman was reluctant to give it too much power. Besides, he blamed British pigheadedness for the crisis in Iran. The CIA, he told Churchill, would not help.

Now the British were truly out of options. Their pressure campaign had failed to shake Mossadegh, they had no agents in place who could overthrow him, and the Americans would not help. They were at their wits' end when Kermit Roosevelt, chief of Mideast operations for the CIA, stopped in London for a chat with his counterparts in the Secret Intelligence Service. They asked him if there was any hope of the Americans reversing their position and agreeing to overthrow Mossadegh.

"I told my British colleagues we had, I felt sure, no chance to win approval of the outgoing administration," Roosevelt wrote years later. "The new Republicans, however, might be quite different."

The election of November 1952 had brought Dwight Eisenhower to power, and with him two brothers who would fundamentally reshape America's approach to the world. John Foster Dulles, who had spent decades as a highly paid lawyer for multinational corporations, became secretary of state. Allen Dulles, five years younger, ran the CIA. This was the first and only time that siblings ran the overt and covert sides of American foreign policy.

Truman had been sympathetic to rising nationalism in poor countries; Eisenhower and the Dulles brothers saw those countries only as bit players in the global cold war drama. They considered any government not fully aligned with the West—and certainly any that dared to nationalize a Western corporation—an enemy to be crushed. This gave the British their chance. They sent an envoy to meet with officials of the incoming administration. Cleverly analyzing the new political landscape in Washington, the envoy decided not to lay out the old British case—Mossadegh must be deposed because he had seized a British oil company—but a new one: Mossadegh was too weak to resist a Communist coup, and must be deposed before the Communists struck.

At this moment the United States was gripped by cold war fears. Soviet forces had crushed democracies in Central Europe and tried to starve West Berlin. Communists had seized power in China. In Korea, Communist soldiers were killing Americans. Communist candidates were winning elections in France and Italy. Senator Joseph McCarthy was telling Americans that their own government was riddled with Communists. In this climate, the British idea of a strike against Mossadegh was an easy sell. Eisenhower agreed to send the CIA to do the deed.

"So this is how we get rid of that madman Mossadegh," John Foster Dulles mused as he read the plan for Operation Ajax several months later.

President Eisenhower and Secretary of State Dulles made their decision to overthrow Iran's democratic government without debate, without reflection, without analysis, without weighing costs and benefits. When the CIA station chief in Tehran, Roger Goiran, warned that deposing Mossadegh might undermine long-term American interests, they had him removed. They never consulted either of the State Department's two Iran specialists. Mossadegh appealed to them, publicly and in private letters, but they brushed him off.

"The intense dislike that Dulles and Eisenhower had toward Mossadegh was visceral and immediate," the American scholar Mary Ann Heiss concluded after studying this confrontation. "They were not interested in negotiation.... It was all very emotional and very quick. There was no real attempt to find out who Mossadegh was or what motivated him."

Never before had the CIA set out to depose a foreign leader. Operation Ajax would open an era of intervention that reshaped the world.

On July 19, 1953, Kermit Roosevelt slipped into Iran using a false passport. His grandfather, Theodore Roosevelt, had helped overthrow Spanish power in Cuba, Puerto Rico, and the Philippines; his mission was to overthrow Iranian power in Iran.

For nearly a century, Iranians had known America's benevolent side. Thousands had attended American schools or been treated at the American Hospital in Tehran. Howard Baskerville and Morgan Shuster were national heroes. This golden age was about to end.

Roosevelt's mission—to overthrow Mossadegh—did not go exactly as planned, but in retrospect it is amazing how easily he accomplished it. He started by bribing newspaper columnists, mullahs, and members of Parliament to denounce Mossadegh; they called him an atheist, a Jew, a homosexual, and even a British agent. Then he suborned key military officers and police commanders. He hired a street gang to rampage through the streets of Tehran, firing pistols and smashing windows while shouting, "We love Mossadegh and Communism!" Then he hired another gang to attack the first one, seeking to portray Mossadegh as unable to control his own capital city. On the evening of August 19 a mob of several thousand, unaware that it was being manipulated by the CIA, converged on Mossadegh's house. Military units arrived and began shelling it. Bodyguards inside returned fire. Three hundred people were killed. When the shooting stopped, the Mossadegh era was over.

The cowardly Mohammad Reza Shah, who had fled Iran in the turbulent days before the coup, was dining at a hotel in Rome when reporters burst in with news that his nemesis, Mossadegh, had been overthrown. At first he was too stunned to speak. Finally he managed a few words.

"I knew it!" he blurted out. "They love me!"

A few days later, the shah returned to Tehran and the Peacock Throne. He ordered Mossadegh, who was then seventy-one years old, tried for treason and sentenced to a prison term followed by house arrest for life. Slowly, using the combination of cajolery and brutality he learned from his father, Mohammad Reza Shah consolidated the power that democracy had denied him. The next era of Iranian history would be his.

During Mossadegh's twenty-seven months in office, the promise of the Constitutional Revolution finally became real. Power was held by elected officials. Parliament addressed people's needs. The grasping shah had been pushed into the background. Iranians enjoyed more freedom than ever in their history.

American leaders should have cheered this, but because of the cold war they could not. They might have looked at Iran's democracy and recognized a partner, a nation whose people were passionately engaged in political life and determined to rule themselves. Instead they looked at its nationalization of an oil company and saw an enemy.

"When Mossadegh and Persia started basic reforms, we became alarmed," wrote Supreme Court Justice William O. Douglas, who had visited Iran before the 1953 coup. "We united with the British to destroy him; we succeeded; and ever since, our name has not been an honored one in the Middle East."

This coup did more than simply bring down Mossadegh. It ended democratic rule in Iran and set the country off toward dictatorship. Mohammad Reza Shah gave the United States a quarter century of dominance in Iran, but his repression ultimately set off an uprising that produced a fanatically anti-American regime.

The coup against Mossadegh also bound Iran and the United States together. Until 1953 the United States had not been a major force in Iran; afterward it became the dominant foreign power. Many Iranians came to blame the United States for their country's modern tragedy. If the CIA had not deposed Mossadegh and thereby ended democratic rule, they reasoned, Iran might have escaped the decades of oppression that followed. When Americans condemn, threaten, and sanction Iran, they lament in reply: We had a democracy once, but *you* took it away from us!

"Iranians of all political persuasions increasingly formed a negative opinion of the United States," wrote James Bill, one of the leading American historians of modern Iran. "They no longer saw the United States as an external, liberating force whose influence would protect Iran from its traditional enemies, Britain and Russia. Instead, they developed a perspective in which the protector had become the exploiter. In the view of many Iranians, the first significant move in this American turnaround was the overthrow of Mossadegh. . . . As Britain retreated from its preeminent role in the Persian Gulf, the United States replaced it as the new, intrusive and intervening external power."

Fierce-looking soldiers with flowing mustaches and curved swords hanging from their belts cemented modern Turkish-American friendship. They came to fight in Korea, sealing with blood the partnership that began when the USS *Missouri* called at Istanbul.

The fifteen thousand soldiers Turkey sent to Korea—all volunteers who signed up after their leaders told them America needed help—comprised as odd a brigade as ever fought alongside the United States Army. Nearly all were from remote Anatolian villages. None spoke English or knew where Korea was. They were the first group of Turks to venture outside their homeland since the founding of the republic, and they did not look like soldiers any American had ever seen. No one knew what to expect from them.

The Turks quickly earned a reputation as ferocious fighters who instantly obeyed orders, willingly advanced through fire, and were near-invincible in close combat. Legend had it that they sometimes severed the heads and ears of their victims. When American officers doubted their high body count reports, the Turks began carrying the bodies of North Korean and Chinese soldiers they killed to American headquarters and piling them outside. The Turkish brigade took three thousand casualties. More than seven hundred of its members lie buried in the cold Korean soil.

"The Turks are the hero of heroes," General Douglas MacArthur, the Allied commander, said as reports of their valor spread. "There is no impossibility for the Turkish brigade."

Americans were accustomed to seeing Turkey as a weak supplicant that needed protection. As both the Korean War and the cold war intensified, Turkey began looking more like a potential partner. That led to a giant step. In 1952 Turkey was admitted to America's most important military alliance, the North Atlantic Treaty Organization. This brought Turkey under the Western defense umbrella, but it also meant something more deeply satisfying. Membership in NATO certified Turkey as a full-fledged European power. Atatürk would have been ecstatic.

For the rest of Turkish history, however, debates over what Atatürk wanted have become steadily more divisive. His ideology, which became known as Kemalism, was not a firm set of principles but rather a diffuse nation-building project. In the years after his death, the military-dominated elite embraced the Kemalist label, insisting that the Gazi's secular nationalism required limits on free speech, a commanding political role for the military, and a state that made decisions on behalf of citizens, against their will if necessary. Others, however, insisted that this was not what Atatürk wanted, and that he would have fought for more democracy, not less. This debate has led many Turks to consider the Kemalist elite an enemy of freedom, a force that weighs Turkey down and holds it back.

Atatürk liked the idea of opposition, but not the reality. He tolerated only his own Republican People's Party. For a decade after his death, the one-party model held. By the time World War II ended, though, the

Turks, like the Iranians, wanted to choose their own leaders. President Inönü was wise enough not to resist. He allowed ambitious members of the Republican People's Party to break away and form a party of their own. Then he called a competitive election.

Inönü had devoted his life to serving his country. He was a key commander in the Independence War, served as Atatürk's foreign minister and then, for more than a decade, as his prime minister, guiding the new nation through a host of crises before becoming its second president. No service he rendered, however, was greater than his decision to hold an open election in 1950. Leaders of one-party states rarely agree voluntarily to turn them into multiparty states. By doing so, Inönü displayed the quality that has allowed Turkey to progress while countries around it stagnated: an ability to change with the times.

Turks flooded to the polls on May 14, 1950. President Inönü insisted that votes be counted fairly, and the result was astonishing. The opposition Democrats won an overwhelming victory. Some urged Inönü to reject the result. He refused. After twenty-seven years, the period of one-party rule in Turkey was over.

The new prime minister, Adnan Menderes, was a jovial, well-to-do lawyer and cotton planter who had been educated at the American College in Izmir and was a decorated veteran of the Independence War. During the campaign he had promised to turn Turkey into "little America," with a millionaire in every district. As prime minister he aided farmers, eased some restrictions on religious practice, and enjoyed the rewards of a worldwide economic boom. The population more than doubled during his decade in office, to twenty-seven million. Per capita income tripled. The number of automobiles increased fivefold. A middle class—the foundation of stability in any country—began to emerge and thrive. Democracy was good to the Turks.

Slowly, however, things began to sour. As Menderes began his third term in 1957, the economy was faltering. So was democracy. Menderes became increasingly arbitrary, censoring the press and arresting critics. Political thugs attacked opposition leaders, including former president Inönü. Then, as tensions were rising, Menderes's plane crashed near

London; fourteen of the twenty-four people aboard were killed, but he walked away unhurt. He and some of his supporters claimed this as a sign of divine favor. They formed an "investigation commission" that met secretly to consider closing opposition parties and banning unfriendly newspapers. People became alarmed. Students rioted. Martial law was imposed.

On May 27, 1960, a group of midlevel army officers staged a coup and overthrew the Menderes government. They said they had acted "to prevent fratricide" and to "extricate the parties from the irreconcilable situation into which they had fallen."

Many Turks may have been relieved by this coup, but nearly all were horrified by its bloody climax. Leaders of the old regime were placed on trial. Fourteen were sentenced to death, and three of these sentences were carried out. One of those executed was Menderes. He attempted suicide in his jail cell, but was revived and hanged the next day.

Military coups became a lamentable motif of Turkish life. Yet some Turks saw each of these coups—there was a second one in 1971 and a third in 1980, plus a "post-modern coup" conducted by ultimatum in 1996—as a rescue mission. Each came at a time when the country seemed to be slipping toward the abyss of instability. In Syria, Iraq, Egypt, and Libya, military coups meant the wiping away of an entire order and the imposition of something radically new. In Turkey, the military withdrew from power soon after seizing it, and coups did not reshape society so profoundly.

Progress toward democracy was irregular but palpable in Turkey during the 1960s and '70s. Political parties were dominated by bosses who deferred to military power, but society steadily opened. New ideas poured into the country, mainly through the emerging intellectual class but also through the hundreds of thousands of "guest workers" who took jobs in Western Europe. Labor unions gained power. On college campuses, leftist and anti-imperialist groups became steadily more militant.

Despite all of this, Turkey still made no impression on the outside world. It discouraged foreign investment, exported little, and had no independent foreign policy. Half a century after emerging as a state, it remained insecure and unwilling to assert itself.

Although Turkey did not try to shape the world during this era, the world crashed into Turkey. Some Turks, especially students and leftist intellectuals, became viscerally anti-American, partly out of anger at the U.S.-led war in Vietnam but also for reasons closer to home. By the mid-1960s, more than twenty-five thousand American servicemen and dependents were living in Turkish cities and towns. The boisterous enlisted men's club in downtown Ankara symbolized their intrusive presence. Some Turks began seeing them as occupiers, and they became targets. Several were kidnapped. Bombs were thrown at American offices.

Anti-American emotions spiked sharply after an outbreak of communal violence on Cyprus. The Greek-dominated government there was trying to abolish provisions protecting the Turkish minority, and at the end of 1963, guerrillas who wanted to make Cyprus part of Greece launched a wave of attacks on Turkish Cypriots. Turkey was about to send troops to protect them, but was dissuaded in part by a startlingly blunt letter from President Lyndon Johnson. Fearing the possibility of war between Turkey and Greece, and even the prospect that the Soviets might become involved, Johnson insisted that the Turks not take a step "fraught with such far-reaching consequence." Then, in what the Turks took as a deeply threatening insult, he added that NATO members "have not had a chance to consider whether they will have an obligation to protect Turkey against the Soviet Union if Turkey takes a step which results in Soviet intervention." Some Turks were disappointed; more were furious.

When the aircraft carrier USS *Forrestal* called at Istanbul in 1969, angry crowds greeted it. Women held up signs reading "Istanbul Is Not a Brothel for the Sixth Fleet." It was a far cry from 1946, when Turks were so happy to see the USS *Missouri* that, according to *Time*, "sailors found it difficult to pay for anything, including prostitutes."

As leftists became more violent in Turkey, so did their counterparts on the far right. Militants staged bank robberies to raise money. Strikes paralyzed the economy. Politicians and university professors were assassinated. On March 12, 1971, eleven years after the army stepped in to depose a civilian government, it did so again.

That calmed Turkey for a while, but by the late 1970s it was swept by another wave of political violence, far worse than that of the 1960s.

The global left-right polarization of the 1970s was especially strong in Turkey. Leftists were intoxicated by promises of revolution. Rightists felt justified using all forms of violence to defend the state. Political parties, which should have been able to channel this passion, proved unable or unwilling to do so. Some even promoted violence. So did outsiders. Much is still unclear about the origins of the violence that shook Turkey in the late 1970s, but some historians believe that both the American and Soviet secret services, recognizing Turkey as a strategic battleground, fed encouragement, advice, and help to factions they favored.

More than two hundred Turks died in political violence during 1977. By 1979 the toll was five times that. Shootouts, bombings, robberies, and kidnappings were daily events. Turkey fell into low-level civil war. Generals began thinking of staging yet another coup. Then stunning, unbelievable news came from Iran.

The ruins of Persepolis, a spectacular imperial capital until Alexander sacked it in 330 BC, served as the backdrop to one of the most mind-boggling displays of excess in modern Middle East history. Five hundred guests from sixty-nine countries joined the bacchanal, sleeping in yellow and blue tents set amid columns erected by Darius and Xerxes. Among them were Emperor Haile Selassie, Marshall Tito, Prince Rainier and Princess Grace of Monaco, King Hussein of Jordan, Vice President Spiro Agnew, the kings of Greece, Denmark, and Norway, the Crown Prince of Sweden, and the fifteen-year-old daughter of Ferdinand and Imelda Marcos, who wore a diamond necklace across her forehead. All food except the caviar, highlighted by partridge with foie gras and truffle stuffing, was flown in from Paris and prepared by chefs from Maxim's. Entertainment was provided by eighteen hundred performers dressed as ancient Persians, along with hundreds of camels, horses, and water buffalo.

The man around whom this carnival revolved, Mohammad Reza Shah, had consolidated a potent dictatorship and become a formidable world leader. His $100 million bash at Persepolis in 1971, which he called "the greatest show the world has ever seen," was styled as a celebration of twenty-five hundred years of Persian monarchy. It was also a way for this son of a stable boy to persuade himself and the world that he was not simply great, but as great as any king who ever lived.

"He is a highly dangerous megalomaniac because he combines the worst of the old and the worst of the new," the Italian journalist Oriana Fallaci wrote after interviewing him. "Thanks to his foolish visions, he is too firmly convinced of being the reincarnation of Darius and Xerxes, sent to this earth by God to rebuild their lost empire."

Eighteen years had passed since the CIA had restored Mohammad Reza Shah to the Peacock Throne. In that time he had worked assiduously to crush Iranian democracy. With help from the CIA and the Israeli Mossad he established a domestic security agency, SAVAK, that became one of the world's most dreaded. In foreign affairs he was unfailingly pro-Western, dutifully bringing Iran into two American-designed security alliances, the Baghdad Pact and its successor, the Central Treaty Organization. At home he ruled by intimidation and corruption.

"The present system," one of the last independent members of Parliament told a British diplomat in 1959, "by which elections were cooked and politicians were forcibly enrolled into fake parties, was worse than a sham; it was corrupting and degrading the whole standard of public life and filling every Iranian who had any concern for the healthy evolution of his country with black despair."

The Eisenhower administration gave Mohammad Reza Shah more than $1 billion in aid. President Kennedy was less enamored, and his reticence led the shah to begin flirting ostentatiously with the Soviets; Leonid Brezhnev was in Tehran on the day Kennedy was assassinated in 1963. Relations warmed again under President Johnson, who saw the shah as a political wheeler-dealer like himself as well as a bulwark against communism. Johnson was impressed by the "white revolution," a series of modernizing reforms the shah decreed in 1963, among them measures to promote rural education, women's rights, land reform, and literacy. These reforms were submitted to a plebiscite. When the government announced that 99.9 percent had voted in favor, tens of thousands of angry protesters poured into the streets. Police killed hundreds.

As in other countries where it maintains bases, the United States had a "status of forces" agreement with Iran to define the rights of its soldiers. In 1964 it imposed a new agreement stipulating that any American soldier or dependent who committed a crime in Iran was immune from prosecution in Iranian courts. The Iranians, highly sensitive to infringements on their sovereignty, erupted in anger. A Princeton professor who was there reported "a bitter and vehement public reaction."

Into this vortex stepped Ayatollah Ruhollah Khomeini, a slight, sixty-two-year-old cleric with quick wits and a modest following in the holy city of Qom. He had been briefly imprisoned for denouncing the "white revolution," and like many Iranians, he saw the "status of forces" agreement as another lash from the imperial whip that had been flogging Iran for generations. After Parliament accepted it, he rose before an assembly of the faithful, denounced it, and called the shah an American stooge:

> They have reduced the Iranian people to a level below that of an American dog.... If the Shah himself were to run over a dog belonging to an American, he would be prosecuted. But if an American cook runs over the Shah, the head of state, no [Iranian] will have a right to arrest him....
>
> The President of the United States must know that he is today the most obnoxious person in the world in the eyes of our people.... American advisors get immunity, and some members of Parliament cry out, "Ask these friends of ours not to do this to us. Don't bribe us. Don't colonize us." But who listened?

Rather than arrest Khomeini for his impertinence or have him killed, the shah decided to expel him from Iran. Perhaps he believed he would never hear again from this troublesome cleric. An American diplomat in Tehran, however, wrote in a prescient dispatch that by exiling Khomeini, the shah "lent him a new aura of martyrdom and has quite likely raised his stature.... Should he return, he would no doubt find a more enthusiastic following than he did before his exile."

In the late 1960s and early '70s, that prospect seemed remote. Oil money flowed in, and life for many Iranians improved steadily. Inflation was low, new job opportunities opened up, and oil revenues fueled a growing economy. There was little in the way of protest. Corruption was rampant, allowing the shah to buy off many potential critics. Those who could not be bought were repressed or left the country. Many Iranians believed protest was pointless because the Americans would certainly rescue their shah in any crisis.

The garish celebration at Persepolis in 1971 announced, among other things, the shah's arrival as a major player on the world stage. This he achieved largely by buying huge amounts of advanced weaponry from the United States. He chose not what Iran needed to defend itself, or even what it needed to project power, but whatever was newest and flashiest. President Richard Nixon, in an extraordinary show of support, ordered that the shah be given access to all conventional weapons in the American arsenal. Between 1972 and 1977, the United States sold Iran a staggering $16 billion worth of weaponry—including systems so complex that the Iranians never managed to master or maintain them.

Mohammad Reza Shah commanded the largest navy in the Persian Gulf, the largest air force in western Asia, and the fifth-largest army in the world. In his arsenal were one thousand tanks, four hundred helicopters, three hundred fighter planes, and three destroyers.

He paid for all of this with oil money. Under an agreement imposed by the United States after the 1953 coup, a consortium of American, British, and French companies kept half the profits from Iranian oil and sent the other half to Iran. This arrangement brought Iran half a billion dollars per year in the mid-1960s, and twice that by the end of the decade. The oil-shock year of 1973–74 pushed Iran's income to $5 billion. The next year it was $18 billion, and the year after that $20 billion.

Mohammad Reza Shah spent the 1970s in a vertiginous fall toward megalomania. American weaponry fed his increasingly irrational fantasies. The rest of the economy groaned.

"Some of the things the Shah purchased from us were far beyond his needs," recalled Henry Precht, an American diplomat who served in Tehran during the 1970s and later became the State Department's desk officer for Iran. "Prestige and his fascination with military hardware played a great part. There was no rational decision-making process. It was the same way on the civilian side. There was tremendous waste and corruption. Shiploads of grain would arrive and there were no trucks to off-load them, so they would just heap the grain in mountains and set it afire."

The United States relied heavily on Iran. Secretary of State Henry Kissinger considered the shah "that rarest of leaders, an unconditional ally." He and other American leaders saw the shah as a bulwark against both the Soviet Union and the rising tide of Arab nationalism—a "regional policeman" always available to do Washington's bidding. At first they worried that by sucking so much money out of the United States through his oil exports, the shah might destabilize the American economy. Once he agreed to send that money back to the United States as payment for weapons, their concern evaporated. This arrangement allowed the shah to pursue his ambitions, gave the United States a faithful partner in the Middle East, and brought great profit to American arms manufacturers. By the mid-1970s dozens of them, including Grumman Aerospace, Lockheed, Bell Helicopter, Northrop, General Electric, McDonnell Douglas, Westinghouse, and Raytheon, had large and busy offices in Iran.

In the same way boorish American soldiers based in Turkey had alienated many Turks, the tens of thousands of American civilians who poured into Iran alienated many Iranians. Lavishly paid and often breathtakingly arrogant, they behaved as if they were occupiers in a backward third-world outpost rather than guests in a nation ten times older than theirs. To them the Iranians were "ragheads," "sand niggers," and "stinkies."

"Companies with billion-dollar contracts needed manpower and, under time pressure, recruited blindly and carelessly," according to one account. "Hatred, racism and ignorance combined as American employees responded negatively and aggressively to Iranian society."

The shah portrayed himself as a modernizing reformer. During his reign, many factories were built, ports were improved, highways and rail lines were extended, and the number of schools in Iran tripled. Close below the surface of national life, though, tensions were building. Some people became ostentatiously rich while many others fell into poverty. As the shah proved unable to meet rising expectations, resentment over his autocratic rule grew.

With the United States firmly behind him, the shah became an absolute dictator; by some estimates no other world leader except Fidel Castro enjoyed as much personal power over his country. He allowed only sycophants to hold government office, and required them to show their fealty by kissing his hand when they approached. On ceremonial occasions he dressed like a character out of Gilbert and Sullivan, in uniforms adorned with braids, ribbons, gold-threaded epaulets, and giant, bejeweled medals. In 1975 he decreed that every Iranian must join his political party and that those who refused would be treated as traitors.

Several members of Congress tried to limit American arms sales to the shah, but without success. Others raised questions about human rights. They were told that the problem was indeed worrisome, but that the shah, as one American official told Congress in 1977, had made "important changes" and that there was a "gratifying trend" toward respect for dissent.

An academic study of Iran during this period, however, described repression there as "simple and brutal."

"All opposition organizations were outlawed," it said. "The security forces also rigged elections.... Mass organizations such as labor unions and student groups were heavily penetrated by SAVAK and their leaders were systematically harassed. Prominent intellectuals, artists and clergymen who criticized the regime were harassed and often arrested. Censorship was quite severe.... At least three hundred Iranians were executed between early 1972 and late 1976 after having been condemned by military tribunals, which were generally reserved for political prisoners. Many more Iranians were killed in shootouts with the security forces, 'shot while trying to escape,' or simply disappeared.... Amnesty International declared in 1975 that 'no country in the world has a worse human rights record than Iran.'"

With the regime becoming steadily more repressive and the United States supporting it ever more fervently, it was inevitable that some Iranian militants would take out their anger on Americans. Bombs exploded at the American embassy, the Peace Corps headquarters, and other symbols of U.S. power. Several American military officers and civilian contractors were assassinated. In Washington, these attacks were easy to dismiss as the work of isolated terrorists. In fact, they were signs that the country was cracking apart—and that when it did, Iranians would take revenge on the United States.

Although the shah banned secular opposition groups, he feared the clergy and left it alone. As a result, mosques became the only places where Iranians could gather to talk of forbidden things. Nationalists and other anti-shah plotters were drawn to them. Mullahs became their mentors. Slowly the dissident movement took on a religious tone. This would decisively shape the course of the rebellion to come.

President Jimmy Carter, who took office at the beginning of 1977, took an odd, contradictory approach to Iran. He zigzagged between praise for the shah's rule and criticism of his repression. When the shah presented him with a new multibillion-dollar wish list, including a request for sophisticated AWACS surveillance planes, Carter endorsed it. He seemed to realize that the shah was a bad man, but believed he could be redeemed and transformed into a good one.

The shah, accustomed to accommodating American presidents, tried to placate Carter by loosening restrictions on free expression.

Immediately dozens of civic and political groups emerged, all anti-shah. By mid-1977 the country was engulfed in protest. People accustomed to living in fear began charging through streets yelling, "The Shah Must Go!"

As Iran burned, Carter and the shah had two bizarre encounters. The first was in Washington, on November 15, 1977. As the two leaders were exchanging compliments on the White House lawn, thousands of enraged protesters, many of them Iranian exiles, fought police nearby. Clouds of tear gas wafted toward the dignitaries. Before long, the president and the shah, along with their wives, were rubbing their eyes. They were forced to cut the pleasantries short and retreat inside.

The empress noticed that protesters were carrying placards bearing the face of a bearded cleric "whose defiant look meant nothing to me." Later she asked aides who he was. An exiled cleric named Khomeini, they told her.

Six weeks later, on the last day of 1977, the shah threw a New Year's Eve party for Carter in Tehran. Carter emerged full of praise for his host.

"Iran, under the great leadership of the Shah, is an island of stability in one of the more troubled areas of the world," he bubbled. "This is a great tribute to you, your Majesty, and to your leadership—and to the respect, admiration and love which your people give to you."

Carter could reasonably plead ignorance about conditions in Iran. The CIA station there had long since ceased to operate independently. Mohammad Reza Shah wished it to accept intelligence only from him and not cultivate other sources; astonishingly, it agreed. In 1977 the State Department, relying in part on CIA analysis, issued a paper predicting that Iran "is likely to remain stable under the Shah's leadership.... The Shah rules Iran free from serious domestic threat."

By the beginning of 1978, however, Iran was ablaze. Protests spread across the country. Many were brutally repressed, but that only intensified popular anger. During the course of that year, police officers and soldiers killed hundreds of "crocodiles," as the regime called protesters. This was the bloodiest rebellion in modern Iranian history.

"I lived for two weeks in November–December 1978 among the so-called crocodiles in southeast Tehran," the scholar James Bill has written. "Here the masses of the Iranian people, crowded in line for their kerosene and rationed meat, shouted slogans against the shah. Taxi drivers spit in the direction of the shah's soldiers, and students combed the city for portraits of the royal couple to tear down and deface. Luxury hotels, cinemas and liquor stores stood silent as dark, windowless, bombed-out hulks. Anti-Americanism was intense, and a wild, powerful sentiment pervaded the crowded sidewalks, markets and streets. This was the heartbeat of the revolution."

The shah, unable to grasp what was happening, careened wildly. On some days he seemed to believe he could crush the rebellion with ruthless repression; on others he tried conciliatory gestures. He sent police to attack students at Tehran University, then apologized, released a thousand political prisoners, and fired the head of SAVAK. Then he made a rambling, emotional appeal on national television.

"I pledge that past mistakes, lawlessness, injustice and corruption will not only no longer be repeated, but will in every respect be rectified," he told his people. "As soon as order and calm have been restored, I undertake to set up a national government to establish fundamental liberties. . . . I guarantee that in the future, the government of Iran will be based on the Constitution, social justice and the people's will."

A revolutionary firestorm had enveloped Iran. Throngs of Iranians were marching through every major city chanting, "Death to the American Shah!" Analysts in Washington, however, continued to report that all was well. On September 28, 1978, the Defense Intelligence Agency predicted that the shah would "remain actively in power over the next ten years." When a reporter asked President Carter about the crisis on December 12, he replied, "I fully expect the Shah to maintain power in Iran. . . . The predictions of doom and disaster that come from some sources have certainly not been realized at all."

Rarely have American leaders been so quickly shown to have been so disastrously wrong.

On January 16, 1979, the unthinkable happened. Mohammad Reza Shah, Light of the Aryans and Commander of All Warriors, fled Tehran aboard a silver and blue Boeing 707. With him he took his family, all the wealth he could carry, and his father's body, which he wished to save from desecration. It was a shattering end to the Pahlavi dynasty.

Two weeks later Ayatollah Khomeini flew from Paris to Tehran on a chartered Air France jet. His arrival set off what has been called "one of the most tumultuous demonstrations in human history." It also plunged Iran into a maelstrom of revolution more violently destructive than anyone could then imagine.

Mohammad Reza Shah's crime was not simply his support of the CIA coup that had ended democracy in 1953, but his refusal to pursue a democratic project of his own. The reforms of which he was so proud emerged from nothing more than his own impulse. He imposed them by decree or through acts of Parliament, which he corrupted and used like a toy. By the end, most Iranians saw him not as a reformer but as an oppressor.

"The revolution erupted not because of this or that last-minute political mistake," the Iranian-American historian Ervand Abrahamian has written. "It erupted like a volcano because of the overwhelming pressures that had built up over decades deep in the bowels of Iranian society."

This rebellion came to be known as the Islamic Revolution, but that name is misleading. It was a broad-based movement of clerics but also of shopkeepers, laborers, intellectuals, students, and others who had no wish to create a religious regime. Ayatollah Khomeini, who became the new government's "supreme leader," understood this. Instead of imposing religious rule immediately, he named a cabinet led by nationalists, many of whom had worked for or admired Mossadegh. It survived for less than a year. On November 4, 1979, militants seized the American embassy in Tehran and took dozens of U.S. diplomats hostage. Cabinet ministers appealed to Ayatollah Khomeini to order them out. When he refused, they resigned. By the beginning of 1980, Iran was under a radical Islamic regime that detested everything the shah had held dear.

Why did mullahs emerge as winners of the fight for postrevolution Iran? First, they had broad and deep support from ordinary Iranians; liberal political parties, by contrast, had atrophied during the shah's repressive rule and lost touch with the masses. Second, religion played a deeper role in Iranian society than the shah understood, and the mullahs' moral authority grew steadily as the regime became steadily more corrupt. Third, the mullahs were more prepared than any other faction to use violence against their rivals. They repressed, imprisoned, and killed with abandon. Ultimately this left them in control of a regime Iranians had hoped would lead them back toward the democracy they lost in 1953.

Both superpowers considered the Islamic Revolution a devastating strategic loss. The Americans saw an instinctively pro-American leader replaced by one who was instinctively anti-American, and feared he would open the way for a Soviet thrust toward Persian Gulf oil fields. The Soviets, for their part, feared that Iranian fundamentalists would foment Islamic uprisings across Central Asia, including in Muslim republics that were part of the Soviet Union itself. At the end of 1979, determined to prevent that from happening, they sent the Red Army to invade and occupy Afghanistan.

The Turks watched this upheaval from across their eastern border, and it terrified them. Turkey was in a crisis of its own during 1979 and 1980, with a weak government unable to stop waves of murderous terror from left and right. The unexpected emergence of a radical religious regime in Iran led some Turks to fear that the fire might spread to Turkey—that fanatics would try to destroy the Kemalist state, and with it both secularism and democracy.

Turkey was falling toward chaos. There were food shortages. Inflation raged. Political violence was taking ten lives a day. A region on the Black Sea coast announced its secession from the Turkish Republic.

Army commanders waited until nearly everyone in the country seemed ready to support a coup. Finally, at four o'clock on the morning of September 12, 1980, they struck. The generals said they were seizing power to end a "state of anarchy," to crush "reactionary and other perverted ideologies," and to wipe away the "extreme" freedoms that allowed them to flourish.

Both Turkey and Iran broke sharply with their pasts in 1980. That filled some people with the thrill of anticipation. Others felt only dread.

5

SOWERS OF CORRUPTION ON EARTH

The senior American diplomat in Iran, Bruce Laingen, was in a dark stone cell on the 430th day of his captivity when the cell door suddenly opened and one of his jailers walked in. He started to speak, but Laingen, boiling with anger built up over months of captivity, exploded at him.

"You are holding people hostage without any kind of respect!" he shouted. "It's totally against every precept of decency, and especially against the Iranian tradition of hospitality. It is wrong, wrong, totally wrong on every count—wrong politically, wrong morally, wrong historically and wrong on the pure basis of human rights. It's immoral and it's illegal!"

Laingen railed until he ran out of breath. When he finished, his jailer stared at him for a few moments and then replied without sympathy.

"You have nothing to complain about," he said. "You took *our whole country* hostage in 1953."

Iran's descent into dictatorship began after the United States overthrew the most democratic government it ever had. The 1953 coup against Mohammad Mossadegh was one of the twentieth century's more significant events, yet few histories of the century published in English give it more than a line or two. For nearly all of Mohammad Reza Shah's twenty-five-year reign, as royal dictatorship became more oppressive and Iranian anger grew, American leaders and most of the American press portrayed the U.S.-Iran relationship as ideal.

"Mr. President, do you think it was proper for the United States to restore the Shah to the throne in 1953 against the popular will within Iran?" a reporter asked President Jimmy Carter at a news conference during the hostage crisis.

"That's ancient history," Carter replied.

For the Iranians, it was not and is not. Their collective consciousness still burns with the sting of conquest by Greeks, Arabs, Mongols, Tatars, Russians, and British. After 1953 many came to see the United States, a nation that once inspired them, as the latest in this line of usurpers.

Washington was stunned when Mohammad Reza Shah fell in 1979. His regime had been the main instrument through which the United States projected power in the Middle East, a rock of stability, armed to the teeth and to all appearances invincible. Its sudden collapse came less than five years after the fall of South Vietnam. In a country accustomed to having its way in the world, these two traumas bred frustration and anger.

When Iranian militants loyal to Ayatollah Khomeini took Bruce Laingen and other American diplomats hostage at the end of 1979, emotions in the United States turned white-hot. Gangs attacked and beat Iranian-Americans. A new evening news program, *America Held Hostage*—which later became *Nightline*—emerged to cover the crisis, and it riveted the nation. Each night the broadcast began with the painful note that this had been "day eighty-seven" or "day three hundred sixteen" of the ordeal. Handcuffed and blindfolded American diplomats shuffled across the screen. A sign on the wall of the occupied embassy compound proclaimed the excruciating truth: "US Can Not Do Anything." This continued for 444 days and seared the American psyche.

To a generation of Americans, Iran became the face of the hateful "other," an incarnation of the predatory barbarism that always threatens civilization. The bitterness of that two-year period—from the shah's fall on January 16, 1979, through the end of the hostage crisis on January 20, 1981—never dissipated. It has shaped American policy toward Iran ever since.

In relationships between nations, as between people, partners who split apart angrily often develop totally different narratives about what happened. So it was with the United States and Iran at the end of 1979.

Americans saw themselves as wronged innocents. Their narrative was simple: We were generous friends to Iran until, after a sudden revolution, a new regime led by nihilist fanatics sent thugs to kidnap our diplomats, without provocation and in violation of every law of God and man.

Many Iranians perceived the relationship quite differently. They saw the United States as a bloodstained predator, a hostile force that had intervened in 1953 to rob them of their democracy, propped up the reviled Mohammad Reza Shah for twenty-five years, and was threatening to intervene again at any moment.

As Iranians celebrated their revolutionary victory, Mohammad Reza Shah wandered the world, a wealthy but nonetheless unwanted refugee. He went first to Egypt and then to Morocco, the Bahamas, and Mexico. Wherever he landed, the Iranian government demanded his return for trial. Finally, in need of treatment for pancreatic cancer, he appealed to President Carter for permission to come to the United States. Against much advice, but perhaps moved by his Christian conscience—and urged on by two of the shah's faithful friends, Henry Kissinger and David Rockefeller—Carter agreed.

Some in Washington may have seen this as nothing more than a final courtesy to a dying comrade. From Tehran it looked far more frightening. Many Iranians instantly flashed back to 1953, when the shah fled, but CIA agents working in the basement of the American embassy staged a coup and brought him back. They feared this history was about to repeat itself.

American diplomats in Tehran had predicted that the Iranians would react this way. Several weeks before Carter decided to admit the shah, the embassy sent a report to Washington warning that "any decision to allow him or his family to visit the US would almost certainly meet with immediate and violent reaction." The Iranian ambassador in Washington warned the State Department that reaction would be "very, very bad," and suggested that the shah be steered to South Africa instead.

This message seemed to have reached Carter and his inner circle, so when Bruce Laingen summoned his embassy staff to an emergency meeting on October 22, 1979, and announced that the shah would be admitted to the United States, everyone was stunned.

"Total silence followed," one of the diplomats later recalled. "In time it was broken by a faint groan. Faces literally went white." Another said he "felt that we had been betrayed by our own people. How could they admit the Shah and leave us in Iran to face the angry wolves?"

Thirteen days later, just as these diplomats had feared, militants stormed the embassy and the anguishing hostage crisis began.

This crisis did more than devastate relations between Iran and the United States. It also allowed Ayatollah Khomeini to rid himself of moderates in his government. These moderates, who believed in the rule of law, made frantic efforts to resolve the hostage crisis. Khomeini rejected them. Their impotence unmasked, they had no choice but to quit.

"Don't listen to those who speak of democracy," Khomeini warned religious students in Qom. "They all are against Islam. They want to take the nation away from its mission. We will break all the poison pens of those who speak of such things as nationalism and democracy."

That such a man, at the head of such a movement, could take control of Iran in the late twentieth century was testimony above all to how grotesquely Mohammad Reza Shah had twisted Iranian politics. By crushing civil society while allowing mullahs to act freely, he all but guaranteed that mullahs would follow him in power. The one who emerged as their leader, Khomeini, was a utopian, a millenarian, an atavistic throwback to an idealized age before Islam was corrupted by worldly things. Iran had been advancing toward democracy for nearly a century; Khomeini wished to pull it back toward religious dictatorship.

"This was an ascetic mystic, fed for a lifetime on a simple diet of yogurt, dates and vengeance.... Savonarola and Calvin combined in a Muslim guise," one Iranian-American scholar wrote. "He was a mystic gone political, a revolutionary ascetic who forced the return of a mutated Islamic mysticism back to the point of its origin."

Two fortuitous crises allowed Khomeini to consolidate power. One was the hostage crisis, which he used to cleanse his regime of moderates. The other was the Iran-Iraq War. They were his fortunate catastrophes.

Saddam Hussein, the Iraqi dictator, considered Iran his great rival for dominance in the Muslim Middle East, and was deeply anti-Iranian; his last words, many years later, would be, "Down with the traitors, the Americans, the spies and the Persians!" For two decades he had to curb his ambition because the United States so fully backed Mohammad Reza Shah. With the shah gone and Iran in upheaval after the 1979 revolution—and especially after mullahs executed dozens of Iran's senior military commanders—Saddam saw his chance. On September 22, 1980, he sent Iraqi troops storming into Iran. He aimed to capture Iran's oil fields and the Abadan refinery; seize control of the strategic Shatt al-Arab waterway, through which much of the world's oil is exported; destroy the religious regime in Tehran; and establish himself as the new regional strongman.

Iran was taken by surprise, but soon counterattacked and drove Iraqi forces out of its territory. The war might have ended there, but Ayatollah Khomeini refused a cease-fire and insisted that his armies fight on until they had deposed Saddam and established a Shiite regime in Iraq. Fighting continued for eight years. This suited Khomeini. People in any country instinctively unite behind their leaders in time of crisis, and Iran proved no exception. The Iran-Iraq War gave mullahs the excuse they needed to reject demands for a more open society and justify ever-fiercer repression. In the first two years after the revolution, tribunals in Iran issued death sentences at the rate of about two per month; over the next four years, as war with Iraq raged, they averaged ten times that number. More than eight thousand "sowers of corruption on earth" were executed.

For those Iranians who believe the West has long conspired to keep their country weak—which means most of them—the Iran-Iraq War provided more infuriating evidence.

As this war intensified, President Ronald Reagan sent a personal envoy to Baghdad to meet with Saddam and offer him American help. The envoy was the former (and future) defense secretary Donald Rumsfeld, then president of the G. D. Searle pharmaceutical company. Blurry photos of Rumsfeld and Saddam shaking hands on December 20, 1983, show two very different men. One was a suave Princeton-bred millionaire and consummate Washington insider, the other a revolutionary Arab nationalist who had shot his way to power. Both, however, were lifelong politicians and short on sentiment. They joined to fight a common enemy: Iran.

Rumsfeld began their meeting by presenting a letter from President Reagan asserting that a victory by Iran in this war would be "contrary to United States interests." Then he asked Saddam to support construction of a billion-dollar oil pipeline from Iraq to the Jordanian port of Aqaba; this project was being promoted by Bechtel, the global construction firm that had formerly employed both Secretary of State George Shultz and Secretary of Defense Caspar Weinberger. Finally Rumsfeld asked Saddam how the United States could help him fight Iran. Saddam asked for two things: helicopters, and access to satellite intelligence that would help his field commanders target Iranian troop concentrations. The United States supplied both.

It was anger at Iran, then, that brought the United States into its death embrace with Saddam—another example of how the U.S.-Iran relationship has reverberated around the Middle East in ways no one could have predicted. Eager to support anyone who would fight Iran, American leaders made Saddam a partner.

During the Iran-Iraq War, Saddam used helicopters to spray poison gas on Iran. This violated international law, but when Iran protested, American officials rejected its charges despite knowing they were true; they also suggested that the Iranians were gassing their own people in order to win sympathy, and blocked a United Nations investigation. The

Iranians learned from this episode that they are vulnerable to attack with unconventional weapons. Many concluded that to defend itself, Iran should have such weapons of its own.

A couple of years after the United States began supplying arms and intelligence to Iraq, it began secretly supplying its enemy, Iran, as well. President Reagan hoped Iran would use its influence to free Americans being held hostage in Lebanon. He was also laying the foundation for the policy of "dual containment"—opposing both Iran and Iraq—that the United States would follow for the next decade and a half.

"I hope they kill each other," Henry Kissinger said in a tart summation of this policy. "Too bad they both can't lose."

While the war raged, Ayatollah Khomeini built a harsh Islamic state. Women were ruled unfit for positions as judges or university professors; so were many men with secular beliefs. Newspapers were censored, civic groups were crushed, and dissidents were arrested and often killed—not only in Iran but abroad. Militants debated the fate of the Persepolis ruins, which they saw as a monument to idolatry: Should they be converted into a public urinal or simply bulldozed?

The Iran-Iraq War ended in 1988 after Khomeini accepted a cease-fire, a decision he called "more deadly than taking poison." Hundreds of thousands had been killed, filling vast cemeteries in both countries. Neither side gained anything of value.

Iran was left devastated. More than a million people lost their homes during this war. Ports, factories, bridges, irrigation works, and industrial complexes, including the refinery at Abadan, were bombed to rubble. Per capita income fell by half.

"The war had two profound effects," the Lebanese-American scholar Fawaz Gerges later concluded. "First, it deepened and widened anti-American feeling in Iran and made anti-American foreign policy a *raison d'être* of the Iranian government. Second, Iraq's use of chemical weapons, and the American role in preventing an investigation and shielding Saddam from criticism, convinced the mullahs that they needed to pursue a program to develop unconventional weapons of their own."

The 1980s were a deeply traumatic period for Iran. Decades of royal dictatorship were followed by a thrilling revolution, a quick fall back into bloody autocracy, and a shattering war. A decade that Iranians hoped would lead them toward liberation led instead to ruin and oppression.

Many Iranians know that the United States was responsible for deposing their last democratically elected leader, Mohammad Mossadegh, in 1953 and setting their country on the road to dictatorship. Even decades later, however, few Americans understood this. In the late 1990s, as Bill Clinton's presidency was drawing to a close, he decided to make a gesture to Iran in the hope of beginning a dialogue. He assigned Secretary of State Madeleine Albright to make a speech admitting American involvement in the 1953 coup.

Rather than deliver this confession before an audience of historians, human rights activists, or Iranian-Americans, Albright chose to do it at a Washington meeting of the American Iranian Council, a lobby group bankrolled by oil companies eager to do business with Iran. Her speech, delivered on March 17, 2000, was a balancing act between the interests of these corporations and those of Israel, which opposed any reconciliation between Washington and Tehran. That doomed it to failure. Nonetheless it marked the first time the United States had admitted what others around the world had known for decades:

> In 1953 the United States played a significant role in orchestrating the overthrow of Iran's popular Prime Minister, Mohammed Mossadegh. The Eisenhower Administration believed its actions were justified for strategic reasons; but the coup was clearly a setback for Iran's political development. And it is easy to see now why many Iranians continue to resent this intervention by America in their internal affairs.
>
> Moreover, during the next quarter century, the United States and the West gave sustained backing to the Shah's regime. Although it did much to develop the country economically, the Shah's government also brutally repressed political dissent.

> As President Clinton has said, the United States must bear its fair share of responsibility for the problems that have arisen in U.S.-Iranian relations. Even in more recent years, aspects of U.S. policy towards Iraq during its conflict with Iran appear now to have been regrettably shortsighted, especially in light [of] our subsequent experiences with Saddam Hussein.

Iran did not respond to this half apology, partly because Albright balanced it with condemnations of the Iranian regime—thought necessary to reassure Israel—for a host of sins including sponsoring terrorism and obstructing American peace efforts in the Middle East. Israel was equally unhappy. The *Jerusalem Post* reported that senior Israeli officials had "sharply criticized the US's more positive attitude toward Iran" and that "the American Israel Public Affairs Committee, Israel's No. 1 lobby in Washington," was against any trade with Iran that would bring that country "large flows of currency." Like previous efforts at reconciliation, Albright's was halfhearted and poorly timed. It raised eyebrows but produced no result.

Much had changed in Iran since the revolution. Its Supreme Leader, Ayatollah Khomeini, died in 1989, provoking a spectacular outpouring of grief. With him was buried the first wave of revolutionary fervor. A new period opened in Iranian history. Theorists of revolution would call it a period of Thermidor: a hesitant retreat from radicalism, a search for stability and normalcy. The new Supreme Leader, Ayatollah Ali Khamenei, launched it in a televised sermon describing the Shiite hero Ali not as an avenging Islamic warrior—the way fundamentalists usually portray him—but as a hardworking, well-dressed plantation owner and businessman. Soon afterward, President Ali Akbar Hashemi Rafsanjani told Iranians that it was time for them to "put away childish things" and end "excesses, crudities and irresponsible behavior." Politicians who had been demanding *jihad* to liberate Jerusalem began demanding better housing and cheaper home appliances.

Rafsanjani's term ended in 1997, and Mohammad Khatami, a reform-minded cleric who had spent years running an Islamic center in Germany, was elected to succeed him. Khatami's call for a "dialogue among civilizations" helped persuade Clinton to try the apology gambit. Neither leader, however, was bold enough to make a dramatic gesture that might have reshaped relations between their countries. Iran and the United States remained frozen in hostility, awaiting some lightning bolt that would change everything. It came on September 11, 2001.

Evening was falling over Tehran when news of that day's terror attacks was first broadcast. Spontaneously, groups of people carrying candles began walking through the streets to express sympathy and support for the United States. They converged at one of the city's main squares and stood in silent witness, reflecting a visceral sense of solidarity that many Iranians, despite the vicissitudes of history, feel with Americans. This vigil was the only pro-American demonstration held that day in any Muslim country.

The September 11 attacks gave reconciliation between Washington and Tehran an urgent political logic. Iran was an implacable enemy of the Taliban and al-Qaeda, whose fanatical leaders wished death to Shiite Islam. Now those forces had attacked the United States. Iran and the United States found themselves facing a common foe.

For several months after the attacks, diplomats from the two countries met regularly. The United States asked Iran to expel hundreds of foreigners it believed were linked to the Taliban or al-Qaeda, tighten security along the Iran-Afghanistan border, and place new names on its watch list of suspected terrorists; Iran did so. When the Americans decided to hire a proxy army to fight their anti-Taliban war in Afghanistan, Iran connected them to the Northern Alliance, with which it had worked for years. Then, after the Taliban was routed, Iran pressed the Northern Alliance to step back and allow Washington's favored Pashtun leader, Hamid Karzai, to become president of Afghanistan. American and Iranian delegations began secret talks in Geneva about how to build on this cooperation.

"The Iranians said, 'We don't like al-Qaeda any better than you, and we have assets in Afghanistan that could be useful,'" the CIA counterterror specialist Flynt Leverett later recalled. "They had real contacts with the players on the ground in Afghanistan, and they proposed to use that influence in continuing coordination with the United States."

As America's anti-Taliban campaign unfolded, the State Department produced a report asserting that the United States had "a real opportunity" to reshape its relationship with Iran. Both the CIA and the White House counterterror office endorsed this report. The prospect of a partnership between these two longtime enemies began to seem realistic.

That prospect evaporated on the evening of January 29, 2002, when President George W. Bush delivered his annual State of the Union address. He not only failed to acknowledge Iran's cooperation in the anti-terror war, but denounced Iran as part of an "axis of evil" along with two of the world's harshest dictatorships, Iraq and North Korea. Iranians were stunned. As so often in the modern history of U.S.-Iran relations, ideology and emotion trumped pragmatic self-interest. A great chance was lost.

Iranian leaders tried once more, a year after the "axis of evil" speech. Early in 2003, they handed a far-reaching proposal to the Swiss ambassador in Tehran, who is the official representative of American interests there. The ambassador, recognizing its importance, hand-carried it to Washington. It is one of the most intriguing diplomatic documents of the young twenty-first century.

Iran proposed comprehensive talks and laid out an agenda. It would ask the United States to end "hostile behavior," lift economic sanctions, guarantee Iran access to peaceful nuclear technology, and recognize its "legitimate security interests." In exchange Iran offered to do both of the things the United States had long demanded: accept "full transparency" in its nuclear program and end "any material support" for militant groups in the Middle East, specifically including Hezbollah, Hamas, and Islamic Jihad.

This was the boldest gesture from Iran in a quarter century. President George W. Bush and his advisers, however, wished to destroy the Iranian regime, not compromise with it. They not only refused to reply to Tehran's proposal but reprimanded the Swiss ambassador for having the temerity to deliver it.

This has been the frustrating pattern of U.S.-Iran relations since 1979. Both sides harbor a deep sense of grievance. Whenever one has seemed ready to compromise, the other was in too militant a mood to respond.

As U.S.-Iran relations atrophied, so did Iranian society. Largely isolated from the rest of the world, partly through its own fault and partly because of the malice of outsiders, Iran has ossified and turned inward. A strong democratic consciousness survives, but civic life is stunted. Many Iranians would like to see the Islamic regime fade into history so they can resume the march toward freedom on which they set off in 1906.

As Iran was reshaped by a revolution, Turkey was reshaped by two, both of them peaceful. The visionaries who led them governed a generation apart and never met. They would have made an odd couple. One was a jovial, backslapping fat man from the provinces, an engineer who had worked for the World Bank but also a practical joker and an enthusiastic glutton with a weakness for Courvoisier. The other was a stern, muscular athlete from Istanbul's mean streets who moved quickly from jail to national leadership.

Both of these Turkish leaders made history. The first of them, Turgut Özal, even said so.

When Özal was elected prime minister in 1983, Turkey was still inward-looking and afraid of the world. Foreign travel was discouraged, few companies produced for export, and possession of most foreign-made products—even a pack of Marlboro cigarettes—was illegal. Özal was determined to smash this protectionist state. One of his many targets was Turkish Airlines, which had been run for decades by a clique of retired generals who treated customers with contempt. He summoned a young, American-educated business executive, named him chief of Turkish Airlines, and assigned him to transform it into "a first-world airline." When the young man protested that the generals were too entrenched and would never work with a pup like him, Özal brushed away his objections.

"We are making history here!" he cried out with a wave of his arm.

Özal was a product not of the Istanbul elite but the earthy Anatolian heartland. His father was a bank clerk, but it was his mother, a powerfully dynamic schoolteacher, who instilled in him the conviction that if he educated himself, there was no limit to what he could become. Like many ambitious Turks who came of age as their country was bounding toward modernity, he chose to study engineering. He worked for one of the country's biggest conglomerates, spent two years in Washington as an economic adviser to the World Bank, and upon his return began dabbling in politics.

The generals who staged the 1980 coup played an inadvertent role in bringing Özal to power. Their coup was welcomed at first, largely because it put a quick end to political violence, but the three-year military regime that followed tore Turkish society apart. The generals not only imposed martial law, suspended the constitution, banned labor unions, dissolved the Grand National Assembly, closed political parties and arrested their leaders, but also launched a campaign of repression more intense than any the Turks had ever seen. Huge numbers of people were arrested, most of them guilty of nothing more than left-leaning politics. Many were tortured. Forty thousand Turks were convicted in special security courts; twenty-five were executed. University faculties were purged and many of the country's best and brightest fled. Nearly six hundred laws, many of them aimed at limiting public freedoms, were proclaimed by decree.

At the end of 1982 the generals announced that they were ready to leave power, but only if the Turks approved a new constitution they had prepared. It prescribed a limited democracy. Free speech was protected, except opinions "contrary to Turkish national interests." Elected leaders would give "priority consideration" to guidance from the National Security Council, which the generals controlled. Turks, eager for whatever democracy they could have, overwhelmingly endorsed this constitution in a referendum.

Once the new constitution was approved, the generals convened elections. All political parties had been banned since the coup, so they created two new ones, and helpfully told voters that one was more rightist, the other more leftist. Both were headed by retired generals. Then, almost as an afterthought—and responding to hints from Washington—they decided to allow a third party to participate. The one that emerged was called Motherland. As its standard-bearer it chose Özal, who had been the generals' chief economic planner.

All of the country's prominent politicians were banned from politics and forbidden to run in this election. Without realizing it, the generals had cleared the decks for the little-known Özal.

The night before the 1983 election, the leader of the outgoing military regime appeared on national television to remind voters that they must choose one of the ex-generals he had nominated. That was the decisive moment of the campaign. Realizing that Özal was the candidate not favored by the military, voters gave him a stunning victory. They wanted their democracy back; he was the only candidate who seemed interested in returning it to them.

The next decade of Turkish history—six years as prime minister followed by four as president—belonged to Turgut Özal. He was the most dynamic leader and most radical reformer his country had known since Atatürk, and also a new kind of figure for Turkey, an upbeat, pragmatic self-made man who had emerged from the masses and spoke their language. He was not a product of the old establishment and did not respect its taboos.

Özal sensed the vibrancy that lay beneath the surface of Turkish society. He realized that if it could be liberated, Turkey would not only break out of its isolation but become dynamic, prosperous, and powerful. He took over a country that was like a musty old house sealed for years, threw open all the doors and windows, and allowed gusts of wind to sweep away thick layers of dust.

Margaret Thatcher was Özal's hero, and like her, he was a free-market zealot. In a hurricane of deregulation, he told the Turks that rules and bureaucracy had crippled them and that the time had come to break free and become rich. Starting a business in Turkey had been a torturous process; suddenly the rules were gone and anybody could start one. Hundreds did, and then thousands. An entire new class of Anatolian entrepreneurs sprang up to challenge the "white Turks" who ran the old, well-connected family firms in Istanbul. Özal scrapped the import-substitution model, under which Turkey tried to produce everything it needed, and embraced a new one driven by export and global trade. Thus liberated, the Turkish economy began a long boom that has continued to this day.

Özal's economic reforms weakened the position of the old rich, but it was his unorthodox social and political views that disconcerted the army. He ordered the body of Adnan Menderes, the former prime minister whom the military had executed in 1961, reburied with full honors, and named an airport after him. He prayed every day and was a member of a Sufi Muslim order that Atatürk had banned. Most startlingly, he did not give military commanders the respect to which they were accustomed. When generals recommended a new chief of staff, he rejected their choice and picked someone else. Once he showed up to review a military parade in shorts. On a visit to the mainly Kurdish southeast, he casually announced that he was part Kurdish; no Turkish leader for half a century had even acknowledged that the Kurds existed.

On key global questions, though, Özal and the generals agreed. They were fiercely anti-Communist. Özal was also instinctively pro-American. That made it easy for him to give President George H. W. Bush everything he asked for in the summer of 1990.

The slim, patrician Yale man and the rotund, earthy Anatolian forged a remarkable bond in the months leading up to the Gulf War. They talked by telephone almost every day. Bush considered Turkey a vital ally because of its standing in the Muslim world. He also asked Özal for three tactical favors: shut down a pipeline that carried Iraqi oil to the Mediterranean, deploy Turkish troops along the Turkey-Iraq border to draw Iraqi soldiers away from Kuwait, and allow American forces to use the Incirlik air base in southern Turkey during the coming war. Özal not only instantly agreed to all three requests but tried to go further and send Turkish troops to fight alongside the Americans. That provoked much anger and led the defense minister, foreign minister, and chief of staff to resign.

Özal believed a new Middle East would emerge after the Gulf War, and he wanted Turkey to be on the winning side. President Bush deeply appreciated his unconditional support. When Özal came to the United States a few weeks after the war was won, Bush took him to Camp David and they talked for hours. Later Bush publicly thanked him for "the best communications I believe two countries could possibly have had."

The payoff Özal had expected, though, never came. A long period of regional instability followed the Gulf War. The United States organized an economic blockade of Iraq, which forced Turkey to close its eastern border, cost the country billions of dollars in trade, and plunged southeastern provinces deeper into poverty. This persuaded many Turks that cooperating with Americans does not always work out well.

Of all the changes that shook the world during Özal's era, none was as shattering as the breakup of the Soviet Union. He reacted to it by proclaiming a typically grandiose project: Turkey would become the godfather and protector of the new Turkic states that had emerged in the Caucasus and Central Asia. In several exhausting trips through the region, he sought to forge a new bloc Turkey could dominate. On his last trip he was his ebullient self, gobbling up fatty food at state banquets that were also all-night brainstorming sessions. On April 17, 1993, soon after returning to Ankara, he had a massive heart attack and died. He was sixty-five.

"For all his many flaws, Turgut Özal leaves Turkey a much more open, tolerant, democratic and colorful society than it was," the British newspaper *The Independent* wrote in its obituary. "Much of this is due to the natural energy his reforms unleashed in the Turks themselves. But he will be sorely missed as an extraordinary, lively leader, who could be both critic and visionary for his country."

History had not known entrepreneurial Turks before. In Ottoman times, trade was in the hands of Greeks, Jews, Armenians, and other non-Muslims. Özal sensed that the Turks, especially those who had returned from jobs as "guest workers" in Europe, were ready to engage the world. He gave them the chance to do so, and by the time he died, an entrepreneurial explosion was transforming Turkey. Businesses sprouted. Exports boomed. Jobs were created by the thousand. Sleepy backwaters became "Anatolian tigers." Pious provincials made tidy fortunes.

Once it had economic power, this new class of Anatolian entrepreneurs sought political power. All it needed was a leader who exemplified its values. Some of these values—democracy, economic freedom, integration with the West—were widely popular. But this new class believed something else as well, something shocking: that limits on religious freedom should be lifted so people could practice their faith as they wished.

Turkey has been reinvented twice since Atatürk invented it in 1923. The first reinventor was Özal, who took over a country that was frozen in time and integrated it into the world of the 1980s. The second pulled Turkey, kicking and screaming, from the twentieth century into the twenty-first.

Kasimpasha, the rough-and-tumble Istanbul neighborhood where Recep Tayyip Erdoğan grew up, is known as a cradle of tough men with prickly senses of honor. Erdoğan (pronounced AIR-doe-wan) was a street fighter who absorbed its values. He attended a religious-oriented *imam hatip* high school, sold lemonade and sesame buns on street corners, briefly played professional soccer, and then found a job with the Istanbul transit authority. He quit after a conflict that may be seen as his first political statement; his boss ordered him to shave his mustache because it could be seen as a symbol of Islam, but he refused. Later he went to work for Ülker, Turkey's biggest candy and snack manufacturer. He spent years dealing with shopkeepers, honing his persuasive skills and building a network of contacts. In 1994 he ran for mayor of Istanbul as a supporter of the Islamic political leader Necmettin Erbakan, and won. He proved distinctly more efficient and honest than most of his predecessors, but also more devout and socially conservative.

Two Americans were early heroes of Iran's struggle for democracy. Howard Baskerville, right, a Nebraska-born schoolteacher, was killed fighting to defend democratic rule against a royalist counterrevolution in 1909. After democracy was reestablished, Morgan Shuster, below, became Treasurer General of the Persian Empire and helped organize Iran's resistance to Russian and British occupiers.

President Kemal Atatürk of Turkey, left, was a fervent modernizer who turned his country into the Islamic world's first secular republic. In Iran, Reza Shah, shown below with his son and heir, Mohammad Reza, was just as radical but set a pattern of repressive rule. Reza traveled to Turkey to meet Atatürk in 1934; a poster showed them as proud nation builders.

After Atatürk and Reza Shah died, their countries became more democratic. President Ismet İnönü of Turkey, above, called a free election in 1950 and willingly surrendered power when his party lost. Prime Minister Mohammad Mossadegh, seated at right in the photo below with U.S. Secretary of State Dean Acheson, was the most democratic leader Iran ever had, but he was overthrown by the CIA after he nationalized his country's oil industry.

Shah Mohammad Reza Pahlavi, at left with President Richard Nixon, was Iran's dictator for a quarter-century and an intimate ally of the United States. His increasingly repressive rule set off the Islamic Revolution of 1979, which brought to power an anti-American regime under the leadership of an Islamic cleric, Ayatollah Ruhollah Khomeini, at center, below.

Turkey has been reinvented twice since Atatürk invented it in the 1920s. Prime Minister (and later President) Turgut Özal, shown cruising on the Bosphorus with President George H. W. Bush, above, smashed the protectionist state and challenged old taboos. Prime Minister Recep Tayyip Erdoğan, right, who took office in 2003, emerged from a background in Islamic politics, but claimed to embrace the ideals of capitalist democracy.

Eleven minutes after Israel proclaimed its independence in May 1948, President Harry S. Truman officially recognized it as a state. His closest friend, Eddie Jacobson, at right, above, helped persuade him to do so. Israel and the United States have been allies ever since, as reflected by street signs at a Jerusalem intersection.

America's other principal ally in the Middle East has been Saudi Arabia. The bond between the two countries was sealed in February 1945 during a secret meeting between President Franklin D. Roosevelt and the Saudi leader, King Abdul-Aziz ibn Saud. Every successive American president embraced this alliance, most visibly President George W. Bush, below, with King Abdullah, a son of Ibn Saud.

As the European Union soured on the idea of admitting Turkey, Prime Minister Erdoğan began deepening his country's ties with Middle Eastern and Asian countries. These ties gave Turkey a new role as a regional broker and peacemaker, while raising fears that it was drifting away from its secular principles and old alliances.

After the disputed presidential election of June 2009, Iranians took to the streets in a wave of protest that electrified the world. Many wished for a return to the democracy their grandparents had enjoyed under Mossadegh. This demonstrator carries a poster showing Mossadegh and the reformist presidential candidate, Mir-Hussein Moussavi, with the caption "We Will Not Let History Repeat Itself."

Over the next few years, Islamic politicians made remarkable gains in Turkey. Society was opening, and people felt more free to express their piety. They were also fed up with the corruption and incompetence of traditional leaders. Islamic mayors who emerged during the 1990s, including Erdoğan, were by comparison paragons of honesty and enterprise.

In such a secular country, however, a religious party could not rise without challenge. When Erbakan emerged as prime minister in 1996 after striking a corrupt deal with one of his rivals, the generals grumbled. They became steadily angrier as Erbakan called for Turkish withdrawal from NATO, a Muslim-oriented foreign policy, and a more religious society, which he wished to anchor by building a mosque facing Istanbul's main square. Finally, on February 28, 1997, the generals struck back, staging what Turks called a "post-modern coup." They did not seize power but simply declared that they would tolerate Erbakan no longer. His party had won just 21 percent of the vote and he had become highly unpopular, so few complained when the army forced him to resign after less than a year in office.

After Erbakan was toppled, Mayor Erdoğan and other young insurgents tried to seize control of the Islamic party. They failed. Rather than stay and fight, they abandoned the party and formed a new one, Justice and Development, known in Turkey as AKP. Soon afterward, in a speech that for a time passed unnoticed, Erdoğan recited a verse from an old Turkish poem:

The mosques are our barracks, their domes are our helmets,
Minarets are our bayonets, and the faithful our soldiers.

Prosecutors, who were under pressure from their friends in the army to come up with a case against Erdoğan, seized on this poem. Claiming that it proved his determination to destroy secularism, they charged him with inciting religious hatred. He was convicted, removed from office, sentenced to ten months in jail, and banned from future political office. After being sentenced, though, he behaved as if he had just won a prize.

"This song is not over yet!" he promised cheering supporters outside the courthouse.

Erdoğan had been stripped of the high office to which voters elected him, and then sent to prison, because the generals wanted to teach him a lesson. In jail, though, he enjoyed a carpeted suite and ate catered meals. By the time he was released four months later, he was a martyr of democracy and a hero to many. He spent the next months crisscrossing the country organizing his new AKP. When the 2002 elections were called, it was ready.

Guided by Erdoğan, who showed a genius for organizing, the AKP waged a modern, grassroots political campaign, something no secular party in Turkey had ever done. Party workers, many of them women, canvassed voters door-to-door, made lists of supporters, and brought them to the polls on election day. The result was a sweeping victory. Erdoğan could not take office immediately because his political ban was still in effect, but the new Grand National Assembly quickly lifted it. Four years after being sent to prison for reciting a poem, Erdoğan was prime minister.

This was Turkey's peasants-with-pitchforks moment. A counter-elite had rebelled and overthrown the established order. The periphery stormed the halls of power. That such a dramatic victory could be won through the ballot box showed the strength of Turkish democracy.

Immediately upon taking office, Erdoğan set off a whirlwind of reform unlike any the Turks had seen since Özal. Repressive laws that had been used to intimidate dissenters were repealed. The constitution was amended to accept the supremacy of the European Convention on Human Rights. Security courts were abolished. So was the death penalty. Prisoners' rights were guaranteed, and torture in Turkish prisons, long a stain on the country's human rights record, all but ended. Most astonishingly, the National Security Council, through which generals had intimidated prime ministers for twenty years, was turned into an advisory board run by civilians.

These reforms decisively weakened the old establishment. To every complaint Erdoğan replied with a simple and deeply resonant refrain: We must change in order to become European.

The story of Turkey's long and frustrating road toward membership in the European Union is an epic of missteps and lost chances. It reflects Turkey's deeply complex relationship with Europe, which is overlaid by centuries of conflict, mythology, and a fluid blend of fear and fascination. Prime Minister Özal submitted Turkey's official application to join the EU in 1987, but during the 1990s Turkish leaders showed little enthusiasm for the project. The EU has a set of democratic standards to which prospective members are expected to adhere: free speech must be guaranteed, minority rights must be respected, government must function transparently, business must be closely regulated, and the military must not meddle in politics. Turkish generals and their comrades in the old elite realized that these reforms would undermine their power. They concluded that their best response was hypocrisy: continue to support the EU project in public, but refuse to take the steps necessary to join.

By the late 1990s, though, an appetite for EU membership had spread throughout society. Liberal-minded intellectuals, politicians, and civic leaders saw the accession process as a way to complete Turkey's democratization. Devout believers saw it as a way to broaden their freedom of religious practice. Groups that felt persecuted by the state, including Kurds and Alawite Muslims, who are often viewed suspiciously by mainstream Sunnis, understood that Turkey would have to guarantee their cultural rights if it hoped to join Europe. Business leaders recognized the immense economic advantages of EU membership. The Grand National Assembly responded by passing a series of reforms, and at the end of 1999, at a summit in Helsinki, European leaders rewarded their efforts.

"The European Council welcomes recent positive developments in Turkey," they said in an official declaration. "Turkey is a candidate State destined to join the Union on the basis of the same criteria as applied to the other candidate States."

Logic suggested that in the 2002 election campaign, a secular leader would emerge as the champion of the EU project. Instead, Erdoğan assumed that role. On the surface it seemed odd; the most religiously conservative of Turkey's political leaders also turned out to be its most fervently pro-European. Western-oriented Turks responded—some more enthusiastically than others—by voting for him despite their distaste for his religiosity.

The first taboo Erdoğan violated after taking office was the one forbidding religious expression in public life. Not only did his wife wear a head scarf—which disqualified her from attending state functions—but he wished to legalize the wearing of scarves in universities. Some secular Turks panicked, fearing that religious rule was at hand and the entire Kemalist project was about to come crashing down. Erdoğan answered that he was doing nothing more than raising Turkey's level of public freedom to European standards—the standards of what Atatürk had called "universal civilization."

Two years after Erdoğan took office, the twenty-five member states of the European Union moved Turkey's membership application to what seemed to be a final stage. At a summit in Brussels, they agreed to open formal negotiations aimed at making Turkey a full EU member. Every country that has ever begun these negotiations, and has remained interested in joining the EU, has ultimately joined.

In 1529 and again in 1683, Turkish armies seeking to conquer Europe were turned back at the gates of Vienna. Now it seemed that Turkey would enter Europe by invitation. Ten generations of Turkish reformers were triumphantly vindicated. Hail *Tanzimat* visionaries! Hail Young Turks! Hail Atatürk! Hail Özal! Hail Erdoğan!

"In the last two years, we have made deep-rooted changes to our society that many countries wouldn't be able to accomplish in ten or twenty years," a jubilant Erdoğan told journalists in Brussels after the EU announced its decision. "We have achieved an extraordinary transformation as a nation."

The old guard, accustomed to dictating the limits of politics, tried but failed to defend its power. Its most humiliating defeat came in 2007, when Erdoğan announced that he would nominate his close comrade Abdullah Gül to be Turkey's next president, a post that had traditionally been a citadel of Kemalist power. The two men shared fundamental beliefs, but in style they were strikingly different. As a true son of the hardscrabble Kasimpasha streets, Erdoğan was imperious, easily offended, and prone to outbursts of temper. Gül, a British-trained economist, smiled often, spoke calmly, and sought consensus whenever possible.

These differences did not impress secular Turks, who believed the new regime was secretly planning to move their country toward religious rule. Hundreds of thousands turned out for protest marches after Gül was named, chanting slogans like "Turkey Is Secular and Will Remain Secular!" Military commanders posted a message on their Web site asserting their determination to "protect the unchangeable characteristics of the Republic of Turkey." Opposition parties boycotted the Grand National Assembly, so no quorum could be reached to elect a president.

In the past, a Turkish leader reprimanded so directly by the army would quickly retreat. Erdoğan, however, sensed that the nation was on his side. The army had been losing moral authority since the 1980 coup, partly through a series of scandals that revealed its collaboration with gangsters and death squads. Turks were reveling in their new freedom. So rather than withdraw Gül's name and nominate someone more acceptable to the generals, Erdoğan called a new election. He won a huge victory, taking even more votes than he won in his first campaign. Abdullah Gül, a devout son of Anatolia, became Turkey's eleventh president. Generals boycotted his inauguration. They had suffered a grievous loss.

Something truly historic happened in Turkey during the first decade of the new century. It was not simply that the country made its decisive breakthrough to democracy; that was certain to happen sooner or later. More remarkable was the fact that for the first time in modern history, a country was led toward democracy by a political party with roots in Islam.

"The Turkish case challenges two dominant Orientalist theses: that Islam and democracy, on the one hand, and capitalism and Islam, on the other, are incompatible," the Turkish-American scholar Hakan Yavuz has concluded. "Contemporary Turkish society is often pragmatic rather than ideological, inclusive rather than exclusive, and essentially nonviolent. . . . The previous paradigm of protecting the state from society has shifted to a paradigm espousing the protection of society from state intervention. The new agent of change in Turkey is not the military but the evolving bourgeoisie [and] the new class of intellectuals."

The success of Erdoğan and his AKP does not represent the triumph of Islamist politics in Turkey, but precisely the opposite: its death. Democracy has become Turkey's only alternative. Even pious Muslims recognize, accept, and celebrate this.

"Our party is the product of continuity," Erdoğan told a Washington audience soon after his election. "In some Western newspapers and publications, my party is described as 'an Islamic party' or 'Muslim democrats.' These characterizations are not correct. This is not because we are not Muslim or not democratic, but because we believe the two must be seen in entirely different contexts. . . . Turkey wants to take its political Magna Carta, which is a synthesis between Muslim identity and modern values, much further by becoming an active leader in promoting modern values, to give the world a new and inspiring 'renaissance' perspective."

In the years after 1980, both the Turks and the Iranians became disillusioned with their authoritarian regimes. They sought a way back to democracy. The Turks found one; the Iranians did not. Why?

The institutions Atatürk and his comrades built proved more flexible, and therefore more durable, than those Reza Shah built. Turkey's democratic system responds, albeit slowly and clumsily, to the people's will. It evolves along with the zeitgeist. Atatürk did not give Turks democracy, but he created conditions that allowed democracy to emerge after his death.

"I am leaving behind no sermon, no dogma, nor am leaving as my legacy any commandment that is frozen in time or cast in stone," the Gazi said as his strength began to fade. "Concepts of well-being for countries, for peoples and for individuals, are changing. In such a world, to argue for rules that never change would be to deny the reality found in scientific knowledge and reasoned judgment."

Here lies the key to Turkey's success as a nation. It has proven able to change with the times. Turkey was founded as an authoritarian state at a time when the authoritarian idea was ascendant. When democracy became the new global faith after World War II, Turkey moved peacefully from one-party to multiparty rule. When the world began using human rights as a measuring stick for nations, Turkey gave its citizens more rights. When many Turks decided they wanted more freedom of religion, the political system gave them a way to express themselves peacefully, and ultimately to elect their champion to lead the country.

In Iran, the opposite happened. Pahlavi absolutism suffocated the natural development of democracy. This produced the explosion that led to Iran's present conundrum.

While Atatürk built institutions, Reza became obsessed with family power. Above all he wanted to assure a clear path to the throne for his son. This made it impossible for him to promote democracy, which rejects hereditary power.

Some American historians believe the United States was fortunate that George Washington had no children, because given the power of the monarchical idea in his time, there might otherwise have been pressure to establish a dynasty. The same might be said for Atatürk. He had no child who might rule Turkey after he was gone. Partly for that reason, he was free to hope that the Turks might one day rule themselves.

Another factor also helps explain the different modern fates of Turkey and Iran: foreign intervention. Midway through the twentieth century, both countries were on the way toward real self-rule. Turkey held its first multiparty election, from which the homespun populist Adnan Menderes emerged. In Iran, the democratic hero Mohammad Mossadegh was elected prime minister. The path to full democracy in both nations seemed clear. What threw Iran offtrack was foreign intervention.

The passionate desire to modernize that drove Atatürk and Reza Shah was the key to their triumphs, but it had a dark side. Both men hated tradition, whether social, religious, civic, or cultural. Both believed there was only one worthy civilization on earth—they called it "universal," but everyone knew they meant European—and demanded that their people embrace it. Their militancy made it inevitable that the Turkish and Iranian pendulums would one day swing back toward deep-rooted habits and beliefs.

Reza Shah rescued Iran from disintegration and imposed a radically new social order, but his dictatorial style set a pattern that has plagued his people ever since. Atatürk's legacy is more positive, but also mixed. His devotion to the army led it to become the dominant institution in Turkey for generations to come, intervening in politics, repressing democratic impulses, and pushing the country into needless confrontations. The education system he built created a nation of readers, but its ethnocentrism and emphasis on rote learning produced narrow and unquestioning minds. His refusal to accept Kurdish identity created a conflict that raged for decades. So did his decision not to investigate the fate of Ottoman Armenians—a more puzzling failure, since the massacres of 1915 were ordered by the Young Turk triumvirate he loathed.

Turkish democracy has developed much like other democracies, in fits and starts, with painful reversals as well as leaps forward. Efforts to reimpose authoritarian rule have ultimately collapsed. Habits of democracy, slowly instilled over generations, have taken deep root in the national psyche.

The Iranians have embraced democracy just as fervently as the Turks—perhaps more fervently, because they have spent so long with so little of it. Both peoples are heirs to a century of struggle for freedom. No other Muslim country in the Middle East has anything close to this history.

Many Iranians judge the 1979 revolution to have failed, as their religious leaders have proved themselves unable to manage either society or the economy. Thousands of the most talented Iranians live abroad, unable to work for the betterment of their own country because the regime has created a society in which they feel constricted and oppressed. Iran, one of the world's oldest and most cultured societies, has become a pariah state. Its religious leaders have led their country into isolation while ravaging the hopes of generations.

In Turkey, democratic consciousness produced democracy. In Iran, this consciousness is just as strong or stronger. The fact that it has not led to the emergence of a democratic regime should not obscure its power. The Iranians, like the Turks, grasp the essence of democracy. To them it is not a set of rules brought from abroad, but part of their indigenous tradition. Their spontaneous uprising after the disputed 2009 election was proof of their democratic passion.

Turkey is the only country in the world that Iranians may visit without a visa. The Turkish Airlines flight from Tehran to Istanbul is a revelation. Women board wearing the drab outfit that is required of them at home. Once the plane is airborne, they begin lining up for the lavatory. Inside, miraculous transformations occur. In goes a veiled and shapeless female; out comes a fashionable woman wearing colorful clothes, jewelry, and makeup. Usually she crowns her outfit with a bright, self-confident smile.

Iranians want the freedom that their Turkish neighbors enjoy. History suggests they will have it, although few would dare to guess when or at what cost. Turkey and Iran are the only Muslim countries in the Middle East where democracy is deeply rooted. That makes their future bright. It also makes them America's logical partners.

PART THREE

• • •

VERY FAR AWAY

· 6 ·

YOU WIN, YOU BALD-HEADED SON OF A BITCH

Slaughtering sheep on the deck of a United States Navy warship is not permitted by military regulations, but it is not forbidden either. That made one of the twentieth century's strangest alliances possible.

As World War II drew to a close, President Franklin D. Roosevelt met with his two wartime allies, Winston Churchill and Joseph Stalin, at Yalta on the Crimean Peninsula. Their conference shaped the fate of postwar Europe. When Roosevelt departed, however, he told neither of his partners that he did not intend to sail straight home. Instead he proceeded to a secret meeting that, in the decades to come, would prove almost as pivotal as the far more famous one at Yalta. Churchill was livid when he learned of it, but by then it was too late.

The leader Roosevelt planned to meet, King Abdul-Aziz ibn Saud, had created a nation on the Arabian Peninsula just thirteen years before. He named it after his family: Saudi Arabia.

Like much of the Middle East, the Arabian Peninsula had been under British dominion for decades. Britain, however, was a declining power. The United States was rising. It needed a Middle Eastern partner, and Ibn Saud, who controlled a vast, oil-rich desert the size of Western Europe, seemed ideal.

Preparations for this meeting were so closely guarded that only five people in the kingdom knew it was to take place: the king and his foreign minister, the American ambassador and his wife, and a cipher clerk at the American embassy. Ibn Saud traveled to the port of Jeddah on the pretense of wishing to visit the nearby holy city of Mecca. In Jeddah he selected two hundred members of his entourage to accompany him. Only after they set out did he order that the party head not to Mecca, but to the harbor. An American destroyer, the USS *Murphy*, was waiting to pick him up and bring him to meet Roosevelt.

Kings of Saudi Arabia travel in a style of their own. Before Ibn Saud boarded the *Murphy*, several large dhows laden with tons of grain, vegetables, and one hundred sheep approached. The captain insisted that taking this cargo aboard was quite impossible. Arguments broke out. Finally the American ambassador, William Eddy, a retired marine colonel, arrived to smooth things over—making him the first of many Americans who have sought to bridge the vast cultural and psychological chasm that separates their countrymen from Wahhabi Arabs. Patiently he explained to the king's protectors that naval vessels carried ample provisions. Ibn Saud, who was unfamiliar with refrigeration, was puzzled, but relented after being told that American officers would be severely punished if they allowed his supplies aboard their vessel. He insisted, however, that fresh meat be available at least to him and his aides. Seven sheep were finally allowed aboard, along with forty-three members of the royal party. As the *Murphy* weighed anchor, one of the sheep was already being skinned—said to be the only time Muslims have ritually slaughtered an animal on the deck of an American warship.

The Saudis covered part of the deck with carpets, set up a tent, which sailors called "the big top," and prayed regularly; the navigator told them which direction they must turn in order to face Mecca, and the royal astrologer confirmed it. Ibn Saud's cooks prepared coffee in gun turrets. Nubian slaves, seven feet tall and with scimitars hanging from their belts, roamed the ship with fascination.

Ibn Saud developed a taste for some American dishes and became especially fond of apple pie with ice cream; later he ordered that apple trees be planted in Saudi Arabia. He was even more impressed with demonstrations of antiaircraft guns and depth charges that the ship's officers staged for him. Apple pie and modern weaponry proved a seductive combination.

On this voyage the king also saw his first motion pictures. He particularly enjoyed a documentary called *The Fighting Lady*, which described the workings of an aircraft carrier. Afterward, though, he told Ambassador Eddy that films were among the many foreign products he did not want in his kingdom.

"I doubt whether my people should have moving pictures, even like this wonderful film," he said. "It would give them an appetite for entertainment which might distract them from their religious duties."

Hypocrisy is the central fact of Saudi life; Ibn Saud's belief in astrology, for example, directly violated Islamic law, as did his weakness for Johnnie Walker Black Label. It was not surprising, then, that the royal party, made up largely of princes, devoured the movies shown to crewmen even as their monarch decreed that they must never be shown to commoners. Ambassador Eddy described the scene in a memoir:

> After the showing of the documentary films on the deck and after the King had retired for the night, the usual ship's movies were shown to the crew below decks. This secret leaked to the ears of the King's third son, Amir Mohammed, who the first morning on board took me aside by the rail and inquired quietly whether I would prefer to be destroyed all at once or to be chopped up in small pieces, bit by bit. I asked him what was the matter, and he said Hollywood pictures were being shown below decks and that he was not invited. Abject with terror, I reminded him that his royal father would not approve of any Arab, much less one of his sons, attending these godless exhibitions of half-naked women, and I begged him to forget the matter. He said very little but what he said was emphatic—to the effect that either he would see these pictures or my children would soon be orphans, and he swore that if I obeyed him he would keep my confidence and not tell his father.
>
> To make a long story short, Amir Mohammed and Amir Mansur,

his younger brother, were in the front row at the late showing for the crew that night of a movie which featured Lucille Ball loose in a college men's dormitory late at night, barely surviving escapades in which her dress is ripped off. The film was greeted by whistles and applauding whoops from the crew, an approval fully shared by the two princes. The following repetition of the film was attended by at least twenty-five Arabs. Fortunately, so far as I know, news of this orgy never reached the ears of the King.

The *Murphy* took two nights and a day to reach its destination, the Great Bitter Lake, a placid lagoon in the Suez Canal. There Roosevelt was waiting aboard the cruiser USS *Quincy*. Before leaving the *Murphy*, Ibn Saud presented its captain with a robe and a golden dagger, gave gold watches inscribed with his name to the officers, and made a cash gift to each sailor. In return he was given the objects he had most admired during his voyage: a pair of binoculars and two submachine guns.

The *Murphy* drew alongside the *Quincy* at midmorning on February 14, 1945. Shortly after ten o'clock, Ibn Saud crossed the gangplank. Roosevelt greeted him warmly. It was Valentine's Day, a fine time to form an alliance.

Roosevelt was weak and sick—he would die just eight weeks later—but in his conversations with Ibn Saud he was, according to Ambassador Eddy, "a charming host, witty conversationalist, with the spark and light in his eyes and that gracious smile which always won people over to him whenever he talked with them as a friend." They began by discussing their physical infirmities, and when Ibn Saud complained about pains in his leg that made it difficult for him to walk, Roosevelt insisted on giving him the spare wheelchair he always kept nearby. Ibn Saud could not fit into it—he was far larger than Roosevelt—but for the rest of his life he took great pleasure in showing it to visitors, calling it "my most precious possession . . . the gift of my great and good friend, President Roosevelt, on whom God has had mercy."

The two leaders spent five hours together, and by all accounts they got on splendidly. Ibn Saud was already favorably inclined toward the United States. American missionary doctors had treated thousands of Saudis free of charge. One of the patients was Ibn Saud himself, who developed a severe eye inflammation, urgently summoned the chief of the American medical mission, and was soon cured. He perceived a vivid contrast that the Iranians and others in the Middle East also saw: Europeans came to oppress and loot, but Americans came only to help.

There was another reason Ibn Saud liked the idea of allying himself with the Americans. He confessed it years later, when an American asked him why he had chosen to embrace the United States rather than accept one of the offers he had received from British, French, and German oil companies.

"You are very far away!" he replied.

After Roosevelt had completed his pleasantries, he asked Ibn Saud whether he could support the idea of a Jewish state in Palestine. The king said he could not, and warned Roosevelt that if such a state were created, "the heavens will split, the earth will be rent asunder, and the mountains will tremble at what the Jews claim in Palestine, both materially and spiritually." Roosevelt asked him what other option might be offered to hundreds of thousands of homeless Jews who were emerging from concentration camps.

"Give them and their descendants the choicest lands and homes of the Germans who oppressed them," the king replied. "What injury have Arabs done to the Jews of Europe? It is the Christian Germans who stole their homes and lives. Let the Germans pay."

The two leaders then moved to the main subject: oil. Saudi Arabia would produce much, Roosevelt said, and would need not just a market but a protecting power. He assured Ibn Saud that whatever happened in the future, the United States would never invade or occupy his country. That was what the king wished to hear. He said he admired the United States as a power that did not colonize, and trusted Roosevelt because he was a proven champion of freedom. As long as the United States would respect Saudi Arabia's independence, he said, Saudi Arabia would be its faithful partner.

"The President," wrote Ambassador Eddy, who served as translator during these meetings, "then gave Ibn Saud the double assurance, repeated just one week before his death in his letter to Ibn Saud, dated April 5, 1945: (1) He personally, as president, would never do anything which might prove hostile to the Arabs; and (2) the U.S. Government would make no change in its basic policy in Palestine without full and prior consultation with both Jews and Arabs. To the King, these oral assurances were equal to an alliance; he did not foresee that Death was waiting in the wings to bear the speaker away before the promises could be redeemed."

With that, a fateful alliance was sealed. Saudi Arabia was soon shown to have one-fourth of the world's oil. It sold vast amounts to the United States, sent much of the money it earned back to America to pay for advanced weaponry, and contributed generously to American-backed anti-Communist movements around the world. In exchange the United States protected the al-Saud family regime and refrained from inquiring into the troubling realities of Saudi life.

The shipboard meeting between Roosevelt and Ibn Saud gave birth to one of America's two key relationships in the Middle East. The other, with Israel, emerged soon afterward. These two relationships have shaped American policy toward the Middle East for more than half a century. In Washington the principle has usually been: What Saudi Arabia wants, Saudi Arabia gets; what Israel wants, Israel gets.

For part of this time Iran was a close American ally, but that alliance collapsed violently after Mohammad Reza Shah was overthrown in 1979. Turkey, as a NATO member, was also an ally of the United States, but it had neither oil nor a distinct security identity. Saudi Arabia and Israel have been Washington's intimate Middle East partners for the last half-century.

These two relationships are frozen in time. They have not evolved as the world has evolved. Worse, they have proven unequal to the challenge of peace. The decades during which the United States has shaped its

Middle East policy according to the perceived interests of Saudi Arabia and Israel have been decades of war, terror, privation, and intensifying hatred. They have also been decades during which the United States has lost much support, influence, and strategic power in the Middle East. This will continue as long as these two relationships remain unchanged.

America's friendship with Saudi Arabia is usually presumed to be based on its need for oil. Its ties to Israel are often described as based on shared values. Both of these clichés are true, but they do not tell the full story.

During the second half of the twentieth century, nothing was more important to the United States than waging the cold war. Many countries joined that fight. Most cooperated in the light of day; they condemned Soviet power, joined or supported NATO, and backed America at the United Nations. But when it came to fighting cold war battles that were waged illegally, in the shadows, without rules, those countries shrank back. Israel and Saudi Arabia never did. This made them Washington's best partners—perhaps even indispensable ones—in the global confrontation of that era.

For much of Harry Truman's life, including his years as president, scornful critics liked to dismiss him as a "failed haberdasher." He and a partner did indeed run a men's clothing shop in Kansas City, Truman & Jacobson, and it did indeed collapse after three years, leaving both men deeply in debt. Truman's rise from this failure to the pinnacle of world power is a familiar, quintessentially American rags-to-riches story. Less familiar is the story of Eddie Jacobson, his partner in failure. Jacobson spent the next twenty years as a traveling salesman, and in 1945—the same year Truman became president following Franklin Roosevelt's death—returned to Kansas City and opened his own haberdashery. History records Truman's decisive role in creating the state of Israel; it was Eddie Jacobson, though, who helped persuade his old friend to play that role.

In the years after World War II, as the scale of the Holocaust became clear, world opinion began to coalesce around the idea of a Jewish state in Palestine. The British, who were retreating from imperial power, decided to end their mandate there and pass this problem to the United Nations—meaning, in essence, the United States. Zionist leaders understood that their most urgent priority was to win President Truman to their cause.

In their search for ways to do it, they found Eddie Jacobson.

The son of Jewish immigrants from Lithuania, Jacobson grew up on the Lower East Side of New York, volunteered to fight in World War I, and at Fort Sill in Oklahoma met another volunteer, Harry Truman. They ran the base canteen together, served side by side, and became lifelong friends, with a relationship like that of brothers. In 1947, as the United Nations vote on partitioning Palestine approached, an official of the Jewish fraternal society B'nai B'rith learned of their relationship. He asked Jacobson, who was also a B'nai B'rith member, to appeal to Truman. The result was a passionate letter from Jacobson to the president "on behalf of my people."

"The future of one and one-half million Jews in Europe depends on what happens at the present meeting of the United Nations," Jacobson wrote to his closest friend. "Tens of thousands of lives depend on the words from your mouth and heart. Harry, my people need help and I am appealing to you to help them."

Jacobson followed up his letter with several private visits to the White House, where Truman received him whenever he wished, no appointment necessary. These meetings had their effect. Truman announced that the United States favored the UN resolution under which a portion of Palestine would be reserved for Jews, and applied America's full power to assure its passage. On November 29, 1947, the resolution passed with thirty-three countries voting in favor, thirteen against, and ten abstaining. Upon hearing the news, Jacobson made a two-word entry in his diary: "Mission accomplished."

Not quite. Six months still remained until the British would withdraw from Palestine. In that time, Zionist leaders had to win Truman's support for the second stage of their plan: to create a full-fledged state on the land the UN had allotted to them, rather than accept some other option like making it part of a federation with a new Arab state in Palestine. They were intense months. "I do not think I ever had so much pressure and propaganda at the White House as I had in this instance," Truman later recalled. Most of it came from Jews in Washington and beyond.

"Jesus Christ couldn't please them when he was on earth," Truman complained, "so how could anyone expect I would have my luck?"

News of Truman's rising anger alarmed Zionists, who feared that the prize they were so close to winning might be snatched from them at the last moment. They decided to bring Chaim Weizmann, the eminence of the Zionist movement and a highly persuasive figure, to the White House. Truman, however, refused to see him. The national chairman of B'nai B'rith, Frank Goldman, asked Jacobson to intercede. Jacobson agreed to write a letter to Truman, but when he did, Truman's answer was still no. That led Jacobson to decide he needed to travel to Washington and plead his case in person.

He came to the White House on Saturday morning, March 12, 1948. The president was in a foul mood, cursing the Jews who were pressuring him as "disrespectful and mean" and, as Jacobson later wrote, coming "as close to being an anti-Semite as a man could possibly be." Truman had just written in his diary that Jews were "very, very selfish" and that "neither Hitler nor Stalin has anything on them for cruelty or mistreatment of the underdog."

Friendship and the urgency of the matter at hand, however, gave Jacobson the courage to persevere.

"Harry, all your life you had a hero," he began, pointing to a painting of Andrew Jackson on the Oval Office wall. "Well, Harry, I too have a hero, a man I have never met, but who is, I think, the greatest Jew who ever lived. . . . He is a sick man, almost broken in health, but he has traveled thousands and thousands of miles just to see you and plead the cause of my people. Now you refuse to see him because you were insulted by some American Jewish leaders. . . . It doesn't sound like you, Harry. . . . I wouldn't be here if I didn't know that if you will see him, you will be properly and accurately informed on the situation as it exists in Palestine, and yet you refuse to see him."

Jacobson was in tears by the time he finished. Truman had been loudly drumming on his table with his fingers. When his friend finished, he turned his swivel chair away and stared out into the Rose Garden. Finally he swerved back.

"You win, you bald-headed son of a bitch," he said. "I will see him."

Jacobson was so shaken by this meeting that before reporting to Goldman at his hotel, he stopped at a bar and chugged two double bourbons, the first alcohol he had ever tasted. When he told Goldman the news, Goldman embraced and kissed him.

Five days later Weizmann was escorted secretly into the White House. He was among the world's most passionately engaged statesmen, and his magic worked on Truman. On May 14, the day before the British mandate over Palestine was to expire, Israel proclaimed its birth as a state, effective at midnight. Eleven minutes after that moment, at 6:11 P.M. in Washington, the United States recognized it as a sovereign nation. That evening Jacobson sent Truman a telegram saying simply, "Thanks and God bless you."

Two weeks later, Weizmann returned to Washington as president of Israel. Instead of sneaking into the White House, he arrived in a motorcade. Truman welcomed him warmly, and at a ceremony on the portico, Weizmann presented him with a scroll of the Torah.

Jacobson's efforts were not all that persuaded Truman. The tragedy of the Holocaust also weighed on him. Zionist groups across the United States held rallies and organized campaigns that brought hundreds of thousands of letters and cards flooding into the White House. Nor was it lost on Truman that, with his reelection campaign in full swing, mobilizing the Jewish vote would help. He decided to recognize Israel over the vigorous objection of the three men on whom he normally relied for guidance in foreign policy: Secretary of Defense James Forrestal, Undersecretary of State Dean Acheson, and Secretary of State George Marshall.

A few months after Truman left office, the Jewish Theological Seminary in New York honored him at a banquet. Eddie Jacobson introduced him. "This is the man who helped create the State of Israel," he told the crowd.

"What do you mean, 'helped create'?" Truman thundered back. "I am Cyrus! I am Cyrus!"

The visionary American gangster Bugsy Siegel, who helped build the mob-run gambling hub at Las Vegas, was not a sentimental man. Nor was the Zionist agent who approached him before the United Nations vote of 1947 and asked for help. The agent told him that the Jews in Palestine believed they would have to fight to defend the country the United Nations was about to give them. Siegel and other Jewish crime bosses like Meyer Lansky, Mickey Cohen, and Moe Dalitz, he said, were bound by their heritage to help.

"Do you really want to tell me that the Jews in Palestine have taken up arms, shoot, fight?" Siegel asked incredulously.

"Yes."

"When you say 'fight,' you mean kill?"

"Yes."

"Then I'm your man."

For months thereafter, Siegel called his friend regularly and told him when bags of cash would be waiting for him at a Los Angeles restaurant. He enlisted gangsters and entertainers to the cause, mostly Jews but also mob-connected celebrities like Frank Sinatra, who one evening in 1948 agreed—over drinks after a performance at the Copacabana in New York—to carry a suitcase of illicit cash to a boat captain waiting at the waterfront. The boat was full of weapons and ammunition for Jewish fighters in Palestine, but the captain refused to sail unless paid in advance. Teddy Kollek, the Zionist agent who ran the arms-smuggling operation— and who later became mayor of Jerusalem—was under FBI surveillance and could not deliver it. He arranged for Sinatra to visit him at his hotel suite, pick up the cash-filled suitcase, and slip out a back door with it while Kollek, his FBI tail close behind him, left through the front door.

Smuggling operations like this one were part of a multifaceted campaign that brought decisive support from America to the Zionist cause. Dozens of former U.S. military pilots and more than one thousand veterans of the U.S. Army, most of them Jewish, were recruited to fight in Palestine. Between 1946 and 1948 the United Jewish Appeal raised more than $350 million for the Zionist cause. Americans helped assure that when war came to the Holy Land, the Jews would be ready.

In the days after Israel proclaimed its independence on May 14, 1948, twenty-five thousand soldiers from Lebanon, Syria, Egypt, Transjordan, and Iraq stormed across its borders. Israel fought back with impressive power. On June 11 a truce brokered by the United Nations came into effect. With Americans at its side, Israel survived an attempt by its neighbors to strangle it at birth.

Once this battle was won, the United States began treating Israel like any other developing country. It was made eligible for aid under the "Point Four" program, which would bring it $3 million to $4 million annually. Israel wanted much more, and Abba Eban, its ambassador in Washington, set out to obtain it. In the early 1950s Eban helped forge a lobby group called the American Zionist Council, later renamed the American Israel Public Affairs Committee, or AIPAC. It won a quick series of victories, persuading Congress to approve $65 million in aid for Israel and another $70 million in low-interest loans, none of it requested by the White House.

During the Eisenhower presidency, there was much talk about "friendly impartiality" in the Middle East and an "even-handed" approach to Arabs and Israelis. Secretary of State John Foster Dulles toured the Middle East in 1953 and told the Israeli prime minister, David Ben-Gurion, that the United States needed good relations with the Arab states as well as with Israel. Later that year, after Israeli soldiers killed dozens of civilians in what the Israeli government called a retaliation raid on the Jordanian town of Qibya, President Eisenhower temporarily suspended American aid. Assistant Secretary of State Henry Byroade pleaded with Israel to change its ways:

To the Israelis I say that you should come to truly look upon yourselves as a Middle Eastern state, and see your own future in that context rather than as a headquarters or nucleus, so to speak, of a worldwide grouping of peoples of a particular religious faith, who must have special religious rights within and obligations to the Israeli state. You should drop the attitude of the conqueror, and the conviction that force and a policy of retaliatory killings is the only policy that your neighbors will understand. You should make your deeds correspond to your frequent utterance of the desire for peace.

Speeches like this, even though they carried no explicit threat, deeply distressed Ambassador Eban. He said they reminded him of a judge who promised a defendant justice, only to have the defendant reply, "That's exactly what frightens me. I'm looking for mercy." Then, in quick succession, two dramatic events reshaped world politics in ways that gave the United States a new appreciation for Israel.

In the spring of 1956, the CIA received reports that the Soviet leader, Nikita Khrushchev, had delivered a secret speech in which he depicted Stalin as an oppressor and mass murderer. Allen Dulles, the CIA director, was desperate to obtain a copy of this speech, but could not. Israel, working through an agent in Poland, came up with one and passed it to the Americans, who spread it around the world. Dulles later claimed this as the greatest triumph of his career. Not for many years did it become clear that the credit was Israel's. Those who knew the story, however, developed a new respect for Israel's value as a strategic partner.

Later in 1956, President Gamal Abdel Nasser of Egypt stunned the world by nationalizing the Suez Canal. Britain and France, the powers that had built and owned the canal, rightly saw this as a fundamental challenge to their imperial rights. They decided to invade Egypt, take back the canal, and if possible depose Nasser's regime. Israel, which considered Nasser its main enemy, joined them. The three powers launched their invasion on October 29. In Washington, President Eisenhower was outraged at what he considered a retrograde attempt to reimpose European colonialism in the Middle East. He directed a global diplomatic effort, focused at the United Nations, that forced the invaders to withdraw.

The Suez crisis showed the Israelis that the United States had become the dominant power in their region, and therefore their indispensable ally. Americans, for their part, developed a new respect for Israel's military strength.

President Eisenhower and Secretary of State Dulles saw the world through a single lens, that of the cold war. They tried to woo Nasser, who was emerging as the most exciting Arab leader in generations, to their side, but he chose to cast his lot with the Soviets. By 1956 Soviet-bloc arms were streaming into Egypt. That made Washington's calculus easy: Egypt is a Soviet client; Israel opposes Egypt; therefore Israel must be America's friend.

Israeli and American leaders shaped a warm relationship in the years that followed. Ordinary Americans also came to admire Israel—but for reasons that had nothing to do with politics.

The bestselling book of 1958 in the United States—it sold two million copies in a matter of months, more than any book since *Gone with the Wind*—was Leon Uris's captivating epic *Exodus*, about the founding of Israel. Its hero, Ari Ben Canaan, is a Jewish freedom fighter whose fiancée has been tortured to death by Arabs. Other characters include an idealistic American nurse whose conscience moves her to join the Zionist cause, a British officer tormented by memories of a concentration camp he helped liberate, and a quiet Polish teenager who becomes an anti-Arab guerrilla and later an officer in the Israel Defense Forces.

"The melodrama sweeps the reader up in a tide of emotional involvement and identification of the heroes [and] neatly divides the world into diametric opposites," the Israeli scholar Rachel Weissbrod wrote. "[Uris] took advantage of the trademark characteristics of melodrama—external rather than internal conflict, hyperbolically drawn black-and-white characters, and allegiance to accepted tenets—to paint a glowing portrait of the Zionist enterprise."

Two years after its publication, *Exodus* was made into a stirring film, directed by Otto Preminger and starring Paul Newman and Eva Marie Saint, that had an even greater impact on the American consciousness. Israel's birth was cast as an archetypal struggle for freedom and redemption, while faceless Arabs seemed to have no motives other than the blind hatred that drove Nazi monsters. The score featured a song that became hugely popular in versions by Andy Williams, Pat Boone, Connie Francis, and a host of others.

"This land is mine, God gave this land to me," the lyrics say. "If I must fight, I'll fight to make this land my own. Until I die—this land is mine!"

There was also a spate of biblical films during this period, most notably the epic *Ben-Hur*, which won a record eleven Academy Awards, including Best Picture of 1959. Together with *Exodus*, these movies had an immense impact on the American popular consciousness. From them Americans took two messages: that Christianity and Judaism are intimately tied, and that Americans and Israelis share values, traditions, and ideals.

After President Kennedy was assassinated in 1963, his successor, Lyndon Johnson, told an Israeli diplomat, "You have lost a very great friend, but you have found a better one." Johnson's grandfather had been a strict Baptist who told him when he entered politics that he must "take care of the Jews, God's chosen people"; his Bible-thumping aunt warned him, "If Israel is destroyed, the world will end."

"Israel, for him, was a latter-day Alamo, surrounded on all sides by compassionless enemies," wrote the historian Michael Oren, who later became the Israeli ambassador to the United States. "Nasser was the reincarnated Santa Ana."

Early on the morning of June 5, 1967, waves of Israeli fighter jets flew in tight formation toward Egypt. They spent the day bombing Egyptian bases. By nightfall they had destroyed more than three hundred war planes on the ground—nearly all of Egypt's air force.

Two days later an Israeli land force captured Jerusalem. A second force stormed across the Sinai Desert to the edge of the Suez Canal. A third occupied parts of Syria. Israel won one of the quickest and most dramatic victories in the history of modern warfare.

The Six-Day War, launched by Israel to preempt what it believed was an imminent Arab attack, was the most crucial episode in the history of U.S.-Israel relations.

Until this moment, even the most pro-Israel of American leaders considered Israel a consumer of American security, a weak ally that the United States was obliged to defend. With its battlefield victories over much larger countries, it suddenly looked like a country that could *provide* security. Rather than a drag on the West—John Foster Dulles called it "the millstone around our necks"—it had become a dominant regional power.

"Incidentally, Israel at war destroys the stereotype of the pale, scrawny Jew," Johnson's special envoy to the region, Harry McPherson, added in his report to the White House. "The soldiers I saw were tough, muscular and sunburned."

Five months after this quick war, the United Nations Security Council passed its famous Resolution 242, which to this day is more widely cited than any other document as the basis for long-term peace in the region. Much of the world considered it a logical compromise, and still does. Not surprisingly, though, it satisfied none of the belligerents.

Israel interpreted the clause requiring it to withdraw "from territories occupied in the recent conflict" as meaning that it should withdraw from some territories, but not all. Arabs insisted that Israel must give up all conquered land. They also refused to accept the resolution's requirement that they recognize Israel's "territorial integrity and political independence."

In the years that followed, the United States made sporadic efforts to push Israel and Arabs toward comprehensive peace. All failed. In October 1973 Syria and Egypt attacked Israel on the Jewish holiday of Yom Kippur. This war went badly for Israel at first, but seven days after it began, the United States launched a massive resupply airlift. Planes full of weaponry landed in Tel Aviv at the rate of nearly one per hour, twenty-four hours a day, for more than a week. While this airlift was under way, Congress approved President Richard Nixon's request for $2.2 billion in emergency arms aid to Israel. Thus reinforced, Israeli troops turned the tide of war and pushed to within fifty miles of Cairo.

In the aftermath of the Yom Kippur War, Israel developed a strategic culture based on the unconventional use of military power. This appealed to American leaders, who were eager to wage covert cold war battles in various parts of the world but were hampered by troublesome legal restrictions. Israel became a prized, semisecret partner of the United States: a trainer of anti-Communist forces that the United States could not directly train, a conduit for arming regimes and rebel groups the United States could not openly arm, and a productive source of intelligence from around the world.

Death came from the air in the lush volcanic highlands of Guatemala, where Mayan Indians have lived since time immemorial. During the 1970s and '80s, soldiers killed more people in Guatemala than in the rest of Latin America combined. Often they attacked from aircraft unlike any these wretched Indians had ever seen.

Storming off their strange-looking planes, soldiers would surround a village, assemble its citizens, and kill the lucky ones—others would be saved for torture—with state-of-the-art assault rifles. Years later a United Nations investigation found that Guatemalan soldiers had rampaged with "extreme cruelty that led to the extermination *en masse* of defenseless Mayan communities." The UN estimated that between 1978 and 1984, Guatemalan soldiers killed about 180,000 people, most of them unarmed peasants.

For nearly all of this period, the United States was banned by an act of Congress from selling weapons to Guatemala's military regime. European countries also refused to arm it. Nonetheless weaponry flooded in. Most remarkable were the short-takeoff-and-landing planes, called Aravas, that ferried soldiers to the villages where they did their killing.

The army also bought helicopters, patrol boats, artillery pieces, grenade launchers, one thousand machine guns, and fifty thousand assault rifles. All came from the same source: Israel.

Guatemalan intelligence officers tracked their victims with help from a computer system that an Israeli firm installed in the National Palace. A veteran of the Israel Defense Forces who had trained security forces in Israel became the Guatemalan army's top military instructor.

"We've indicated we're not unhappy they're helping out," a spokesman for the U.S. State Department said when asked about Israel's support for Guatemala.

President Ronald Reagan considered the guerrilla insurgency in Guatemala part of the global Communist offensive he was sworn to fight. Determined to crush it, he asked Israel to sell the Guatemalan army whatever it wanted. Israel eagerly agreed. During the height of the Guatemalan civil war, Israeli companies supplied nearly all of the army's weaponry—$20 million worth in 1984 alone.

"The Uzi submachine gun is the preferred weapon of the liquidation units operating in the early hours against dissidents, Indians and non-Indians, or against *campesinos*, the poor farmers, whenever they take the initiative to organize agricultural cooperatives or attempt to find out the fate of disappeared relatives," the Israeli newspaper *Ha'aretz* reported in 1985. "Israelis who visit Guatemala are shocked to see the special Army units wearing Israeli uniforms and armed with Israeli weapons."

While the Guatemalan highlands were being drenched with blood, the same thing was happening in nearby El Salvador. Israel became El Salvador's main arms supplier after President Jimmy Carter cut off military aid in 1977. Israeli advisers trained the Salvadoran secret police and elite army units. The director-general of the Israeli foreign ministry insisted that Israelis in El Salvador were "agricultural advisers," but their real job was so widely known that a Tel Aviv newspaper published a petition signed by 144 high school students protesting their country's role in the Salvadoran civil war.

The third conflict raging in Central America during the 1980s was in Nicaragua, where American-backed "contra" guerrillas were fighting to depose the leftist Sandinista regime. President Reagan felt a visceral tie to the contras, whom he called "the moral equivalent of our founding fathers." After Congress cut off aid to the contras, he turned to Israel. Thus began Operation Tipped Kettle, under which, according to Lieutenant Colonel Oliver North, one of its organizers, Israel "secretly provided several hundred tons of weapons" to the contras. To cover their tracks, the Israelis sent no weapons of their own, only supplies they had captured from Palestinians or bought through middlemen from Poland and Czechoslovakia. As compensation, Colonel North asserted in a court deposition, the United States assured Israel "that in exchange for the weapons, the U.S. government would be as flexible as possible in its approach to Israeli military and economic needs, and that it would find a way to compensate Israel for its assistance."

The contras maintained bases in Honduras, which made the Honduran army another essential U.S. ally. That army, however, like those of Guatemala and El Salvador, behaved with a brutality that repelled many in Congress. Israeli contractors stepped into the breach. They sent advisers to train elite Honduran units, including the notorious Battalion 316, which was later found to have kidnapped and murdered scores of Honduran labor organizers, antiwar protesters, and other dissidents. In 1982, at the height of this repressive campaign, Israeli minister of defense Ariel Sharon visited Honduras and announced that Israel would sell tanks and jet fighters to its army.

"We had Israeli advisors in the Honduran special forces," General Walter López, commander of the Honduran army, said after leaving office. "They were seconded to our special forces by the Israeli ministry of defense, although they came officially as 'non-governmental.' Their front was that they were training special security groups for the president and military chiefs, but behind that was everything else: special operations courses, courses on how to take over buildings, planes, hostages.... There was coordination between them and the CIA."

Washington's other main client on the Central American isthmus was General Manuel Antonio Noriega, the Panamanian strongman.

Noriega amassed a fortune from drug trafficking while the CIA was paying him $200,000 per year as a prized "asset." His chief adviser and alter ego was the most flamboyant Israeli agent in Latin America, Mike Harari, a former Mossad officer famous for having headed the death squad that tracked and killed the Palestinian terrorists who murdered Israeli athletes at the 1972 Munich Olympics. In Panama, "Mad Mike" arranged a money-laundering operation by which Noriega deposited his drug profits in Swiss banks, designed eavesdropping and surveillance systems that allowed Noriega to spy on his enemies, and served as a well-paid middleman for Noriega's purchase of half a billion dollars' worth of Israeli weapons.

"In Central America, Israel is the 'dirty work' contractor for the U.S. administration," General Matityahu Peled, a member of the Israeli Knesset, said as his country's operations in the region were at their peak. "Israel is acting as an accomplice and arm of the United States."

Central American armies were not the only ones that turned to Israel for help. Dictators around the world, from Bolivia, Chile, and the Dominican Republic to Burma, the Philippines, and Indonesia, equipped their soldiers with Galil assault rifles and Uzi submachine guns.

Israel also became the principal arms supplier for the apartheid regime in South Africa, which President Reagan fervently supported but could not arm because of congressional restrictions. Israelis trained South Africa's elite police and military units, sold tanks and aviation technology to its army, licensed the production of Galil rifles at a factory in South Africa, and even advised the regime on developing nuclear weapons. In 1976 Prime Minister John Vorster of South Africa, whom the British had jailed during World War II for his pro-Nazi activities, was given a red-carpet welcome in Israel, laid a wreath at the Yad Vashem Holocaust memorial, and heard Prime Minister Yitzhak Rabin praise him at a state banquet for creating a "prosperous atmosphere of cooperation" between their two countries.

Israelis trained more than a dozen guerrilla and paramilitary forces blessed by Washington. They established private security forces in

Colombia that ranchers and drug traffickers used to protect themselves and dispatch their enemies, and did the same in the Philippines during the Ferdinand Marcos dictatorship. In 1986 Israeli and American advisers worked together to shape two thousand Libyan exiles into a guerrilla force to fight Muammar Qadaffi's regime. After Congress banned U.S. aid to anti-Marxist rebels in Angola, Israel sent them trainers, paid for indirectly by the Reagan administration.

"Israel's main role in the partnership was as a go-between," Prime Minister Shimon Peres later told his biographer. "There were countries . . . that the United States wanted to assist. It was very convenient in cases such as this to give the aid via Israel, or to encourage Israel to step up its exports to these countries."

All of these unsavory countries had powerful friends in Washington, but those friends could not embrace them publicly. Israel had no such reservations. Whatever country the United States wanted to help but could not, Israel could and did.

"We maintained a very, very intimate dialogue on various parts of the world," David Kimche, the top Israeli diplomat of the era, later recalled. "We used to discuss what one should do in third-world countries, in the Middle East, etcetera. We'd give our opinion and they would give theirs. It was a *very* intimate dialogue."

One day at the beginning of 1984, President Reagan's national security adviser, Robert MacFarlane, told Prince Bandar bin Sultan, the urbane, worldly Saudi Arabian ambassador in Washington, that they needed to have a "no-conversation conversation." Bandar had access to the kingdom's checkbook and knew what was coming.

"What do you want?" he asked.

One million dollars a month for the contras in Nicaragua, came the reply.

This was a pittance for a country that, in the year just ended, had earned $36 billion from oil sales. Prince Bandar said Saudi Arabia would provide it. Soon afterward MacFarlane asked him to double the contribution; he agreed to that, too. Saudi Arabia contributed a total of $32 million to the contra cause, all of it collected clandestinely at the margins of American law.

Nicaragua was not all the United States had on its mind during the 1980s. Another anti-Communist war was under way half a world away, in Afghanistan, where CIA-backed guerrillas were fighting the mighty Red Army. This was the costliest operation the CIA had ever launched. To finance it, the United States turned to Saudi Arabia. The Saudis responded by opening their treasury in a way no country ever has for a covert American war.

Here Saudi Arabia vividly affirmed its cold war commitment to the United States: our checkbook is your checkbook.

Saudi princes so admired CIA director William Casey that they provided him with his own villa in the capital, Riyadh. Its special feature was a set of thirty artistically designed bowls, each holding a different kind of cashew, Casey's favorite snack. When Casey made a secret trip to the kingdom at the beginning of 1984, though, he was looking for more than nuts.

The *mujahideen* insurgency in Afghanistan had already become the most ambitious and expensive operation in CIA history. Casey wanted to expand it further. He told King Fahd that this was the crucial battle of the age, a chance for Americans and Saudis to join in destroying the Soviet power they both detested. To do that, more money would be needed than the United States government could provide.

"What can you do to help us?" Casey asked King Fahd.

"Do what you can," Fahd replied. "I'll match it."

Soon afterward, a senior Saudi intelligence officer flew to Pakistan, where the Afghan rebels were based. The Pakistani dictator, General Muhammad Zia ul-Haq, received him personally. Zia was not interested in hearing what he had to say, but rather in seeing what was inside the boxes he had brought with him. The general ordered a couple of aides to take the boxes to another room and open them. They returned soon afterward with good news: just as Zia had hoped, the boxes were packed with bundles of fresh hundred-dollar bills, $1.8 million worth.

From that moment, the Saudis faithfully matched every dollar the CIA sent to Afghan rebels. That meant $470 million in 1985, $630 million in 1986, and steadily increasing sums for the next several years. Ultimately Saudi Arabia contributed more than $6 billion to support the Afghan insurgency.

"We don't do operations," the longtime Saudi intelligence director, Prince Turki al-Faisal, once explained. "We don't know how. All we know how to do is write checks."

Besides their considerable contribution to the *mujahideen*, the Saudis also sent hundreds of millions of dollars to the Pakistani army and intelligence service. Further afield, they aided whatever government, rebel force, or individual leader they and their American friends considered worth aiding. They sent President Anwar Sadat of Egypt, Washington's favorite Arab leader, an annual subsidy of $200 million; gave the conservative regime in Yemen money to buy American weapons when it faced a leftist uprising; paid for an emergency airlift of Moroccan troops to Zaire when rebels threatened the dictator Mobutu Sese Seko; contributed $15 million to pro-American rebels in Angola; and provided what the *New York Times* called "sizable amounts of money to the government of Somalia in the late 1970s that helped switch that country's allegiance from the Soviet Union to the West."

"Often I found through other channels a helpful Saudi footprint placed so unobtrusively that one gust of wind could erase its traces," Henry Kissinger later wrote.

While supporting projects around the world favored by American leaders, the Saudis never forgot American leaders themselves. Anytime a president or other influential figure wanted money for a pet project, from the John F. Kennedy Center for the Performing Arts to the "Just Say No" antidrug campaign, they were happy to help. Saudis have contributed to the building of every presidential library since Jimmy Carter's, with gifts in the $10 million range. Upon realizing that Nancy Reagan had a weakness for jewelry, the Saudi government sent her a briefcase containing $2 million worth of diamonds, which she had mounted onto a tiara by the New York designer Harry Winston. Soon afterward Mrs.

Reagan asked Prince Bandar if he could find a job for Michael Deaver, a former White House aide who had fallen on hard times; Bandar hired him as a consultant, paying him $50,000 per month but never asking him to do any work.

Saudi Arabia had become so rich that these contributions barely dented its treasury. Its income skyrocketed with the price of oil. In 1969–74 its five-year budget was $9.2 billion; for the next five-year period it was $142 billion.

The money Saudi Arabia sent to Afghan rebels brought handsome returns. It helped the rebels deal a blow to the Soviets, whom the arch-conservative Saudis detested. It also won them much gratitude in the United States, where they wished to buy advanced weaponry. Their first payoff came quickly, when they asked President Reagan to supply them with four hundred Stinger antiaircraft missiles, a transfer forbidden by law. Reagan invoked an emergency provision and sent the missiles.

"We don't put conditions on friends," he told Prince Bandar.

Over the decades that followed, Saudi Arabia bought more weaponry from the United States than any other country. In 1972 it bought $305 million worth; by 1975 the sum had increased more then tenfold, to $5 billion. The political alliance that pushed these sales through Congress—the U.S. defense industry, the White House, and the Saudis themselves—even managed to deal the Israel lobby the only significant defeat in its history. It came when Congress narrowly approved an $8.5 billion sale of AWACS early-warning planes to Saudi Arabia in 1981, over strenuous objection from Israel.

"If you knew what we were really doing for America," Bandar said during this debate, "you wouldn't just give us AWACS, you'd give us nuclear weapons."

As the world changed, these arms sales never stopped or even slowed. A 1990 headline in the *New York Times* read "U.S. to Sell Saudis $20 Billion in Arms; Weapons Deal Is Largest in History." A headline seventeen years later was almost identical: "U.S. Set to Offer $20 Billion Arms Deal to Saudi Arabia and Other Gulf States."

These deals gave Saudi Arabia great military power, but they cast the regime in a dubious light at home because they proclaimed its intimacy with the United States. Some Saudis saw this partnership—between a regime that considers itself the defender of pure Islam and the world's most powerful Christian nation—as a symbol of the regime's hypocrisy. They were also repelled by the lifestyle of some Saudi princes, which they associated with yachts, private jets, opulent estates, casino gambling, multimillion-dollar shopping sprees, and corrupt debauchery.

Anger over this hypocrisy began turning some young Saudis, inculcated with the militant principles of Wahhabi Islam, into enemies of the regime. What better way for the regime to protect itself against this threat than by sending these passionate idealists to fight abroad? Thousands of Saudis traveled to Afghanistan to fight alongside the *mujahideen*. Others fought in Kashmir, Bosnia, and Chechnya. At least some might have turned against the Saudi regime if they had not found other causes far away.

The al-Saud family's balancing act—preaching austere Islam while embracing the United States and allowing princes to live notoriously un-Islamic lives—requires a special arrangement. This arrangement is a bargain between the family and Wahhabi clerics. It brought the regime to power and has sustained its rule ever since.

Wahhabi Muslims, who prefer to call themselves *muwahhidun*, or "unifiers," reject everything that smacks of ostentation, from music to tiled mosques to nail polish. Some oppose the use of any device invented after the seventh century, when the Prophet Muhammad lived. They abhor the use of "graven images," and with it painting, photography, and television. Although they scorn Christians and Jews, they even more fiercely condemn those they consider apostate Muslims, especially Sufis and Shiites.

The allied forces of the al-Saud and al-Wahhab families waged a series of wars that shook the Arabian Peninsula for nearly two hundred years. In the early twentieth century, with British help, they overran most of Arabia, and in 1932 they established their state, Saudi Arabia.

Their leader, Abdul-Aziz ibn Abd al-Rahman ibn Faisal al-Saud, became known in the West as Ibn Saud; it was he who met Franklin Roosevelt aboard the USS *Quincy* as World War II was ending.

American leaders felt blessed to have a partner nation that generously provided oil, returned much of its profit to the United States in the form of weapons purchases, and faithfully supported American interests around the world. This relationship became a bedrock of American foreign policy. It transcended politics. Jimmy Carter was probably not exaggerating when he said there "has not been any nation in the world that has been more cooperative than Saudi Arabia." George W. Bush had just as much reason to pledge "eternal friendship" to the al-Saud monarchy a generation later.

This monarchy governs in a power-sharing agreement with Wahhabi clerics. The ruling family allows the clerics to enforce harsh religious law. It also gives them great sums of money, which they use to build fundamentalist religious schools in Saudi Arabia and throughout the Muslim world. In exchange, the clerics ignore the al-Saud family's un-Islamic ways and bless its alliance with the United States.

The essence of this deal is, as former CIA director James Woolsey put it, "for the Wahhabis to be given all of the money in the world they could ever remotely dream of needing or wanting to spread their sect's beliefs, and for them to leave the House of Saud alone." Saudis frustrated by this arrangement have shaken the kingdom several times. Forbidden to speak as they might in a more open society, they have several times exploded in violence.

The most stunning blow ever struck against the Saudi state was delivered as the call to prayer floated through Mecca's hot desert air at 5:18 on the morning of November 20, 1979. A conspirator named Juhayman al-Otaybi moved silently among the faithful. He was a fugitive who had quit the National Guard because he felt unable to serve the impure al-Saud family, and had written a stream of tracts denouncing the family as a font of "evil and corruption."

For months Juhayman had been furtively traveling to towns where he knew passionate believers, some of them veterans of a religious uprising the regime had crushed years before. He assembled several hundred followers and brought them to Mecca. Groups of them carried shroud-covered litters like those used to bring corpses to the Grand Mosque for final blessings. Beneath the shrouds were pistols, automatic rifles, and stores of ammunition.

When the mosque's imam began his morning call on November 20, the barefoot figure of Juhayman burst from the crowd.

"Behold the Mahdi! Behold the Right-Guided One!" his followers cried out from the vast courtyard. As they shouted, they sealed the mosque's twenty-five gates, pulled weapons from beneath their robes, and shot every security guard and police officer who tried to resist.

The Grand Mosque, toward which Muslims everywhere turn when they pray to God, had been captured—not by infidels, but by believers. They had three demands: that the al-Saud family be deposed, that ties to the United States be cut, and that strict religious law be imposed upon all in the kingdom.

It took fourteen days for Saudi soldiers, aided by French commandos armed with paralyzing gas grenades, to retake the Grand Mosque. The rebels retreated into the maze of tunnels and compartments that honeycomb the earth below.

"Not a single rebel surrendered voluntarily; they sprang ambushes and fought viciously to the bitter end," the British author Robert Lacey wrote in his account of this siege. "Finally, on Tuesday, December 4, 1979, two weeks to the day from the beginning of the siege, the attackers burst through a metal door to find a huddled group of men, their faces blackened with soot, their ragged clothes soiled with blood and vomit. The gas had had its effect. Some were shivering uncontrollably. But one, hidden among crates of weapons and piles of colored pamphlets, retained the wild and now surprisingly frightened eyes of a cornered beast of prey. 'What is your name?' asked the Saudi captain, pointing his gun. 'Juhayman,' came the reply."

By official accounts, more than one hundred men on each side died inside the Grand Mosque; other estimates place the number in the thousands. Soon afterward, Juhayman and sixty-two of his followers were beheaded in eight public squares around the country. Citizens were called to witness the fate of those who believe they know God's will better than the al-Saud family.

"You know what they have done!" one of the victims shouted to the crowd as his executioner's sword was about to fall. "You have witnessed their sins and their corruption! May their end be most horrible!"

The Grand Mosque seizure deeply shook the al-Saud regime. It had to decide how to respond: by trying to crush religious zealots, or trying to placate them. To no one's surprise, it chose to placate. Determined to prove its fidelity to Wahhabi principles, the regime ordered a crackdown on creeping modernity, including closing all hairdressing salons and dismissing all female television announcers.

"We killed the extremists of 1979, but later on, a few months after we killed them, we adopted their ideology," one Saudi journalist lamented years later. "We gave them what they wanted when they were alive."

The Saudi regime's next great crisis came in 1990, after Saddam Hussein sent Iraqi troops to invade and occupy Kuwait. The al-Saud family feared that if Saddam was not stopped, he might invade Saudi Arabia next. King Fahd was in a state of controlled panic when high-level aides to President George H. W. Bush arrived in Riyadh. Whatever a war against Saddam would cost, Fahd told them, Saudi Arabia would pay.

"What is money between friends?" he reasoned. "You just go to the finance minister and you tell him what you think is appropriate, or what you need."

Saudi Arabia paid $50 billion to underwrite the Gulf War. Hundreds of thousands of American soldiers and huge amounts of military equipment flooded into the kingdom. The war was fought from bases there. Some Saudis were embittered by the royal family's decision to side with the United States against a brother Muslim state. After the war ended, terrorists began striking inside the kingdom. Among their successes was the 1996 suicide bombing of the Khobar Towers residence near the Persian Gulf, in which nineteen American servicemen were killed and nearly four hundred injured.

Then came two attacks outside Saudi Arabia that were attributed to al-Qaeda, an emerging terror group led by the Saudi millionaire Osama bin Laden. In 1998 the American embassies in Kenya and Tanzania were bombed; 244 diplomats and others were killed. Two years later a bomb attack on the destroyer USS *Cole*, which was anchored off the coast of Yemen, took the lives of seventeen American sailors.

This made it unsurprising that fifteen of the nineteen hijackers who carried out the terror attacks of September 11, 2001, along with the man who sent them on their mission, were from Saudi Arabia. The al-Saud family's balancing act had become unsustainable. Its twin pillars of support—the United States and Wahhabi Islam—were so inherently antagonistic that one had to strike out virulently against the other. The products of Saudi Arabia struck first.

"Don't lie to me!" an enraged President Ronald Reagan shouted into the White House telephone.

Prime Minister Menachem Begin of Israel, not accustomed to being addressed this way by American leaders, tried to calm the president. If Reagan believed that Israeli forces were bombing Beirut and killing its people, Begin told him, he was sorely mistaken. On the contrary, he assured his friend, the Israeli invasion force had left Beirut after a quick operation and was retreating back toward its own territory.

Reagan had always been pro-Israel, but he knew Begin was being untruthful. He had just heard by telephone from his personal envoy in Beirut, Philip Habib, who was watching the carnage and described it in horrifying detail. If any more evidence was needed, it was being broadcast live on American television stations, whose correspondents in Beirut were giving breathless commentary as the city was shattered by Israeli bombs.

"I'm sitting here watching it on CNN!" Reagan yelled at Begin. "What one world leader says to another is his word. And you told me yesterday you were pulling out. You're now telling me you *did* pull out, and I'm sitting here watching it!"

The long Israeli war in Lebanon, and especially the killing of several hundred Palestinian civilians by a militia under Israeli protection at the Sabra and Shatila refugee camps, led some Americans to begin reshaping their perceptions of Israel. In the years that followed, Jewish settlements in Israeli-controlled territories steadily expanded. Palestinians launched two uprisings, the *intifadas,* which Israel harshly repressed. At the end of 2008, three years after pulling out its troops and abandoning civilian settlements in Gaza, and provoked by Palestinian rocket attacks, Israel launched a devastating attack on Gaza and then imposed a harsh blockade that United Nations investigators called "a deliberately disproportionate attack designed to punish, humiliate and terrorize a civilian population." American admiration for an idealized Israel—sometimes called "the *Exodus* factor"—began to fade.

During these years, negotiations between Israel and the Arabs produced important results, notably decisions by Israel to withdraw its forces from the Sinai Peninsula and grant limited self-government to Palestinians in the West Bank and Gaza. Prime Minister Begin and President Sadat shook hands on the White House lawn in 1979, and their accord brought them the Nobel Peace Prize. Fourteen years later, also at the White House, Prime Minister Yitzhak Rabin and the Palestinian leader, Yasser Arafat, shook hands on another deal, and they too won Nobel Prizes. Some Arab governments began to accept, however grudgingly, that Israel's existence had become a permanent fact of Middle East life. For all the fanfare that attended them, though, these turned out to be only momentary successes. The world heard a series of catchphrases—Camp David Accords, Madrid Conference, Oslo Process, Road Map, Wye River Memorandum, Annapolis Peace Conference—but to many Palestinians, this was no more than background noise. The crisis dragged endlessly on. It will continue as long as the United States—the most influential player in the Middle East—continues to act as it has in the past.

While the cold war raged, partnerships that bound the United States to Israel and Saudi Arabia served a clear strategic purpose. The world has changed decisively since then. Freed from the constraints of superpower rivalry, America has a chance to reimagine these partnerships. Could they change in ways that might reshape the Middle East? Should the United States be looking for new strategic partners? It so, where should it look? The American political system is notoriously bad at answering complex questions like these.

Old approaches to the Middle East bring only repetition of past failures. Negotiation has become the enemy of peace. The region is crying out for something new. What might it be?

7

SO DEEPLY ENTWINED

It's better for you if I'm neutral. Don't force me. Don't push me to betray my neighbors. Don't make me do things that turn my friends and family into enemies.

Sitting late one summer night at an outdoor restaurant beside the Red Sea in Jeddah, my friend Khaled Batarfi answered that way when I asked him how the United States should treat his country. Our evening was as close to fun as one may legally enjoy in Saudi Arabia. Stars shone above and waves lapped below. Behind us flashed the neon signs of more popular restaurants—Friday's, Applebee's, Ruby Tuesday, Burger King—but we had the pleasure of delicately flavored local seafood.

The very idea of fun—carefree moments, sensual pleasure, escape from the tyranny of routine and obligation—is highly suspect in Saudi Arabia. Drinking alcohol is forbidden. No man may dine publicly with a woman unless they are married. Although conversation is free, unorthodox ideas are not to be broadcast. Khaled used to be a journalist, but he gave it up after his editors, enforcing the government's many unwritten rules, rejected too many of his columns. Now he teaches business at a school for hotel managers.

Some believe the United States should push Saudi Arabia to break out of its reactionary shell, renounce its alliance with Wahhabi fundamentalism, wipe away restrictions on free speech, and let citizens live as they wish. Others believe the United States should warn the al-Saud family against reform because it could lead to upheaval, revolution, and fundamentalist rule. Which is the right path?

Neither.

What do Americans want Saudi Arabia to be? To do? To promote? To suppress? Which leaders in the Middle East should it sponsor, support, oppose, or fight? Which countries should it supply with oil? Which should it boycott? Is absolute monarchy the best form of government for Saudi Arabia? What political system might be better? How should the United States push the al-Saud family in the direction it must go?

In the nearly three-quarters of a century since Franklin Roosevelt met Ibn Saud aboard the USS *Quincy*, American policy makers have devoted enormous energy to debating questions like these. While Washington was fixated on the cold war, those debates may have made sense. They no longer do. Imagining, shaping, and guiding Saudi Arabia is no longer America's business. It is Saudi Arabia's.

Resetting America's approach to the Middle East requires not only building new partnerships but reshaping old ones. The two oldest are those that tie the United States to Saudi Arabia and Israel. Both of these relationships have brought Americans much of value, and will continue to do so in the future. Breaking them off would hardly be in America's interest, not just for evident political, economic, and moral reasons but also because big powers weaken themselves when they are seen as willing to change partners whenever political winds shift. It is right for the United States to remain friends with both Saudi Arabia and Israel. As times have changed, however, the way to be their friend must also change. What served these relationships well for half a century no longer serves them well.

America's challenge is not to find ways out of its friendships with Saudi Arabia and Israel, but to find new ways to be friends with those countries that will, in the changed circumstances of the post–cold war era, truly serve the interests of all parties. The key to making this change is for American leaders to dare something new. For different reasons, neither Saudi Arabia nor Israel is able to articulate or promote policies that serve its own long-term strategic interests. Both are caught in self-destructive patterns. So is the United States. The difference is that the United States, because of its power, its distance from the region, the richness of its strategic options, and the importance of peace in the Middle East for its own security, has the capacity to break away from old patterns. Unless it does so, nothing in that benighted region will change. That will be bad for the United States and for its friends.

Nowhere else on earth does the United States maintain an alliance that requires it to guarantee the right of one family's male heirs to rule indefinitely as they see fit. This was the essence of Franklin Roosevelt's commitment to Ibn Saud in 1945. Since then the relationship has grown wildly out of control, reaching a grotesque peak under the presidency of George W. Bush. The famous photo of Bush holding hands with King Abdullah during the king's visit to Texas repelled many people in both countries. It crystallized an intimacy that grew from state-to-state friendship into a uniquely dense web of political and economic ties.

"In all, at least $1.476 billion had made its way from the Saudis to the House of Bush and its allied companies and institutions," Craig Unger wrote in his damning book *House of Bush, House of Saud*. "Never before had a president's personal fortunes and public policies been so deeply entwined with a foreign nation."

During the cold war, the United States and the Soviet Union enforced tight discipline on their clients. Societies could not develop freely because they were twisted to the whims of Washington and Moscow. The Middle East was terribly deformed by this suffocating global competition. It has been painfully slow to find a new paradigm for the post–cold war era.

"By failing to help foster gradual paths to democratization in many of our important relationships—by creating what might be called a 'democratic exception'—we missed an opportunity to help those countries become more stable, more prosperous, more peaceful, and more adaptable to the stresses of a globalized world," Richard Haass, director of policy planning at the U.S. State Department, asserted in 2002. "It is not in our interest, or that of the people living in the Muslim world, for the United States to continue this exception."

A profound tragedy lies behind the phrase "democratic exception." It is shorthand for the lamentable fact that Arab countries are the only ones that, as a group, have failed to join the worldwide march to freedom. Not long ago a democratic South Korea, a democratic Brazil, a democratic Poland, or a democratic Liberia seemed almost unimaginable. All these fantasies have become real. As this wave of freedom has washed so many shores, the Arab world has languished under the rule of corrupt autocracies. Keeping them in place may have made sense during the cold war. Now, however, it is past time for the United States to loosen the bonds that have bound it to these regimes, and allow the Arabs to shape their own destiny.

Saudi Arabia would be a fine place to start.

Much American analysis of Saudi Arabia has been painfully simplistic. For decades the American press, its perceptions shaped by Washington, portrayed the Saudi regime as a close and valued ally of the United States, a beacon of moderation and stability in a region that seemed ever more radical and incomprehensibly anti-American. Suddenly, after the September 11 attacks, the pendulum swung wildly to the other extreme. Saudi Arabia was demonized as a cauldron of terror and hatred. Members of Congress who had eagerly supported massive arms sales to Saudi Arabia began denouncing its leaders and opposing its effort to join global institutions like the World Trade Organization.

Saudi Arabia is a richly complex country. It is ruled by a family that holds absolute power but must balance the interests of many groups, factions, tribes, and regions. The family's alliance with Wahhabi Islam has had horrific effects, but has also given the country almost unbroken domestic peace while many of its neighbors have collapsed into violence and poverty. Beneath all the political conflicts of the moment, and beyond the wealth that has flooded into the kingdom since the discovery of oil there, this land is the birthplace of Islam. Its people feel their inheritance profoundly and embrace it fervently. Whatever government rules the Arabian Peninsula will always play a central role in the Muslim consciousness.

Should that government continue to be the al-Saud family? If so, should the family continue to hold absolute power? If not, what kind of regime should replace it? Publicly debating these questions is illegal in the kingdom. At least some Saudis, however, would like to do so.

Oil workers launched a wave of protests in 1956, demanding workers' rights and closure of the U.S. air base at Dhahran; organizers were arrested and beaten. In 1962 several members of the royal family publicly called on the family to accept a constitution, and even produced a draft; the ruling group rejected it. Seven years later the family cracked down on air force officers it believed were plotting a coup, executing several, arresting hundreds of civil servants who were thought to sympathize with them, and crushing what the *New York Times* called a "revolutionary movement" that was "the largest ever uncovered in Saudi Arabia."

In 1990 forty-seven women violated one of the country's many deadening restrictions on female freedom by driving cars in an illegal caravan through Riyadh. A few months later, four hundred mullahs and religious scholars issued a "letter of demands" asking the regime to abandon corruption and end foreign alliances that they said violate Islamic law. In 2003 pro-democracy activists sent the royal family a proposal called "Strategic Vision for the Present and the Future," calling for greater public freedoms and a constitutional monarchy; their leaders were imprisoned. Later that year several hundred protesters were arrested at a demonstration against the government's human rights commission, which they denounced as a fraud. In 2007 ten men were arrested in Jeddah on charges of plotting to form a political party. In 2009 seventy-seven Saudis, identifying themselves as human rights advocates, sent a petition to King Abdullah asking that a commoner be named prime minister, that a parliament be elected and given a role in selecting future monarchs, and that all criminal defendants be given "fair and public trials."

The persistence of these protests should not be taken to mean either that the kingdom is ablaze with reformist passion or that the royal family resolutely rejects it. For every terrifying incident—like the 2002 deaths of fourteen girls who perished when religious police refused to allow them to flee their burning school because they were not properly veiled—there are encouraging ones, like the limited municipal elections of 2005 or the opening in 2009 of a university where male and female students may mix freely. Nor can the Saudis ignore the terrors of democracy, which they see in neighboring Kuwait, where an elected parliament feuds constantly with the monarch, and even more vividly in Iraq, where the introduction of democracy at the point of a gun brought death and horror beyond imagining.

There is widespread agreement, both within the kingdom and beyond, that the al-Saud family needs to progress toward reform. Beyond that general consensus, many debate "the speedometer"—how fast reform can proceed without jeopardizing stability. Setting the pace of change is Saudi Arabia's central challenge. But it is and must remain Saudi Arabia's challenge, not America's. If the United States pushes for sweeping change, it delegitimizes Saudi reformers by making them seem to be America's pawns. If it warns against change, it places itself in opposition to those reformers, many of whom embrace values that Americans hold dear. The best course is to abandon the idea that setting the speedometer is America's job. It is Saudi Arabia's.

Rather than change its view of what is best for Saudi Arabia, the United States should simply stop trying to shape and guide it. The greatest service Americans could render to the cause of reform in Saudi Arabia would be to loosen ties between Washington and Riyadh. This is the one option the United States has never tried in Saudi Arabia—or in Egypt, Iraq, Syria, Jordan, or Lebanon: to allow politics to evolve without interference. The best way for outside powers to help Saudi Arabia and other Arab countries develop regimes that are popular and legitimate is to be neutral toward them. Do not try to guide their internal development. Just as important: do not press them to become allies in foreign wars, especially against other Muslim countries. Doing so only weakens their legitimacy in the eyes of their people.

This does not mean the United States should cut its ties to Saudi Arabia. The two countries have common interests, especially in promoting regional peace and fighting terrorism. That should not require, however, that they maintain the intensely intimate "special relationship" that bound them during the cold war. This relationship stains both countries. It has turned the United States into an enemy of Saudi reformers and given it a share of the blame for the violent militancy that has emerged from Saudi society. At the same time, it weakens the Saudi regime by stigmatizing it as a collaborator with American policies that many Saudis and other Arabs consider anti-Islamic and sinfully biased toward Israel.

Let Saudi society mature in its own way; let it make its own mistakes; let it find its own path. Loosen the informal "special relationship" that has bound the United States to Saudi Arabia since 1945. This approach will serve both countries' interests in the twenty-first century.

Might the United States suffer economically if it takes this course? Perhaps. Saudi arms purchases over the last quarter century have pumped huge amounts of money into the American economy; a congressional report in 2003 found that these purchases created thousands of jobs and "helped maintain the U.S. industrial base." Less known but at least as important is the huge investment Saudi Arabia has made in U.S. government securities. The amount is secret—not even diplomats at the U.S. embassy in Riyadh are allowed to know it—but it certainly reaches tens of billions of dollars and probably much more.

Loosening ties between the United States and Saudi Arabia could lead to increased oil prices for Americans, though that is far from certain since oil is increasingly sold on a global market rather than through country-to-country deals. If Saudi Arabia were to squeeze the United States this way, though, it would be doing Americans a great favor. Americans desperately need reasons to reduce their dependence on foreign oil, and if rising world prices provide such a reason, they should be welcomed. The Saudi oil minister suggested in 2009 that a crash program by Western nations to develop alternative energy sources would be a "nightmare scenario" for oil-producing countries. That is doubtful, but it would be a dream scenario for the United States.

Would a loosening of U.S.-Saudi relations lead the Saudis to stop fighting terrorism? Certainly not. The Saudi regime was slow to awaken to the involvement of Saudi citizens in global terror, but the decision of terrorists to begin launching attacks inside the kingdom roused it to action. The most potent burst of these attacks, in 2003–4, took nearly two hundred lives and included bombings, decapitations, drive-by shootings, an attack on the American consulate in Jeddah, and a horrific raid on oil installations near the Persian Gulf. The regime responded with a vigor that impressed even officials in Washington who had for years been frustrated with its refusal to face this threat.

Saudi society faces looming challenges. Half the population is under the age of twenty. Many young Saudis are studying abroad, including eighteen thousand in the United States, where they absorb ideas radically different from those promoted in their homeland. They return to a society that lives under stifling restrictions. Women are increasingly frustrated. Saudi Arabia desperately needs critical thinkers, but the regime is deeply conservative and fears critical thinking. Like other Arab countries, the kingdom is a bystander on the highway of progress.

The al-Saud family also faces difficult choices about succession to the throne. Every king since Ibn Saud has been one of his sons. More than a few princes wish for reform, but there is no sign the gerontocracy will allow them to come to power—much less skip a generation so a monarch could emerge who embodies the aspirations of a young and impatient population.

Both the Saudi regime and the Saudi population are weary of demands from Washington. A decision by the United States to stop pushing Saudi Arabia this way and that would be widely welcomed. The impact this decision would have on the course of Saudi politics is not entirely predictable, but the United States cannot and should not insist on predictability in the politics of foreign countries.

During the cold war, the United States considered it vitally important to keep friendly regimes in power around the world. Those days are over. Saving governments whose people do not support them should no longer be America's job. Being the ultimate protector of regimes in the Middle East may have made sense during the cold war; today it serves neither American nor Arab interests. What the al-Saud family decides, or what history decides for it, should no longer be America's urgent concern.

This does not mean there is nothing the United States can do to help encourage democratic progress in Saudi Arabia. It can, in fact, take three steps that will immeasurably benefit Saudi Arabia while serving America's strategic interests. It can work intensely to pacify Iraq, which many Saudis see as an example of the tragedy that befalls a country when the United States arrives with its own blueprint; refrain from starting new wars in the Middle East; and do whatever is necessary to resolve the Israel-Palestine conflict.

Saudi Arabia and the United States still share interests—though not nearly as fully as they did during the cold war—but their societies share precious little in the way of values. This is a marriage gone wrong, with spouses who sleep in the same bed but have different dreams. If it does not change, it will lead both parties to grief.

"Anyone who wants to change the Arab world needs a success story," Khaled Batarfi told me as we finished our long seaside dinner. Could it be Saudi Arabia? Perhaps—but only if the United States loosens its suffocating embrace and allows Saudi Arabia to go its own way.

All we want is the basic human right to live safely and freely; brutes attack and terrorize us; we must defend ourselves in order to survive.

This is the essence of both the Israeli and Palestinian narratives. Six decades of war, and of suffering beyond measure, have been the product of this mirror-image conflict.

Some Israelis and Palestinians fear peace. Some use violence to make peace impossible. They do so for two reasons. First, the wounds of history are exceedingly deep, and justice cries out for their redress.

Second, no nation or people makes security concessions unless it feels safe, and the maddeningly vague concept "peace" does not guarantee safety.

It is easy to understand why radical strains have emerged so powerfully in Israeli and Palestinian politics. In such a poisoned climate, there is always a political market for militancy and irredentism. For some factions in both societies, sixty years of conflict are not enough. Far from being exhausted, they are ready to fight for another sixty, or more.

The remarkable aspect of this conflict is not that some on both sides want to keep fighting, but that so many want to stop. Generations have come of age knowing nothing but conflict and hatred. They long for the normal life that a secure peace will bring. Yet the internal dynamics of their societies prevent them from reaching that goal. Israel's electoral system is skewed in ways that give radical factions wildly disproportionate power and make decisive steps toward peace impossible. Palestinian society is distorted in an even more frightening way: life under occupation has given power to angry men with guns and marginalized those who believe in peace. Left to their own devices, these enemies may not make peace in the lifetime of anyone now on earth.

What makes this paralysis so frustrating is that unlike some other deep conflicts, the outline of a solution to this one is clear. Mediators do not have to start fresh. All they need to do is make real the promise of "land for peace." It is a formula enshrined in United Nations Resolution 242, which was adopted after the Six-Day War of 1967 and reaffirmed with another resolution after the Yom Kippur War of 1973.

Using these resolutions as a framework, Israeli and Palestinian negotiators designed a peace plan at a conference in 2000, held at the town of Taba on the Israel-Egypt border; it came to nothing because both the Israeli and American governments changed hands soon afterward. Two years later the Arab League, acting at the urging of King Abdullah of Saudi Arabia, produced a version of the same plan. Leaders of the Palestinian Authority immediately accepted it. Some Israeli leaders also found it appealing; former prime minister Shimon Peres welcomed it as a "U-turn," and Ehud Olmert, a future prime minister, called it "a new way of thinking—the willingness to recognize Israel as an established fact and to debate the conditions of the future solution is a step that I can't help but appreciate." Absolutists on both sides, among them leaders of the militant Palestinian group Hamas and the then-opposition leader in Israel, Benjamin Netanyahu, rejected it.

The way to peace between Israelis and Palestinians is clear to all and has been for years. Israel will evacuate nearly all of its settlements in the West Bank, and give Palestinians land elsewhere to compensate for the settlements it keeps. A demilitarized Palestinian state will be created in the West Bank and Gaza. Its capital, like Israel's, will be Jerusalem. Palestinians will have the right to return to this state from wherever they are, and to be compensated for land and homes they lost in what is now Israel. All states in the region will recognize each other and pledge to resolve future disputes peaceably.

Arabs and Israelis cry peace, peace—but there is no peace. Deeply divided among themselves, paralyzed by fear and mistrust, and trapped by memories of excruciating pain, they cannot move beyond the paradigm of conflict. Both societies have learned, however unhappily, to live with conflict and war. Peace is an unknown country full of terrors. This much, however, is clear about peace between Israel and the Palestinians:

- It is the essential precondition to security in the world's most explosive region.
- Although it seems very far away, even unachievable, in fact the opposite is true: it is within reach.
- It will not be reached if the warring parties are left to shape it themselves.

No president of the United States will ever abandon Israel. This is as it should be. Far from being illegitimate, Israel may be seen as having a stronger legal claim to existence than many Arab states; its creation was, after all, blessed by the United Nations, while modern Syria, Iraq, Kuwait, Jordan, and Lebanon were called into existence by European diplomats who drew lines on maps at meetings no one in the Middle East even knew were being held. If Israel was born in sin, as some Arabs insist, so were many of the world's nations. In any case, Israel has established itself as a permanent fact of Middle East life. History, morality, and *realpolitik* bind the United States to Israel, and always will. For this reason, only the United States can be the long-term guarantor of peace between Israelis and Palestinians—and only the United States can impose it.

Most Israelis, Arabs, and Americans, along with nearly all world leaders, agree on the shape Middle East peace must take. The paralyzing question is how to get there. In no other world crisis is the outline of a solution so clear while the prospects of reaching it seem so bleak. That is because one factor is missing: an outside power to impose the solution on parties who cannot accept it any other way. Only the United States can play this role.

If a president of the United States announced that he intended to impose a comprehensive peace on Israelis and Palestinians—and made clear what his imposed plan entailed—absolutists would howl with protest. An "iron triangle" of opposition would quickly emerge. First would be the settler lobby and others in Israel who fear that any peace accord poses a mortal danger to their state. Second would be the highly organized supporters of Israel in the United States, many of whom have convinced themselves that the best way to defend Israel is to support its government unconditionally. Third would be those Arabs, especially Arab leaders, who want to keep American influence out of their region and fear what might happen to their societies when they can no longer wave the death-to-Israel banner.

This chorus should be welcomed for what it is: proof that the parties to this conflict are unable to make peace on their own. Consumed by internal feuds and day-to-day political bickering, they have lost the ability to do what they must to guarantee their future.

If an American president could hold firm in the face of this outrage, leaders from every corner of the globe might rush to support him—and their support would be crucial, since it would turn this from a unilateral initiative into one that much of the world endorsed. In the end, militants on both sides would have an entirely new form of political cover: the ability to tell their constituents, "I hate this, but the world is forcing us to accept it."

Does the United States have the power to impose a solution on Israel and the Palestinians? It may—as long as it is committed to using all of the enormous political, economic, and diplomatic resources at its disposal. Israel, after all, rightly expects the United States to be its friend and protector; in its first sixty years of national life, it received more than $100 billion in aid from the United States, more than half of it in the form of weaponry provided free of charge. Palestinians also recognize, and in some cases even welcome, the fact that the United States must be the guiding force behind any peace settlement.

It would not do for the United States to come in shooting—to announce that it has devised a formula for Israel-Palestine peace and is sending the 82nd Airborne Division to enforce it. More plausible would be a coercive version of the smoke-filled room, with a powerful president of the United States at the head of the table. He should come armed with everything short of a sidearm, determined to twist limbs, squeeze appendages, and not stop when he hears cries of pain.

Who would guarantee Israel that a land-for-peace deal truly delivers peace? Who would guard borders? Who would pay compensation to Palestinians who must give up their right of return to what is now Israel? The United States would either have to play these roles itself or arrange for the world community to play them. If it is ready to do this—if it imposes a peace plan and remains determined to see it succeed at all costs—it may succeed. If it is tentative or halfhearted, if the president is swayed by the protests it would certainly provoke, or if he opens his plan to the kind of endless negotiation that has prevented a solution for so long, it will fail.

In 1956 it took only a single message from the president of the United States—backed by a 65-to-1 vote at the United Nations—to force Israel to withdraw its army from the vast Sinai Peninsula, even though just days earlier, Prime Minister Ben-Gurion had promised his people that Sinai would forever be "part of the third Kingdom of Israel." For years thereafter, Israel carefully weighed the possible response from Washington before every military operation. As for the Palestinians, they too would have nowhere else to go if the United States decided to become the peace enforcer. Both sides would have powerful incentives to comply, however reluctantly, with what the United States demanded.

This approach would also allow the United States to sidestep the difficult question of with whom it should negotiate. American leaders regularly assert that this or that regime or faction is beyond the civilized pale and cannot be invited to peace talks. These include regimes and factions without whose cooperation there can be no peace. The way to resolve this dilemma is simple: talk to no one. The Middle East crisis has dragged on for so long that everyone's position is painfully clear. No more negotiations are necessary. They drag on endlessly, used by absolutists to buy time and rarely producing decisive results. The time for negotiation is past. Not another round of talks but a clarion call from the president of the United States would be the way to end this tragic conflict.

A president who takes this bold step would be taking political risks. The American body politic has become comfortable with the Middle East status quo. In the United States there is no political cost, and often much benefit, to repeating the "Israel-right-or-wrong" mantra. The alternative would not be politically palatable, but it is clear and simple. Israel is unable to find its way out of the terrifying labyrinth in which it finds itself. Its only hope for long-term security is peace with its neighbors. By imposing peace and guaranteeing it, the United States will be doing Israel, as well as its neighbors, a *mitzvah* of historic proportions.

Peace between Israel and the Palestinians has seemed so distant for so long that some have lost sight of the enormous impact it could have. Its possible benefits—not certain ones, to be sure, but possible nonetheless—are deeply tantalizing.

- It would do more to weaken anti-Western terror movements than any war the United States has ever fought.
- It would make resolving other Middle East problems infinitely easier.
- It would free Israel from its looming demographic threat; by 2050 eight million Jewish Israelis will be living next to twenty million Palestinians, a recipe for explosive danger if there is no peace.
- It would dry up refugee camps that are breeding grounds for hatred.
- It would make Israel a fully respected member of the world community, freeing it from the opprobrium of occupying territory.
- It would destabilize every Arab government, which would be disconcerting at first but in the end would produce a more democratic and secure Middle East.
- It would isolate radical regimes and undermine militant movements that feed off Muslim anger and frustration.
- It would allow two peoples whose religious traditions have strongly secular aspects—Jews and Palestinians—to give the Middle East an alternative to fundamentalism.
- It would show the world that in the twenty-first century, the United States wishes to be a peacemaker, not a warmonger.
- It could lead to regional security arrangements, and then to cooperation in a host of areas, from education and health care to tourism, water supply, and energy development.
- Most important, it could give Israelis the long-term security that is their fervent wish, while returning to Palestinians their dignity and self-respect.

By imposing a peace accord on Israelis and Palestinians, the United States would not be weakening its friends, appeasing aggressors, or rewarding enemies of freedom. On the contrary, it would serve its own strategic interests, guarantee a safe future for a close and valued ally, and give millions of deprived men, women, and children the prospect of new life.

Some would construe a powerful American initiative like this to be anti-Israeli or anti-Palestinian. They might argue that warring parties have the sole right to decide when and how to make peace. Only a people's own leaders, they would insist, are equipped to make the most delicate decisions about their future.

History, however, has made painfully clear that neither Israel nor its Arab adversaries can make those decisions. Their failures have contributed to a series of ever-escalating crises around the world, some of which have ballooned into terrifying global threats. Allowing this process to continue poses deep risks to Americans and people around the world. This is not a dispute that can be confined to one region without affecting others. It is the most overwhelmingly destabilizing of all the world's conflicts. Without confronting it directly, the United States cannot preserve its own security or that of its allies.

Would it be an act of arrogance for the United States to presume to impose a settlement this way? Perhaps, though it would be less arrogant than other recent and far more violent American intrusions into the Middle East and nearby regions. But the cold war is over, and the United States need no longer embrace other countries' policies as its own in exchange for their support against a global adversary. No step the United States could take anywhere in the world would have such a sudden, wide-ranging, and positive effect on global security, or hold as much potential to broaden humanity's freedom, as imposing peace on Israelis and Palestinians. It would electrify the world.

If an agreement like this could be made, how would it be enforced? With difficulty. Spoilers on both sides would seek to undermine it, and not always nonviolently. An armed peacekeeping force would probably be necessary, at least for a period of years. Undoubtedly this force would face difficult and perhaps bloody challenges, like pulling Israeli settlers from their homes or repressing militant Arab factions.

The daunting military challenges of imposing peace would not even be the most complex. There is an enormous economic challenge: How can Israelis and Arabs cooperate when their levels of development are so vastly different? Even more challenging is the psychopolitical barrier posed by the fact that many Arabs have never come to consider Israel a legitimate player in Middle East politics, much less a partner. Arab countries have trouble cooperating with each other; asking them to work with Israel is asking a great deal.

Normal relations between Israel and the Palestinians would not create a regional lovefest. Israelis would neither trust Arabs nor happily accept restrictions on their freedom of military action. Arabs would not easily recognize the permanent presence of Israel, nor would Arab societies cease to be dysfunctional. Palestinian factions would not forget their deep differences. Religious extremism, which is growing in both societies and poses a serious obstacle to peace, would not fade away. Powerful leaders—including the prime minister of Israel and the president of the Palestinian Authority—would wonder if accepting an accord might cost them their jobs. If it did, no one could guarantee that they would be replaced by more moderate figures. The opposite might happen.

It is also possible that one side or the other would reject this plan so categorically that no amount of pressure and persuasion will have any effect. This possibility should not dissuade the United States from trying.

The search for peace between Israel and Palestinians has dragged on for so long that it has created its own class of professionals. Some are earnest diplomats who have immersed themselves in the conflict's minutiae with the sincere hope of reaching a breakthrough. Others use endless negotiating as a tactic to assure that nothing substantial ever changes. What they all have in common is failure.

It may not be realistic to imagine that an American president would wish to try imposing a settlement on Israelis and Palestinians, or feel able to do it. Only this or some other comparably radical break from diplomatic convention, though, has a chance of breaking the Middle East deadlock in our time.

PART FOUR

THE DOOR IS
SO WIDE OPEN

8

WHERE THEY COME TOGETHER

Communication and dialogue is the path to peace and compromise.
—Prime Minister Recep Tayyip Erdoğan of Turkey

A scene never before imagined played out in Ankara at midmorning on an autumn day in 2007. President Shimon Peres of Israel strode purposefully to the podium of the Grand National Assembly and began speaking in Hebrew. This was the first time an Israeli leader had addressed the legislature of any Muslim country.

"Turkey instills trust," Peres told the hushed hall. "I came here to express my gratitude to Turkey."

Instilling trust has become Turkey's global mission. In the first decade of the twenty-first century, a visionary group of Turkish leaders led their country into the world. They not only broke out of the shell within which Turks had been hiding for generations, but drew on unique historical, geographic, cultural, and political assets to turn Turkey into a highly promising new player on the global scene.

Turkey has been a political and military ally of the United States for more than half a century. This relationship has not been free of trouble, but it has always fit the needs of the moment. The longest moment was the cold war, and during that period the two countries' strategic needs meshed well. The United States wanted allies who fully embraced its basic foreign policy principles. Turkey was a reliable frontline state in the confrontation with Soviet power.

In every other way, though, Turkey was a country on the periphery. It was near the Middle East, the Balkans, the Caucasus, North Africa, and the Slavic world, but not part of any of them. Partly by its own choice and partly as a result of that era's political geography, Turkey was a cold war outlier, a strategic afterthought with no distinct role in the world or even its own region.

After giving itself what one scholar has called a "historical lobotomy," the Republic of Turkey spent three-quarters of a century denying and hiding from its Ottoman past, when the Turks ruled a vast empire that spread from Algiers to Mecca to Budapest. That may have made sense; Turkey had urgent challenges at home, did not want to be seen as neo-imperialist, and embraced Western security goals as its own.

Since the end of the cold war, few countries have so completely redesigned their approach to the world.

On the new world map, Turkey is no longer on the edge of anything. Instead it is once again what this piece of geography has been since time immemorial: the epicenter of the immense Eurasian landmass. The combination of Turkey's location, its Ottoman heritage, and its successful blend of Islam and democracy gives it enormous strategic potential. It is seizing that potential in ways that benefit not only itself, but also the United States and the West.

Turkey has taken on the role of mediator, conciliator, and arbitrator. The world urgently needs some country to play that role. Few are better equipped to do so than Turkey.

When Israel wished to begin secret talks with Syria, it asked Turkey to arrange them. After Sunnis in Iraq decided to boycott national elections, Turkey persuaded them to change their minds and participate. Whenever Turkish officials land in a bitterly divided country like Lebanon or Pakistan or Afghanistan, every faction is eager to talk to them. Turkey is working to calm tensions between Iran and the United States, between Syria and Iraq, between Armenia and Azerbaijan. No country's diplomats are as welcome in both Tehran and Washington, Moscow and Tbilisi, Damascus and Cairo. No other nation is respected by Hamas, Hezbollah, and the Taliban while also maintaining good ties with the Israeli, Lebanese, and Afghan governments.

Foreign Minister Ahmet Davutoğlu's grand concept, which he calls "strategic depth," envisions Turkey as a hyperactive peacemaker. His first project was to resolve all of Turkey's disputes with its neighbors; in this he has been largely successful. His next ambition is grander, not just "zero problems with neighbors" but "zero problems *between* neighbors." Every dispute in Turkey's extended neighborhood, he argues, threatens peace and limits chances for regional development; all are therefore of urgent concern to Turkey.

For most of Turkey's modern history, the Muslim world has seen it as an apostate. Atatürk's reforms pulled it so far from Islam that it seemed to have no religious legitimacy. Besides, it was perceived as Washington's lackey, stigmatized by its embrace of American policies that many Muslims found abhorrent.

Neither of those objections applies to Turkey today. It is governed by pious Muslims and has its own foreign policy. Its leaders are warmly welcomed in many places where, in the past, they would not even have cared to visit.

Turkey has found remarkably little resistance to its new ambition. By intervening only when asked and maintaining good relations with such a wide range of governments and factions, it plays a role no other country can. It has unique credentials. Turkey is big—seventy million people with the largest economy in the Middle East. Its Ottoman past gives it enormous historical weight. It is also a highly alluring model, not just because of its relative prosperity but also because its society is so free.

The Lebanese scholar Fares Braizat spoke for many Middle East intellectuals when he called Turkey "a role model that has successfully balanced tradition and modernization." Mahmoud Abbas, the Palestinian leader, admires Turkey as "a model on the way to democracy." Sedat Laçiner, an influential adviser to the Turkish foreign ministry who runs a think tank in Ankara, goes even further. "Problems like Palestine, the occupation of Iraq, Chechnya, Afghanistan and the occupation of Karabakh by the Armenians have created a great hopelessness," he asserts. "The majority of Muslim people do not trust their own governments to solve their political, economic and social problems. They need to see a miracle—and Turkey is the miracle they need to see."

Turkey has escaped from America's orbit. In the language of geostrategists, the two countries have become "decoupled." Turkey's new role, however, holds great promise for the United States. As a Muslim country intimately familiar with the region around it, Turkey can go places, engage partners, and make deals that America cannot. What it has done to separate itself from the United States—refusing to allow American troops to invade Iraq from Turkish territory, for example, or denouncing Israel's actions in Gaza—has enhanced its reputation in other Muslim countries. That strengthens its ability to influence them.

Turkey's foreign policy, though independent, reinforces America's. Both countries share key strategic goals. Both are essentially conservative. The existing world order has been good to them. They want to strengthen it, not radically reshape it.

Both countries want to see a peaceful, democratic Iraq; a moderate Iran that does not threaten its neighbors; an end to the Israeli-Palestinian conflict; a stable Middle East free of radical forces; a weakening of religious fundamentalism; a coordinated global anti-terror strategy; a pipeline network that brings oil and gas to the West without the danger of political or economic blackmail; an end to "frozen conflicts" from Cyprus to Kashmir; stability in Afghanistan and Pakistan; and genuine independence for the nations of the South Caucasus. Not only does Turkey share these American goals, it is well placed to help achieve them.

"Turkey's new search for independence in its foreign policy, however complicating or irritating for the United States, will nonetheless serve the best interests of Turkey, the Middle East, and even the West," the former CIA analyst Graham Fuller has concluded. "The Muslim world is in search of a leader. In view of its present leadership deficit—there is hardly a single leader who commands broad respect across the region—Turkey is being listened to more carefully as an increasingly respected, independent and successful Muslim voice.... Enlightened American observers will come to appreciate the presence of this new Turkey, strengthened and rooted in democratic process, as an anchor of stability in the troubled and tempestuous region of the Middle East."

Around the same time Fuller wrote those words, the American strategic prognosticator George Friedman published a study called *The Next 100 Years: A Forecast for the 21st Century*. "When we look at the wreckage of the Islamic world after the American invasion of Iraq in 2003 and consider what country must be taken seriously in the region, it seems obvious that it must be Turkey," he wrote. Accompanying his prediction was a map of the Middle East, North Africa, and southeastern Europe captioned "Turkish Sphere of Influence 2050." It looks strikingly like a map of the Ottoman Empire.

Under other circumstances, Egypt, Pakistan, or Iraq might have emerged to lead the Muslim world. Their societies, however, are weak, fragmented, and decomposing. Indonesia is a more promising candidate, but it has no historic tradition of leadership and is far from the center of Muslim crises. That leaves Turkey—which, by happy coincidence, is eager to play this role.

Although Turkey is on its way to becoming one of the world's indispensable powers, it still has one important hurdle to leap. Having resolved nearly all of its international disputes, it must now finish putting its domestic house in order. Turkish law still limits freedom of speech. The military still plays a role in politics that is unacceptable in a democratic country. Minorities are still less than fully protected—not just Kurds, whose culture was brutalized by decades of official repression before Prime Minister Erdoğan persuaded the Grand National Assembly to restore many of their rights in 2009, but also Christians, non-mainstream Muslims, and unbelievers. A streak of chauvinistic nationalism still runs through Turkey's political culture. The press is weak and corrupted. Political parties are closed autocracies. The education system is rigid and discourages free thinking. Until Turkish democracy is made whole, its ability to serve as a beacon of freedom will be limited.

Some of the other drags on Turkish power are technical; its diplomats are renowned for their sophistication, for example, but there are barely one thousand of them, hardly enough to carry their country's message around the world. Other challenges come in the form of rival nations. Turkish leaders like to say that their goals conflict with no one else's, but that is never true for an ambitious country. When Turkey encourages Georgia, Armenia, and Azerbaijan to claim their full independence, it irritates Moscow. When it rallies to the defense of Chinese Muslims, it challenges Beijing. As Turkey's global reach grows, it must learn to manage these conflicts and assure that they do not grow into confrontations.

The Turks are emotional people, and this poses another challenge because emotion is the enemy of sound foreign policy. Turkish leaders have at times allowed emotion to affect their attitude toward Israel. They are understandably angry over Israel's actions in occupied territories, especially the destruction wrought in Gaza by its 2008–9 invasion and the punishing blockade that followed. If Turkey is to be a bridge among nations, though, it cannot afford gratuitously to alienate any. The United States has brought itself much grief by isolating Iran; it would be just as foolish for Turkey to reject Israel. Like Iran, Israel is a pariah in many circles and is frozen out of Middle East security arrangements. This is bad for all parties. Pushing Israel into a corner, or making Israel feel that it is alone and friendless, does not serve the cause of peace. Turkey has a history of excellent relations with Jews, and in 1949 it became the second Muslim country—after Iran—to recognize Israel. Turning its back on that legacy would contradict its new diplomatic role as a broker of compromise.

This drift, however, does not disqualify Turkey as a uniquely valuable partner for the United States. Nor does its new focus on the Middle East and Asia. By widening its policy sweep, Turkey strengthens its geopolitical appeal.

Americans have come to realize that they lack some of the historical and cultural tools necessary to navigate effectively through the Middle East and surrounding regions. They need a guide. Turkey is their best choice. As the United States shapes and carries out its policies toward Muslim countries, it should do so with Turkey at its side.

But is the United States, so long accustomed to acting on its own, ready to be guided?

A successful partnership requires partners to listen to each other, accept each other's counsel, and adapt to each other's needs. The Turks may be ready for this kind of relationship with the United States, but America has little experience in listening to other powers. Shattering events of the last decade, however—including the September 11 attacks, the bloody aftermath of the Iraq invasion, the daunting challenges emerging from Afghanistan and Pakistan, and the emergence of global terror networks—have shaken Americans' sunny "can-do" mentality. For the first time in their history, they see that there are some things in the world they cannot achieve by themselves, no matter how determined they are or how much money they spend. Many now realize that they need help in understanding and resolving global crises. If they accept this truth, and if they agree that the place they most need help is the Muslim world, Turkey becomes America's next best friend.

Why has Turkey turned away from its traditional foreign policy, which was based on relations with Europe and the United States, and become so much more active in the Middle East and Asia? It has matured as a country and now has the self-confidence to play a global role; the end of the cold war has freed it from a policy straitjacket and given it the chance to pursue broader interests; it sees a wide range of political and economic opportunities and wants to seize them. Another reason, however, underlies all of these. Europe is slamming its door in Turkey's face. Turkey, a proud country that does not react well to insults, is responding by seeking friends elsewhere.

The romance between Turkey and Europe, never passionate, has cooled decidedly. Officially the consummation is still just a matter of time. How much time, though, is now quite unclear. Some European leaders have directly contradicted the European Union's promise to Turkey—that it is "a candidate state destined to join the Union"—by asserting that they do not want Turkey ever to join. As Europe's change of heart became painfully evident during the first decade of the new century, the pace of reform in Turkey slowed. That, in turn, gave Europeans more reason to criticize Turkey. This downward spiral has hurt both sides.

It is bad for Turkey because the EU has for years been the principal outside force pushing Turkey to complete its march toward democracy. Turkey has its own reasons to broaden minority rights, lift restrictions on free speech, and end military influence in politics. The prospect of EU membership, though, gave it an especially powerful incentive to do so. As that prospect has faded, so has the pressure for reform.

Turkey needs the power of Europe to maximize its strategic clout. With Europe behind it, Turkey can help reshape the world. Without Europe it can increase its influence, but its power will remain limited.

Europe also suffers from this breach. With Turkey as a member, the European Union can become a major world power; without Turkey it has less chance. Turkey is a vibrant country full of young people eager to work and pay the taxes that will fill the pension funds of graying European countries. Most important, Turkey is Europe's best hope to calm radicalism in the Islamic world, which threatens Europe as it does every other region. By admitting Turkey, the EU would send a clear message to Muslim countries: if you become democratic, the world is open to you. By rejecting Turkey, it sends the opposite message: we don't want you, no matter what you do.

"Should Turkey join the EU, then this will have a profound effect on the entire Muslim world and on the Arab world in particular," the Moroccan commentator Abdullah Turkmani has written. "This process will contribute to their political and intellectual modernization. In the future, near or far, they will all be forced to imitate what Turkey is doing."

Not only Arabs but Muslims everywhere place great hope in the Turkey-EU relationship. "Turkey, as a model of tradition and modernity, draws a lot of attention from intellectuals, politicians and policy-makers in Pakistan and other Muslim states," asserts the Pakistani scholar Rasul Bakhsh Rais. "The formal, institutional integration of Turkey with Europe will strengthen secular democratic forces in Muslim states that are locked in a struggle with traditional Islamist groups for defining the identity of states and societies in the modern world."

Given these advantages of embracing Turkey, why has the EU lost so much of its enthusiasm for the idea? Part of the answer is that ordinary Europeans were never keen on it. The EU has always been an elite project, and now that its citizens are slowly gaining some say in its decisions, they are expressing their unhappiness with the idea of Turkish membership. Many believe that a Muslim country has no place in the EU; others fear the cost of future European subsidies to Turkey; still others are overcome with "enlargement fatigue" after admitting so many other countries to the EU in recent years. Politicians in some European countries have realized there are votes to be gained by promising to keep Turkey out of the EU. That may change, but not overnight. Until it does, Turkey has little prospect of joining.

Given this reality, Turkey is looking elsewhere. It would probably be seeking to broaden its horizons in any case, but Europe's unfriendliness gives it another reason to do so. That has led some to fear that Turkey, stung by Europe's insults, is trading its Western orientation for a different one.

President Barack Obama addressed that fear when he spoke to the Grand National Assembly in 2009, making Turkey the first Muslim country he visited after taking office. He strongly restated American support for Turkish membership in the EU, asserting that Turkey "has been a resolute ally and a responsible partner in transatlantic and European institutions" and that "Turkish membership would broaden and strengthen Europe's foundation." Then he addressed "those who like to debate Turkey's future."

"They wonder whether you will be pulled in one direction or another," Obama said. "But I believe here is what they don't understand: Turkey's greatness lies in your ability to be at the center of things. This is not where East and West divide. This is where they come together."

Turkey's road to membership in the European Union is strewn with obstacles, some of them stemming from Europe's shortsightedness and others of Turkey's own making. Perhaps Turkey will be admitted by 2023, when it celebrates its hundredth year of existence as a sovereign state. In the meantime, though, Turkey can help the United States achieve some of its most urgent goals. President Obama mentioned one—arguably the most urgent—in his speech to the Grand National Assembly.

"We share the goal of a lasting peace between Israel and its neighbors," he told his Turkish hosts. "The United States and Turkey can help the Palestinians and Israelis make this journey."

America's long-term strategic interests coincide with Turkey's. Each country has its own set of tools with which it can promote those interests. That alone would be enough to make this a promising partnership. But there is more.

These countries are also well suited to each other for a second reason: their people share a democratic approach to politics and life. The Turks have internalized democratic values that Americans also embrace: human rights, free elections, and the right of people to live their lives as they wish. Democracy has become so entrenched in Turkey that even military coups have been unable to shake it. The Turks understand that they can only progress by moving ever closer to Western ideas of modernity and freedom.

An ideal partnership between countries is based on two foundations. First, the two countries must share strategic goals. Second, their societies must share values, because partnerships based only on relations between ruling elites are inherently unstable. On both counts, Turkey qualifies as the best partner the United States can find in the world's most troubled region.

> A government that is in danger from the outside will take any chance to accelerate nationalism inside the country.
> —Shirin Ebadi, winner of the 2003 Nobel Peace Prize

One fact jumps from any map of the Middle East: Iran is the big country in the middle. It stands out the way Germany stands out on a map of Europe.

Many Americans see Iran the way their grandparents saw Germany, as a bad actor that causes nothing but trouble. Their grandparents realized after World War II that unless Germany was somehow calmed down, Europe would never be stable. Today Americans realize the same about Iran and the Middle East.

For a time in the mid-1940s, Allied leaders considered the option of punishing Germany by cutting it into pieces, demolishing its factories, and forcing it to earn its living from agriculture alone. That plan was based on emotion: anger at the horror Germany had inflicted on the world and determination to make its people suffer. Cooler heads prevailed, though, and an opposite plan emerged. Germany was divided by the cold war, but West Germany was brought into the European family. Four decades later, Germany was peacefully reunited. It has become a normal country, a promoter of peace instead of a maker of war.

The parallel to today's Iran is not exact, since Germany had been defeated in war, while Iran is intact and self-confident. Nonetheless the underlying dilemma is the same. Is it better to sanction and punish a troublemaker, or entice it toward normality?

Beneath that question lies a deeper one: Does the United States shape its foreign policy according to emotion, or by cool calculation of self-interest?

This is the essence of the conundrum that has turned relations between Washington and Tehran into one of the world's longest-lasting confrontations. Some powerful Americans are still trapped by their anger at Iran, stemming from the deeply traumatic hostage crisis of

1979–81 and Iran's largely successful efforts over the next thirty years to make trouble for the United States wherever possible. These Americans have spent decades trying to punish Iran. Negotiating, reconciling, and perhaps even building a partnership with Iran seemed to them a form of surrender. Henry Kissinger crystallized this view when asked how the United States should deal with its Muslim enemies.

"They want to humiliate us," he said. "We need to humiliate them."

But the goal of diplomacy—or of avoiding diplomacy—should not be to punish, inflict pain, extract tribute, or redeem festering emotions. Nor should it be seen as a way to make friends. Its essential purpose is to advance interests. The tragedy of America's long estrangement from Iran is that it has undermined America's own interests.

There are a host of abstract reasons to negotiate with Iran, and just as many others not to do so. None are truly important. What matters is that none of the chief American goals in the Middle East—pacifying Iraq, stabilizing Lebanon, ending the Israel-Palestine stalemate, weakening Islamic fundamentalism, crushing al-Qaeda, moderating nuclear competition, reducing the threat of future wars—can be achieved without Iran's cooperation. As the last thirty years of history amply prove, an isolated Iran is a spoiler. A calm and prosperous Iran can be to the Middle East what a calm and prosperous Germany has been to Europe: a stabilizing power, a provider of security, and a motor of economic development.

During the first years of the twenty-first century, Iran's power in the Middle East dramatically increased. This happened largely because of spectacularly ill-conceived actions taken by the country that has posited itself as Iran's greatest enemy: the United States. Crippling American sanctions turned out to be not so crippling after all; they impoverished ordinary Iranians, enriched a class of smugglers tied to the regime, and led Iran to develop a web of new economic ties to more pragmatic countries, including Russia, China, Japan, and India. Then, during the presidency of George W. Bush, the United States deposed the two regimes in neighboring countries that were Iran's most bitter enemies: Saddam Hussein's in Iraq and the Taliban's in Afghanistan.

With its rivals gone, Iran quickly emerged as a regional power with hegemonic ambition.

The toppling of Saddam Hussein did more for Iran than simply removing a powerful enemy. It also led to the establishment of a Shiite-dominated government in Iraq that has warm ties to Tehran. When Iranian president Mahmoud Ahmadinejad visited Baghdad in 2008, he toured the city in an open car, waving to cheering crowds, and ridiculed President Bush for having to sneak into Iraq unannounced for fear of being attacked. It was a painfully potent sign that Iran, the enemy Bush claimed to hate, had emerged from his invasion of Iraq as the big winner.

"To us, it seemed out of the world that you would do this," the baffled Saudi foreign minister, Prince Saud al-Faisal, marveled after the United States overthrew Saddam. "We are handing the whole country over to Iran!"

America's strategic miscalculations were based in part on ignorance. Bruce Riedel, a former CIA analyst who advised three presidents on Iran, has asserted that "for thirty years, the United States has tried to deal with Iran and its revolutionary ideology without a well-grounded understanding of what motivates and inspires Iranians." American policies aimed at isolating Iran have had precisely the opposite effect, isolating Americans from the information and contacts they need in order to deal effectively with Iran. "I was the point person on Iran from 2005 to 2008 and I never once met an Iranian official," former undersecretary of state Nicholas Burns has recalled. Blinded by emotion, the United States sank into willful ignorance. Secretary of State Condoleezza Rice seemed almost proud of it.

"We don't really have people who know Iran inside our own system," she admitted when asked about the prospects for a changed relationship. "We don't really have very good veracity or a feel for the place."

As a new president seeks to reshape American foreign policy, and as new concerns about Iran emerge, especially about its nuclear program, the United States is reconsidering its approach. The emotions that prevented a rapprochement in the past have not evaporated. For the first time, however, there are signs that Washington is considering the advantages that might emerge from a new understanding between the United States and Iran.

- Iran can do more than any other country, including the United States, to assure long-term peace in Iraq.
- Iran can also help stabilize Afghanistan, where it has been engaged for centuries.
- A stable and secure Iran, no longer in need of a scapegoat, might stop threatening Israel.
- Iran can tame militant groups like Hamas and Hezbollah, which would contribute to Israeli security, help stabilize Lebanon, and dramatically improve the prospects for peace between Israel and its Arab neighbors.
- Reconciliation between Iran and the United States would decisively improve relations between the United States and the Muslim world.
- Iran will have less incentive to invite Russian power into the Middle East, something the United States is rightly eager to avoid.
- Iran is an enemy of al-Qaeda and would cooperate in a transnational effort to crush it.
- Iran has 7 percent of the world's oil reserves and 16 percent of its natural gas; if the United States does not exploit and buy it, Russia and China will, thereby increasing their strategic leverage in the region.
- Iran's oil infrastructure is in pitiful shape and desperately needs modernizing that will cost billions of dollars; American companies are ideally placed to do the job.
- An Iran that no longer feels threatened by the United States might be more willing to compromise on nuclear issues.

What would the United States have to do in order to secure these results? Above all, it would have to recognize Iran as an important power with legitimate security interests. Successive American presidents have rejected the idea of compromise for exactly this reason. They wished to punish, contain, and isolate Iran, not reward it with a promotion to regional-power status. That ignored the reality that Iran needs no promotion. It is already a regional power. The United States may wish that this were not the case, but self-delusion is an unsound basis for foreign policy.

No aspect of Iran's behavior during the first decade of the new century has been more troubling to outsiders than its pursuit of a nuclear program. It is not unreasonable for Iran to want the capacity to generate nuclear energy. Most Iranians believe it is their natural right. Their country's nuclear program, in fact, was first begun with American encouragement, during Mohammad Reza Shah's regime.

What troubles the outside world, though, is that Iran's drive for nuclear power is shrouded in secrecy and subterfuge, leading to the eminently reasonable suspicion that its true goal is not nuclear power but nuclear weaponry. Just as troubling is the fact that as Iran presses ahead with its nuclear program, it is broadening its regional ambitions and recklessly threatening Israel. Even Israeli leaders may not truly fear that Iran would attack their country with nuclear weapons; that would bring instant retaliation and lead to Iran's death as a nation. The Israelis and others realize, however, that a nuclear-armed Iran would be able to intimidate its neighbors in ways that would ultimately endanger Israel's security. A nuclear-armed Iran might well set off an arms race in the region, with Egypt, Saudi Arabia, Turkey, and perhaps other countries pressing for nuclear weapons of their own—a race that would also be deeply threatening to Israel. If Iran seems about to test a nuclear weapon, or does test one, Israel or Saudi Arabia might attack it, with or without American permission. That, in turn, could set off a regional conflagration. So seeking to curb Iran's nuclear program, or at least force it into the open as Iran's treaty obligations require, is a legitimate and urgent task for the outside world.

Attacking or bombing Iran is unlikely to stop this program. It could even have the opposite effect, convincing Iranians that only a nuclear deterrent will prevent future attacks. The U.S. secretary of defense, Robert Gates, was right when he asserted in 2009 that "there is no military option that does anything more than buy time."

The world needs Iran to make an important security concession, just as it needs Israel to make security concessions. No country, however, makes such concessions unless it feels safe. The goal of peacemakers in the Middle East should be to design regional security accords that will reassure both Iran and Israel that their survival is not endangered. Until that happens, Iran will continue to believe that it needs nuclear weapons—which means that it will continue to pursue its highly destabilizing nuclear program.

It is far from certain whether negotiation can produce a new security architecture for the Middle East. Not making an all-out effort, however, plays into the hands of those who want to intensify regional tensions. Every day that the United States and Iran continue their standoff is a day that the centrifuges at Iranian nuclear plants continue spinning. In the years since the United States refused to reply to Iran's offer to negotiate in 2003, the number of Iranian centrifuges at those plants has increased tenfold; this cannot be considered a policy success.

The intensifying danger that Iran's nuclear program poses to regional and global security is not a reason to continue isolating Iran, but a reason to do the opposite: engage urgently with its government in the hope of avoiding its emergence as a full-fledged nuclear power. Threats and sanctions will not achieve this, nor will military attack. Negotiation may also fail, but the stakes are so high that refusing to try is folly.

There need not be losers if the United States and Iran find a way to become partners. That does not mean, however, that everyone would cheer. Saudi Arabia might fear that a stable, prosperous Iran would replace it as Washington's Middle East favorite. If Iran is freed from sanctions and able to resume its old role as a regional trading center, Dubai might lose business. Azerbaijan, ruled by a pro-American dictator, might not like the emergence of a new powerhouse on its southern border. Israel might fear that any gain for Iran threatens its future.

All of these fears are reasonable. A wide-ranging accord between the

United States and Iran, however, would dramatically enhance Middle East security, and that would benefit every country in the region. Countries that are inside a security system have an interest in maintaining and strengthening it; those that are kept out have the opposite interest. Lyndon Johnson tartly enunciated this principle when explaining why he decided not to fire J. Edgar Hoover, the troublesome FBI director: "It's probably better to have him inside the tent pissing out than outside the tent pissing in."

In some diplomatic negotiations, it is best to start slowly, seeking small-scale agreements and "confidence-building measures" before addressing more important issues. That approach will not work with Iran. Instead the opposite is required. The United States should aim for a global accord that will give Iran every right to which its size and power entitle it, while securing from it concessions on every issue the United States considers important. Iran has no incentive to cooperate with the United States on isolated matters; why, for example, should it help stabilize Iraq as long as it fears that the United States might use a stable Iraq as a platform from which to attack it?

The world's concerns about Iran are interlocking. So are Iran's fears of the world. They can only be resolved by a far-reaching accord.

In the months after the terror attacks of September 11, 2001, the United States sought Iranian help in dealing with Afghanistan, and Iran gave plenty. The Bush administration, however, was preoccupied with the idea of deposing Saddam Hussein and then perhaps moving on to overthrow the regime in Iran. Propelled by these triumphalist fantasies, the U.S. government refused to clasp Iran's tentatively outstretched hand. This was one of recent history's most lamentable missed opportunities.

The shocking violence that Iranian leaders used to suffocate protests after the 2009 presidential election does not change the strategic logic of reconciliation between Washington and Tehran. It must, however, remind Americans that they cannot fall into the trap that has soured their relationships with some other countries: making deals between ruling elites that exclude the citizenry. As the United States pursues its strategic interest by seeking an accommodation with Iran, it must do nothing to undermine Iran's brave democratic movement.

Iran is the only Muslim country in the world where most people are reliably pro-American. This pro-American sentiment in Iran is a priceless strategic asset for the United States. For practical as well as moral reasons, American negotiators should make no concessions to Iran's regime that weaken Iranians who are persecuted for defending democratic values.

Opposition figures in Iran find themselves in a difficult situation in which there are no good options. The best of the bad options is for the regime to become integrated with the outside world, to be lured out of its fear, to build bridges to countries where debate, dissent, and protest are considered healthy signs of stability. If Iranian democrats change their minds about that—if they begin asking other countries to cut off their contacts with the regime—the United States will have to reconsider the logic of engagement. Until then, it should press ahead.

The harshness with which Iranian leaders repressed postelection protests in 2009 reflects their nastiness. At least as important, though, was the symbolism of the protests themselves. There are never postelection protests in Egypt, because Egyptians expect elections to be rigged, and none in Saudi Arabia because there are no national elections at all. The months of protest in Iran reflect the legacy of Iran's hundred-year march toward democracy. Today's Iranians believe they are entitled to their vote and voice. They are the heirs to five generations of freedom fighters, including those Howard Baskerville gave his life to support after the 1906 Constitutional Revolution and those who defended Mohammad Mossadegh nearly half a century later. Their sacrifice shows how brightly the flame of freedom still burns in Iran—although, unlike in Turkey, it is not allowed to burn in public.

Iran, despite the persistence of its theocracy, is a potential long-term partner for the United States for the same reasons Turkey is. The two countries share strategic goals, and their societies share democratic values.

The political evolution of Iran has not ended. The regime now in power will not be in power forever. When it changes, evolves, or falls, the Iranian people will demand the democracy for which so many of them yearn. This cannot be said for other countries in the region, because they do not have long democratic traditions.

Democracy cannot emerge overnight. It can only flower after years, decades, even generations of experience. Iran is one of only two Muslim countries in the Middle East that has this experience. It has a vibrant though besieged civil society and is full of democratic potential. Under the right circumstances, it might even emerge from its half-century of dictatorship as more democratic than Turkey. When and if it does, its people should know that the United States has always stood by them.

Direct, bilateral, comprehensive, and unconditional negotiations hold the only hope for a diplomatic breakthrough between Iran and the United States. Iran has incentives to make a deal. It craves legitimacy. It has security needs that only the United States can meet. Its government is unpopular, its economy is reeling from a combination of high inflation and low oil prices, its society is groaning under a host of social ills, its young generation is deeply alienated, and many of its most talented sons and daughters have either emigrated or hope to do so.

Is this enough to assure that Iran will negotiate seriously? Is a breakthrough possible while Iran is ruled by a repressive clique that brutally supresses peaceful protest and seems bent on building nuclear weapons? No one can say for sure, but the prospects are hardly bright. Engagement may have to wait until a new regime, or at least a new group of leaders, emerges in Tehran. The potential benefits are so great, however, that it would be self-defeating for the United States not to try.

If the United States makes a genuine effort to engage Iran and fails, it will at least have shown the Iranian people that Americans are not implacably hostile to them. Its goal should not be to reach a deal at any cost, but rather to realize that as soon as a good deal becomes possible— whether under the current regime or another one—it is in America's interest to make it. Even if no accord is possible now, the United States should recognize that in the mid- to long-term future, Iran can be a highly valuable partner.

Negotiations with Iran, no matter which group of Iranians comes to the table, will be difficult because the two countries are separated by chasms of perception and history. There will also, however, be another obstacle, one posed by psychology. Americans will seek practical concessions from Iran. Iranians will seek something more diffuse: respect, dignity, a restoration of lost pride. They nourish a collective sense of grievance, a culture of resistance, and a profound belief that the rest of the world has spent centuries trying to keep them down. Themes of betrayal and dispossession run deep in their religious as well as political culture.

Many of the most accomplished American diplomats, including some now retired, would like nothing more than the chance to see what they might achieve in negotiations with Iran. If they are turned loose to test their skills, they should bring with them someone who understands both countries and is trained in psychology and philosophy—someone like Nassir Ghaemi, director of the mood disorder program in the Department of Psychiatry at Tufts Medical Center in Boston. Here is some of what he has written about the differences between the American and Iranian mentalities:

- Americans are willing to compromise principle for results; Iranians are willing to sacrifice results to principle.
- Americans worship the future, Iranians the past.... America's history has been an upward arc, justifying, perhaps, the belief that the future will be better than the past. Iranians have a deep historical doubt about whether tomorrow will be a better day.
- Americans value forthrightness, Iranians complexity.... Iranian culture values politeness above all: even if one disagrees with another person, long phrases of praise precede any expression of dismay. Rarely are one's motivations stated frankly and clearly.

- Americans have imbibed science, Iranians literature.... Americans have a positivistic mindset: they seem to think that most problems can be fixed in the same way as the sum of two numbers can be determined. Iranians have a poetic sensibility: they feel concrete problems deeply, often painfully, but they have trouble determining what to do about them.
- Ultimately the average Iranian and the average American share much more in common than not. Indeed they likely share much enlightened self-interest. But to get there from here requires navigating some bumpy currents of emotion.

These "bumpy currents" are not simply the product of American ignorance or prejudice. Iranians have good reason to be angry at the United States, but American anger is also justified. The regime in Tehran has maintained ties, sometimes frighteningly direct, to groups that have carried out bloody crimes—not just crimes against its enemies, like the assassination of Iranian dissidents in Europe, or against humanity, like the 1994 bombing of a Jewish community center in Argentina that took eighty-seven lives, but against Americans. Pro-Iranian militants committed the 1985 torture-murder of William Buckley, the CIA station chief in Beirut, and are believed to have carried out the 1996 truck bombing of the Khobar Towers complex in Saudi Arabia. Iran has supported groups responsible for terror attacks inside Iraq. At many points in its recent history, it has seemed eager to do whatever possible to hurt the United States. In this campaign it has scored several murderous successes.

The desire for vengeance—the desire to punish Iran for its taking of American diplomats hostage in 1979 and for a litany of other outrages—has decisively shaped U.S. policy toward Iran. More recently, Washington has found three other reasons to justify its hostility:

- Iran has carried out a clandestine nuclear development program in repeated violation of its treaty obligations. This program introduces a new destabilizing factor into a region that is

already highly unstable. It unsettles other countries in the region and threatens to set off a nuclear arms race that could lead to apocalypse.
- Iran has used state power to brutalize citizens seeking to make use of fundamental rights guaranteed to them by Iranian law. Repression of protests following the 2009 election is only the most recent example. Show trials, coerced confessions, jailhouse torture, closure of newspapers, and the use of thugs to beat demonstrators have become normal aspects of public life.
- Iranian leaders, most notoriously President Ahmadinejad, have publicly denied the reality of the Holocaust and cast loathsome aspersions on the Jewish people. While demanding respect for their culture and recognition of historical outrages perpetrated upon their nation, they deny these to Jews.

This is not a peaceable regime that suffers international isolation simply because it is misunderstood. It is an irresponsible and deeply disturbing factor in global politics. Underestimating its capacity for violence, repression, and mendacity would be foolish. Wise leaders do not delude themselves about their adversaries—but they also resist the pull of emotion, and shape their policies according to their national interests.

If Americans are brought to realize that Iran is not fated to be their enemy forever, and indeed can be their partner, how should they proceed? First, they should stop making public demands and threats, including thinly veiled ones like the warning that "all options are on the table." They should abandon the carrot-and-stick mentality, which may be appropriate for donkeys but not for dealing with a nation ten times older than their own. Then they should reflect on how President Nixon launched his diplomatic breakthrough with China.

The first document that emerged in that normalization process was the Shanghai Communiqué of 1972. It was signed at a time when China was engaged in extreme "bad behavior"—supplying weapons to North Vietnamese soldiers who were killing Americans every day. Nixon did not make good behavior a condition of negotiation. He recognized that diplomacy works in precisely the opposite way. Agreement comes first; changes in behavior follow.

The Shanghai Communiqué was not an accord—that came later—but a simple statement of each side's concerns. It ended with a joint declaration asserting that "it is desirable to broaden the understanding between the two peoples"; that "economic relations based on equality and mutual benefit are in the interest of the peoples of the two countries"; that the parties would "stay in contact through various channels"; and that they hoped "the gains achieved during this visit would open up new prospects for the relations between the two countries."

If the Shanghai Communiqué suggests how diplomats could start building a partnership between the United States and Iran, the Helsinki Accords, signed in 1975 by thirty-five countries on both sides of the Iron Curtain, suggest where the process might end. These accords were complex and comprehensive, the product of long, painstaking negotiation. The Soviets were jubilant at the result because the accords recognized their legitimacy and required the West to stop interfering in their affairs. Americans and their allies understood that they too had achieved something profound: a pledge that Communist governments would show "respect for human rights and fundamental freedoms." All signatories pledged to settle future disputes peaceably.

If there could be a motto for future Iranian-American talks, it might be "From Shanghai to Helsinki." That could be printed on the front of T-shirts negotiators might hand out at their first meeting. On the back would be a line from Shakespeare that might push them toward agreement.

"I do not know why yet I live to say 'This thing's to do,'" Hamlet tells himself. "I have cause and will and strength and means to do't."

Historians have a target-rich environment when they look for mistakes the United States has made in dealing with the Middle East. The greater challenge is to find a new approach for the future. Remaining imprisoned by old policies, old alliances, and old assumptions will produce only a repetition of old failures. The stakes have become too high for Americans to accept that option. It may well prove impossible for the United States to make Iran a partner as long as the current regime is in power, but Americans should do nothing that will make that partnership more difficult to achieve when conditions are right. Instead they should ask, as the thirteenth-century Persian poet Rumi did, "Why do you stay in prison when the door is so wide open?"

NOTES

INTRODUCTION

1 Howard Baskerville: Mark F. Bernstein, "An American Hero in Iran," *Princeton Alumni Weekly*, May 9, 2007; Robert D. Burgener, "Iran's American Martyr," *The Iranian*, August 31, 1998; S. R. Shafagh, *Howard Baskerville 1885–1909, Fiftieth Anniversary: The Story of an American Who Died in the Cause of Iranian Freedom and Independence* (Tabriz, Iran: Keyhan, 1959). Shafagh places Baskerville's death on April 19 rather than April 20.

3 "perhaps the most perverted": Morgan Shuster, *The Strangling of Persia: A Record of European Diplomacy and Oriental Intrigue* (London: T. Fisher Unwin, 1912), p. xxi.

3 Scores of deputies: Hamid Dabashi, *Iran: A People Interrupted* (New York: The New Press, 2007), p. 79.

7 Voltaire and Tolstoy: Deane Fons Heller, *Atatürk: Hero of Modern Turkey* (New York: Julian Messner, 1972), p. 39.

7 "all bad": Vamik D. Volkan and Norman Itzkowitz, *The Immortal Atatürk: A Psychobiography* (Chicago: University of Chicago Press, 1984), p. 53.

7 "For the first time": Lord Kinross, *Atatürk: The Rebirth of a Nation* (New York: William Morrow, 1985), p. 23.

8 One day while wandering: Ibid., pp. 23–24.

9 Young Turks: Caroline Finkel, *Osman's Dream: The History of the Ottoman Empire* (New York: Basic Books, 2007), p. 510.

9   "blood will be shed": Ibid., p. 511.
9   "The city's Muslim holy men": Volkan and Itzkowitz, *Immortal Atatürk*, p. 60.
10 Turkish life changed: Finkel, *Osman's Dream*, p. 514.
10 an Armenian, a Jew, and two Muslims: Ibid., p. 517; Andrew Mango, *Atatürk: The Biography of the Founder of Modern Turkey* (London: John Murray, 1999), p. 88.

1. THE REAL LIFE AND SOUL OF THE SHOW

19 "The United States at this stage": Michael Axworthy, *A History of Iran: Empire of the Mind* (New York: Basic Books, 2008), p. 209.
20 "I had never even dreamed": Morgan Shuster, *The Strangling of Persia: A Record of European Diplomacy and Oriental Intrigue* (London: T. Fisher Unwin, 1912), p. 4.
22 Shuster on Parliament: Ibid., p. 219.
22 Russian ultimatum: Ibid., p. 167.
22 "The thief is out for theft": Yahya Aryanpour, *Az Saba ta Nima: Tarikh-e 150 Sal Adab-e Farsi [From Saba to Nima: A History of 150 Years of Persian Literature]*, vol. 2 (Tehran: Jibi, 1350 [1971]), pp. 167–68.
23 "It was an hour before noon": Shuster, *Strangling of Persia*, p. 182.
24 "Our task in Persia": Ibid., p. 226.
25 D'Arcy concession: Daniel Yergin, *The Prize: The Epic Quest for Oil, Money, and Power* (New York: Simon and Schuster, 1991), pp. 119–21; Mostafa Elm, *Oil, Power, and Principle: Iran's Oil Nationalization and Its Aftermath* (Syracuse, N.Y.: Syracuse University Press, 1992), pp. 6–7.
25 "Such was the contract": Firuz Kazemzadeh, *Russia and Britain in Persia, 1864–1914: A Study in Imperialism* (New Haven, Conn.: Yale University Press, 1968), pp. 357–58.
26 "Fortune brought us a prize": Winston S. Churchill, *The World Crisis* (New York: Scribner, 1928), p. 134.
26 "Mastery itself": Ibid., p. 136.
26 "floated to victory": *The Times* (London), November 22, 1918.
26 twenty-five hundred soldiers to Iran: Mohammad Gholi Majd, *Great Britain and Reza Shah: The Plunder of Iran, 1921–1941* (Gainesville: University Press of Florida, 2001), p. 25.
26 "Anglo-Persian Agreement": Ibid., p. 37; Ervand Abrahamian, *A History of Modern Iran* (New York: Cambridge University Press, 2008), pp. 61–62; Axworthy, *History of Iran*, pp. 215–16; Cyrus Ghani, *Iran and the*

Rise of Reza Shah: From Qajar Collapse to Pahlavi Power (London: I.B.Tauris, 1998), pp. 44–46, 76–77, 89, 113.

26 Curzon on chessboard: Foreign and Commonwealth Office, *Documents on British Foreign Policy 1919–1939*, first series, vol. 4 (London: Government Printing Press, 1971), pp. 1119–21.

27 "It does not appear to be realized": Ghani, *Iran and the Rise of Reza Shah*, p. 95.

27 Reza froze: Ibid., p. 162.

28 "a first-rate soldier": F. A. C. Forbes-Leith, *Checkmate: Fighting Tradition in Central Asia* (London: G. G. Harrap, 1927), p. 22.

28 "the real life and soul": Karl E. Meyer and Shareen Blair Brysac, *Kingmakers: The Invention of the Modern Middle East* (New York: W. W. Norton, 2008), p. 312.

28 "well over six feet tall": Ghani, *Iran and the Rise of Reza Shah*, p. 147.

29 Sayyed Zia on British payroll: Majd, *Great Britain and Reza Shah*, p. 62.

29 "I have interviewed Reza": Ghani, *Iran and the Rise of Reza Shah*, pp. 153–54.

29 "I have seen only one man": Edmund Ironside, *High Road to Command: The Diaries of Sir Edmund Ironside, 1920–1922* (London: Leo Cooper, 1972), pp. 177–78.

29 "Dear comrades!": Ghani, *Iran and the Rise of Reza Shah*, p. 167.

30 "I fancy that all the people think": Richard Ullman, *The Anglo-Soviet Accord*, vol. 3 of *Anglo-Soviet Relations 1917–1921* (Princeton, N.J.: Princeton University Press, 1973), p. 388.

2. AWAY WITH DREAMS AND SHADOWS!

31 Corinne: Lord Kinross, *Atatürk: The Rebirth of a Nation* (New York: William Morrow, 1985), pp. 60–61, 97, 100; Vamik D. Volkan and Norman Itzkowitz, *The Immortal Atatürk: A Psychobiography* (Chicago: University of Chicago Press, 1984), pp. 74–75.

32 his eyes: Gordon Taylor, *The Pasha and the Gypsy: Writings on Turkey, Kurdistan, and the Eastern Mediterranean*, part 4, April 6, 2008, accessible at http://pashagypsy.blogspot.com/2008/04/pasha-and-gypsy-part-iv.html.

32 "The Turkish nation has fallen far behind": Andrew Mango, *Atatürk: The Biography of the Founder of Modern Turkey* (London: John Murray, 1999), p. 95.

33   *Carmen* is wonderful: Kinross, *Atatürk*, p. 60; Volkan and Itzkowitz, *Immortal Atatürk*, p. 77.
34   Kemal observes Bulgarian parliament: Kinross, *Atatürk*, p. 63.
34   "I have ambitions": Ibid., p. 61.
34   "jealous as a lover": Ibid., p. 10.
34   Kemal's childhood: Ibid., pp. 6–10; H. C. Armstrong, *Grey Wolf: An Intimate Study of a Dictator* (London: Arthur Barker, 1932), pp. 18–20; Mango, *Atatürk*, pp. 32–38; Barbara K. Walker et al., *To Set Them Free: The Early Years of Mustafa Kemal Atatürk* (Grantham, N.H.: Tompson & Rutter, 1981), pp. 13–80.
34   "inflated and grandiose self-concept": Volkan and Itzkowitz, *Immortal Atatürk*, p. xxiii.
35   Enver believes in German victory: Kinross, *Atatürk*, pp. 65–66; Mango, *Atatürk*, p. 68.
35   Enver named a German general: Kinross, *Atatürk*, p. 72; Volkan and Itzkowitz, *Immortal Atatürk*, p. 86.
35   Allied casualties during Gallipoli landing: http://samilitaryhistory.org/vol064sm.html.
36   "I am not ordering you to attack": Mango, *Atatürk*, p. 146.
36   "fought like a man possessed": Volkan and Itzkowitz, *Immortal Atatürk*, p. 88.
36   "Prior to being swept": Ibid., p. 93.
37   Killing Armenians was shameful: Taner Akçam, *A Shameful Act: The Armenian Genocide and the Question of Turkish Responsibility* (New York: Holt Paperbacks, 2007), p. 12.
38   Mudros armistice: Kinross, *Atatürk*, p. 128; Mango, *Atatürk*, p. 190.
38   "News of the Mudros armistice terms shocked Kemal": Alan Palmer, *Kemal Atatürk* (London: Sphere, 1991), pp. 43–44.
38   Arrival at Haydarpasha: Sina Akşin, *Turkey from Empire to Revolutionary Republic: The Emergence of the Turkish Nation from 1789 to Present* (New York: New York University Press, 2007), pp. 120–21; Kinross, *Atatürk*, p. 136; Mango, *Atatürk*, p. 190; Volkan and Itzkowitz, *Immortal Atatürk*, p. 110; Turkish Ministry of Press Broadcasting and Tourism, *The Life of Atatürk* (Istanbul: Dizerkonca Matbaazi, 1961), p. 48.
39   "mangle all thy provinces": Christopher Marlowe, *Tamburlaine* (London: Ernest Benn, 1971), p. 9.
39   "If I obtain great authority": Volkan and Itzkowitz, *Immortal Atatürk*, p. 104.

NOTES

40 "jutting out into the Mediterranean": Selected poems of Nazim Hikmet, accessible at http://www.nazimhikmetran.com/english/pages/siirleri/davet.shtml.
40 "a human cancer": H. W. V. Temperley, ed., *A History of the Peace Conference of Paris*, vol. 4 (New York: Oxford University Press, 1969), p. 24.
40 "It was not European military occupation": Mango, *Atatürk*, pp. 193–94.
41 Karabekir and Ismet visit Kemal: Ibid., pp. 208–9.
42 "What a wonderful feeling!": Kinross, *Atatürk*, p. 151.
42 "I am going to do something": Turkish Ministry, *Life of Atatürk*, p. 55.
42 "The Greek civilian population": Kinross, *Atatürk*, p. 154.
43 "You are too late": Ibid., p. 158.
43 "The Mustafa Kemal who now embarked": Ibid., p. 163.
44 Amasya Circular: Ibid., pp. 171–72; Armstrong, *Grey Wolf*, p. 130; Mango, *Atatürk*, pp. 230–31.
45 "insubordinate, disrespectful and illegal": Mango, *Atatürk*, p. 232.
45 "When we have independence": Armstrong, *Grey Wolf*, p. 133.
45 "the achievement of our sacred national purpose": Mango, *Atatürk*, p. 177.
45 "It is essential": Stanford J. Shaw and Ezel Kural Shaw, *History of the Ottoman Empire and Modern Turkey*, vol. 2: *Reform, Revolution and Republic: The Rise of Modern Turkey 1808–1975* (Cambridge: Cambridge University Press, 1977), p. 345.
46 "Wretches, murderers, traitors!": Mango, *Atatürk*, pp. 250–51.
46 "The first phase is at an end": Kinross, *Atatürk*, p. 196.
46 Meeting with Harbord: Ibid., p. 189.
47 British arrest leaders of Parliament: Akşin, *Turkey from Empire to Revolutionary Republic*, pp. 149–50; Kinross, *Atatürk*, pp. 202–9.
47 "Today the Turkish nation is called": Mango, *Atatürk*, p. 272.
47 fatwas: Ibid., p. 275; Akşin, *Turkey from Empire to Revolutionary Republic*, p. 155.
49 "A sinister death sentence": Mango, *Atatürk*, p. 223.
49 Sèvres Treaty: Akşin, *Turkey from Empire to Revolutionary Republic*, pp. 156–58; Deane Fons Heller, *Atatürk: Hero of Modern Turkey* (New York: Julian Messner, 1972), pp. 179–81; Harry N. Howard, *The Partition of Turkey: A Diplomatic History, 1913–1923* (Norman: University of Oklahoma Press, 1931), pp. 242–49; Kinross, *Atatürk*, pp. 230–32; Mango, *Atatürk*, pp. 284–85.
49 "Loaded with follies": Kinross, *Atatürk*, p. 184.
50 "He bullied": Ibid., p. 237.

51	Comparison of army strengths: Mango, *Atatürk*, p. 315.
51	plans to flee if necessary: Ibid., p. 316; Erik J. Zürcher, *Turkey: A Modern History* (London: I.B.Tauris, 1993), p. 162.
51	they demanded help: Zürcher, *Turkey*, p. 162; Mango, *Atatürk*, p. 318.
52	"The Greek army was a long black dragon": Kinross, *Atatürk*, p. 277.
52	"the ugliest sort of fate": Ibid., p. 279.
53	"As at Gallipoli": Volkan and Itzkowitz, *Immortal Atatürk*, p. 193.
53	"Men and horses looked spectral": Kinross, *Atatürk*, p. 321.
54	"The surface of the sea shone": Ibid., p. 325.
54	"Aren't you the people": Ibid., p. 323.
55	"In her forceful style": Ibid., p. 329.
55	Lloyd George wouldn't run away: Ibid., p. 139; Mango, *Atatürk*, p. 351.
55	"Stop This New War!": *Daily Mail* (London), September 15, 1922.
56	"that member of the Ottoman family": Kinross, *Atatürk*, p. 348.
56	"sovereignty and the Sultanate are not given": Kinross, *Atatürk*, p. 348; Bernard Lewis, *The Emergence of Modern Turkey* (London: Oxford University Press, 1961), p. 258.
56	"Several deputies demanded a vote": Armstrong, *Grey Wolf*, pp. 226–27.
57	"ghost of a monarch": Kinross, *Atatürk*, p. 349.
57	"Away with dreams": Heller, *Atatürk*, p. 111.
57	new caliph: Mango, *Atatürk*, p. 366.
58	"Mustafa Kemal seems at no point": Volkan and Itzkowitz, *Immortal Atatürk*, p. 223.
58	"They think that this is the end": Kinross, *Atatürk*, p. 343.

3. WE HAVE NO CHOICE BUT TO CATCH UP

60	Kemal elected president: Feroz Ahmad, *The Making of Modern Turkey* (London: Routledge, 1993), pp. 53–54; Sina Akşin, *Turkey from Empire to Revolutionary Republic: The Emergence of the Turkish Nation from 1789 to Present* (New York: New York University Press, 2007), p. 190; Lord Kinross, *Atatürk: The Rebirth of a Nation* (New York: William Morrow, 1985), p. 381; Bernard Lewis, *The Emergence of Modern Turkey* (London: Oxford University Press, 1961), pp. 261–62; Andrew Mango, *Atatürk: The Biography of the Founder of Modern Turkey* (London: John Murray, 1999), pp. 396–97.
60	A traveler who passed through: Hassan Arfa, *Under Five Shahs* (London: John Murray, 1964), pp. 150–51.

NOTES

61 "The civilized world is far ahead of us": Mango, *Atatürk*, p. 438.
61 "The beloved face of Freedom": Donald N. Wilber, *Iran Past and Present* (Princeton, N.J.: Princeton University Press, 1975), p. 77.
61 Kemal on abolishing caliphate: Kinross, *Atatürk*, pp. 404–5.
62 "it would be better": Wilber, *Iran Past and Present*, p. 79.
62 "more backward than Zanzibar": Fakhreddin Azimi, *Iran: The Crisis of Democracy* (London: I.B.Tauris, 1989), p. 65.
63 "Linen bags vomited emeralds and pearls": Karl E. Meyer and Shareen Blair Brysac, *Kingmakers: The Invention of the Modern Middle East* (New York: W. W. Norton, 2008), p. 303.
63 coronation: Ali Ansari, *Modern Iran Since 1921: The Pahlavis and After* (London: Pearson, 2003), pp. 41–42; Cyrus Ghani, *Iran and the Rise of Reza Shah: From Qajar Collapse to Pahlavi Power* (London: I.B.Tauris, 1998), pp. 385–86.
63 gifts: Wilber, *Iran Past and Present*, p. 113.
63 He stopped briefly before the throne: Ibid., pp. 113–14; Ghani, *Iran and the Rise of Reza Shah*, p. 61.
63 "I must make known my wish": Wilber, *Iran Past and Present*, p. 115.
63 "We now have as king of Persia": Ghani, *Iran and the Rise of Reza Shah*, pp. 390–91.
64 "History has proven": Mango, *Atatürk*, p. 237.
64 "I am not an ordinary man": Wilber, *Iran Past and Present*, p. 220.
64 Gabor was a conquest: Zsa Zsa Gabor with Gerold Frank, *Zsa Zsa Gabor: My Story* (Cleveland, Ohio: World, 1960), pp. 69–81; Gordon Taylor, *The Pasha and the Gypsy: Writings on Turkey, Kurdistan, and the Eastern Mediterranean*, part 4, April 6, 2008, accessible at http://pashagypsy.blogspot.com/2008/04/pasha-and-gypsy-part-ii.html.
65 Kemal was also a dandy: Mango, *Atatürk*, p. 490.
65 A normal night for Kemal: Arfa, *Under Five Shahs*, p. 281; Kinross, *Atatürk*, p. 478.
65 "the dark forces of religious fanaticism": Wilber, *Iran Past and Present*, p. 180.
66 "Islam, this absurd theology": Paul Fregosi, *Jihad in the West: Muslim Conquests from the 7th to the 21st Centuries* (Amherst, N.Y.: Prometheus Books, 1998), p. 407.
66 "an emblem of ignorance": Hunt Janin, *The Pursuit of Learning in the Islamic World 610–2003* (Jefferson, N.C.: McFarland, 2005), p. 149.
66 "A civilized, international dress": Kinross, *Atatürk*, p. 415.
67 Kemal becomes Atatürk: Mango, *Atatürk*, p. 498; Vamik D. Volkan and

Norman Itzkowitz, *The Immortal Atatürk: A Psychobiography* (Chicago: University of Chicago Press, 1984), p. 302.
67 "incomprehensible signs": Volkan and Itzkowitz, *Immortal Atatürk*, p. 284.
67 Alphabet Reform: Kinross, *Atatürk*, p. 444; Mango, *Atatürk*, p. 465.
67 Iran's clergy fought back: Janet Afary, *The Iranian Constitutional Revolution, 1906–1911: Grassroots Democracy, Social Democracy and the Origins of Feminism* (New York: Columbia University Press, 1996), pp. 148–49.
68 Reza storms mosque in Qom: Azimi, *Iran*, p. 78; Ghani, *Iran and the Rise of Reza Shah*, pp. 63–64.
68 Karabekir asks respect for religious opinions: Akşin, *Turkey from Empire to Revolutionary Republic*, p. 199.
68 "Every one of the Muslim elements": Sylvia Kedourie, ed., *Seventy-Five Years of the Turkish Republic* (London: Frank Cass, 2000), p. 11.
69 Sheik Said rebellion: David McDowall, *A Modern History of the Kurds* (London: I.B.Tauris, 1996), pp. 94–96; Robert W. Olson and William F. Tucker, "The Sheikh Sait Rebellion in Turkey (1925): A Study in the Consolidation of a Developed Uninstitutionalized Nationalism and the Rise of Incipient (Kurdish) Nationalism," *Die Welt des Islams* 18, no. 3–4 (1978): 195–211; Jonathan C. Randal, *After Such Knowledge, What Forgiveness?: My Encounters with Kurdistan* (Boulder, Colo.: Westview Press, 1998), p. 121.
69 "population exchange": Mango, *Atatürk*, p. 390.
69 "It is not becoming": Wilber, *Iran Past and Present*, p. 99.
70 nomads repressed: Ansari, *Modern Iran Since 1921*, pp. 49–51; Azimi, *Iran*, pp. 72–73; Nikki R. Keddie, *Modern Iran: Roots and Results of Revolution* (New Haven, Conn.: Yale University Press, 2006), p. 91.
70 Atatürk used martial law powers: Ahmad, *Making of Modern Turkey*, pp. 49, 58; Kinross, *Atatürk*, p. 430.
71 "One should not wait": Kinross, *Atatürk*, p. 398.
71 Jews build new university: Arnold Reisman, *Turkey's Modernization: Refugees from Nazism and Atatürk's Vision* (Washington, D.C.: New Academia, 2006), pp. 19–310.
71 "At a stroke": Akşin, *Turkey from Empire to Revolutionary Republic*, p. 216.
71 "the meanness of his language": Kinross, *Atatürk*, p. 460.
72 "I proclaim to you": Bernard Lewis, *The Jews of Islam* (Princeton, N.J.: Princeton University Press, 1987), p. 136.

NOTES 227

72   more Jews lived in Ottoman territory: Soner Cağaptay, "The Turkish Prime Minister Visits Israel: Whither Turkish-Israeli Relations?" Policywatch 987 (Washington, D.C.: Washington Institute for Near East Policy, April 27, 2005).

72   sultan rejects blood libel: *The History of the Turkish Jews*, accessible at http://naqshbandi.org/ottomans/protectors/protectors.htm.

73   "A university should have been established": Amin Banani, *The Modernization of Iran* (Stanford, Calif.: Stanford University Press, 1961), p. 40.

73   changes in Tehran: Ervand Abrahamian, *A History of Modern Iran* (New York: Cambridge University Press, 2008), p. 90; Afary, *Iranian Constitutional Resolution*, p. 142.

74   eighteen women elected: Jenny White, "State Feminism, Modernization, and the Turkish Republican Woman," *NWSA Journal* 15, no. 3 (2003): 151.

74   Atatürk divorces: Kinross, *Atatürk*, p. 250.

74   "I was married": Mango, *Atatürk*, p. 458.

74   Reza promotes women: Afary, *Iranian Constitutional Revolution*, p. 151.

74   "The women of this country": Wilber, *Iran Past and Present*, p. 173.

75   "I am always dissatisfied": Ibid., p. 136.

75   "He gets straight to what he has to say": Meyer and Brysac, *Kingmakers*, p. 322.

76   "The real cause of the setback": Wilber, *Iran Past and Present*, pp. 85–86.

76   Reza visits Turkey: Afshin Marashi, "Performing the Nation: The Shah's Official Visit to Kemalist Turkey, June to July 1934," in Stephanie Cronin, ed., *The Making of Modern Iran: State and Society Under Riza Shah 1921–1941* (London: RoutledgeCurzon, 2003).

76   specially commissioned opera: Kathryn Woodard, "Music Mediating Politics in Turkey: The Case of Ahmed Adnan Saygun," *Comparative Studies of South Asia, Africa and the Middle East* 27, no. 3 (2007): 552–62.

77   "The platform was full of people": Arfa, *Under Five Shahs*, pp. 250–51.

77   "Eastern Night": Volkan and Itzkowitz, *Immortal Atatürk*, p. 325.

78   "I admire your sovereign so much": Arfa, *Under Five Shahs*, p. 252.

78   killings at Mashad: Abrahamian, *History of Modern Iran*, p. 94; Wilber, *Iran Past and Present*, pp. 166–67.

78   Reza bans veil: Abrahamian, *History of Modern Iran*, p. 95; Azimi, *Iran*, p. 93.

79   Atatürk gently faded: Kinross, *Atatürk*, p. 413.

79   "I'm bored to tears": Mango, *Atatürk*, p. 489.

80   "I have devoted all of my energies": Wilber, *Iran Past and Present*, p. 215.
81   "I would be afraid of death": Ibid., p. 221.
82   "Atatürk emerged from his childhood": D. M. Birger, "The Psychoanalytic Study of Society: 'Immortal' Atatürk—Narcissism and Creativity in a Revolutionary Leader," *Psychoanalytic Quarterly* no. 53 (1984): 491.
83   Gunther article: John Gunther, "King of Kings: The Shah of Iran—Which Used to Be Persia," *Harper's*, December 1938, pp. 60–69.
84   "I have been able to teach the people": Kinross, *Atatürk*, p. 482.

4. THIS DIZZY OLD WIZARD

88   "Russia knocks threateningly": Samuel Loring Morison and Norman Polmar, *The American Battleship* (Osceola, Wis.: Zenith Press, 2003), p. 134.
89   Stalin withdraws troops from Iran: Yonah Alexander and Alan Nanes, eds., *The United States and Iran: A Documentary History* (Frederick, Md.: University Publications of America, 1980), pp. 161–89; Ali Ansari, *Modern Iran Since 1921: The Pahlavis and After* (London: Pearson, 2003), pp. 94–97; Richard W. Cottam, *Nationalism in Iran* (Pittsburgh, Pa.: University of Pittsburgh Press, 1979), pp. 118–31.
91   "He is not credited with much strength": Fakhreddin Azimi, *Iran: The Crisis of Democracy* (London: I.B.Tauris, 1989), p. 123.
91   Mossadegh was one of four: Nikki R. Keddie, *Modern Iran: Roots and Results of Revolution* (New Haven, Conn.: Yale University Press, 2006), p. 88.
92   "fainting fanatic": *Newsweek*, August 15, 1953.
93   British pressure on Iran: Mostafa Elm, *Oil, Power, and Principle: Iran's Oil Nationalization and Its Aftermath* (Syracuse, N.Y.: Syracuse University Press, 1992), pp. 146–50, 155–68, 271–72; James Goode, *The United States and Iran: In the Shadow of Mussadiq* (London: Macmillan, 1997), p. 33; Mary Ann Heiss, *Empire and Nationhood: The United States, Great Britain, and Iranian Oil, 1950–1954* (New York: Columbia University Press, 1997), p. 130; Stephen Kinzer, *All the Shah's Men: An American Coup and the Roots of Middle East Terror* (New York: Wiley, 2003), pp. 110, 115–17, 137–38.
94   "the block headed British": Henry Grady papers, box 2, 1952, Harry S. Truman Presidential Library, Independence, Missouri.
94   Mossadegh addresses Security Council: *New York Times*, October 16, 1951.
94   Man of the Year: *Time*, January 7, 1952.

95 "I told my British colleagues": Kermit Roosevelt, *Countercoup: The Struggle for the Control of Iran* (New York: McGraw-Hill, 1979), p. 107.
96 envoy meets with incoming officials: C. M. Woodhouse, *Something Ventured* (London: Granada, 1982), pp. 117–18.
96 "So this is how we get rid of that madman": Roosevelt, *Countercoup*, p. 8.
96 Goiran opposes coup: Stephen Dorril, *MI6: Inside the Covert World of Her Majesty's Secret Intelligence Service* (New York: Free Press, 2000), p. 584.
97 Heiss on intense dislike: Stephen Kinzer, "Inside Iran's Fury," *Smithsonian*, October 2008.
98 "I knew it!": *The Times* (London), August 20, 1953.
98 Douglas on basic reforms: James A. Bill, *The Eagle and the Lion: The Tragedy of American-Iranian Relations* (New Haven, Conn.: Yale University Press, 1988), p. 94.
99 "Iranians of all political persuasions": Ibid., p. 5.
99 Turks in Korea: Stanley Sandler, *The Korean War: No Victors, No Vanquished* (Lexington: University Press of Kentucky, 1999), pp. 163–66.
100 MacArthur on Turks: "The Turkish Brigade," accessible at http://www.korean-war.com/turkey.html.
101 Democrats win overwhelming victory: Feroz Ahmad, *The Making of Modern Turkey* (London: Routledge, 1993), pp. 108–9; Bernard Lewis, *The Emergence of Modern Turkey* (London: Oxford University Press, 1961), pp. 312–19; Erik J. Zürcher, *Turkey: A Modern History* (London: I. B. Tauris, 1993), pp. 227–28.
101 Turkey under Menderes: Sina Akşin, *Turkey from Empire to Revolutionary Republic: The Emergence of the Turkish Nation from 1789 to Present* (New York: New York University Press, 2007), pp. 253–67; Andrew Mango, *The Turks Today* (Woodstock, N.Y.: Overlook Press, 2006), pp. 47–48; Stanford J. Shaw and Ezel Kural Shaw, *History of the Ottoman Empire and Modern Turkey*, vol. 2: *Reform, Revolution, and Republic: The Rise of Modern Turkey, 1808–1975* (Cambridge: Cambridge University Press, 1977), p. 408; Zürcher, *Turkey*, pp. 231–52.
101 things began to sour: Akşin, *Turkey from Empire to Revolutionary Republic*, pp. 252–64; Mango, *Turks Today*, pp. 49–52; Zürcher, *Turkey*, pp. 241–45.
102 coup of 1960: Zürcher, *Turkey*, pp. 253–56; Ahmad, *Making of Modern Turkey*, pp. 120–27; Akşin, *Turkey from Empire to Revolutionary Republic*, pp. 262–65.
103 Cyprus crisis and Johnson letter: Ahmad, *Making of Modern Turkey*, p.

225; Parker T. Hart, *Two NATO Allies at the Threshold of War: Cyprus: A Firsthand Account of Crisis Management, 1965–1968* (Durham, N.C.: Duke University Press, 1990), pp. 163–66; Mango, *Turks Today*, pp. 60–61.

103 "sailors found it difficult": *Time*, March 1, 1971.

103 As leftists became more violent: Ahmad, *Making of Modern Turkey*, pp. 144–47; Mango, *Turks Today*, pp. 76–80.

104 party at Persepolis: "All the Grandeur of an Evening: The Persepolis Celebrations," accessible at http://www.angelfire.com/empire/imperialiran/persepolis3.html; Michael Axworthy, *A History of Iran: Empire of the Mind* (New York: Basic Books, 2008), p. 251; Bill, *Eagle and the Lion*, pp. 183–85; *New York Times*, October 12, 15, 19, 1971.

105 "a highly dangerous megalomaniac": Oriana Fallaci, *Interview with History* (Boston: Houghton Mifflin, 1976), p. 264.

105 SAVAK: Azimi, *Iran*, pp. 174–77, 190–209, 235–36, 250–57, 303–18; Bill, *Eagle and the Lion*, pp. 98–99, 186–92, 210–11, 402–3; Cottam, *Nationalism in Iran*, pp. 325–27; Hamid Dabashi, *Iran: A People Interrupted* (New York: The New Press, 2007), pp. 106–10; William H. Forbis, *Fall of the Peacock Throne: The Story of Iran* (New York: McGraw-Hill, 1981), pp. 132–38.

105 "The present system": Azimi, *Iran*, p. 163.

105 turmoil under the shah: Cottam, *Nationalism in Iran*, p. 121; Goode, *United States and Iran*, pp. 185–87.

106 "a bitter and vehement public reaction": Bill, *Eagle and the Lion*, p. 159.

106 "They have reduced the Iranian people": Ibid., pp. 159–60.

107 "lent him a new aura of martyrdom": Azimi, *Iran*, p. 184.

107 $16 billion in arms sales: Bill, *Eagle and the Lion*, p. 202.

108 oil income rises: Ervand Abrahamian, *A History of Modern Iran* (New York: Cambridge University Press, 2008), pp. 123–25.

108 "Some of the things the Shah purchased": Kinzer, "Inside Iran's Fury."

108 American companies in Iran: Bill, *Eagle and the Lion*, pp. 209, 381.

109 every Iranian must join his political party: Ibid., p. 196.

109 "important changes" . . . "gratifying trend": Alexander and Nanes, *United States and Iran*, pp. 452–53.

109 academic study: Mark J. Gasiorowski, *U.S. Foreign Policy and the Shah: Building a Client State in Iran* (Ithaca, N.Y.: Cornell University Press, 1991), pp. 156–57.

111 country was engulfed in protest: Abrahamian, *History of Modern Iran*, p. 181; Keddie, *Modern Iran*, p. 226.

111 tear gas on the White House lawn: Bill, *Eagle and the Lion*, p. 232; Dabashi, *Iran*, p. 156.

111	empress noticed protesters: Patrick Tyler, *A World of Trouble: The White House and the Middle East—From the Cold War to the War on Terror* (New York: Farrar, Straus and Giroux, 2009), p. 213.
111	Carter praises shah: Bill, *Eagle and the Lion*, p. 233.
111	Iran "is likely to remain stable": Richard W. Cottam, *Iran and the United States: A Cold War Case Study* (Pittsburgh, Pa.: University of Pittsburgh Press, 1988), p. 172.
112	"I lived for two weeks": Bill, *Eagle and the Lion*, p. 241.
112	shah careens wildly: Cottam, *Iran and the United States*, pp. 155–88; Gasiorowski, *U.S. Foreign Policy and the Shah*, pp. 209–22.
112	"mistakes... will be rectified": Azimi, *Iran*, pp. 212–13.
112	"Death to the American Shah!": Bill, *Eagle and the Lion*, p. 97.
112	shah will "remain actively in power": Ibid., p. 258.
112	Carter asked about crisis: Ibid., p. 259.
113	"The revolution erupted": Abrahamian, *History of Modern Iran*, p. 155.
114	Political violence was taking ten lives a day: Hugh Pope and Nicole Pope, *Turkey Unveiled: Ataturk and After* (London: John Murray, 1997), p. 139.
115	"state of anarchy"... "perverted ideologies": Ibid., p. 143; Akşin, *Turkey from Empire to Revolutionary Republic*, p. 280.

5. SOWERS OF CORRUPTION ON EARTH

116	Laingen shouts at captors: Author's interview with Bruce Laingen, 2009.
117	"That's ancient history": American Presidency Project, "The President's News Conference of February 13, 1980," accessible at http://www.presidency.ucsb.edu/ws/index.php?pid=32928#.
118	warnings against admitting shah: James A. Bill, *The Eagle and the Lion: The Tragedy of American-Iranian Relations* (New Haven, Conn.: Yale University Press, 1988), pp. 323–27.
119	"Don't listen": Jalal Matini, "Quotes from Ayatollah I Khomeini," accessible at http://www.iran-heritage.org/interestgroups/government-article2.htm.
120	"an ascetic mystic": Hamid Dabashi, *Iran: A People Interrupted* (New York: The New Press, 2007), pp. 160–61, 177.
120	Saddam's last words: *New York Times*, December 31, 2006.
120	"sowers of corruption": Ervand Abrahamian, *A History of Modern Iran* (New York: Cambridge University Press, 2008), p. 181.
121	Rumsfeld promotes pipeline: *New York Times*, April 14, 2003.

122   "I hope they kill each other": Dabashi, *Iran*, p. 170.
122   debates over Persepolis: Abrahamian, *History of Modern Iran*, p. 178.
122   Iran was left devastated: Ibid., pp. 171–75; Michael Axworthy, *A History of Iran: Empire of the Mind* (New York: Basic Books, 2008), p. 274.
123   Albright speech: American Presidency Project, "Secretary of State Madeleine K. Albright: Remarks before the American-Iranian Council, March 17, 2000, Washington, D.C.," accessible at http://www.fas.org/news/iran/2000/000317.htm.
124   Israel was equally unhappy: Sasan Fayazmanesh, *The United States and Iran: Sanctions, Wars and the Policy of Dual Containment* (London: Routledge, 2008), p. 94.
124   Rafsanjani told Iranians: Abrahamian, *History of Modern Iran*, p. 184.
125   The United States asked Iran: *New York Times*, May 24, 2009; Gareth Porter, "Burnt Offering," *American Prospect*, May 21, 2006.
125   Leverett later recalled: Porter, "Burnt Offering."
126   Iran proposed comprehensive talks: Trita Parsi, *Treacherous Alliance: The Secret Dealings of Israel, Iran, and the U.S.* (New Haven, Conn.: Yale University Press, 2007), pp. 341–42.
126   reprimanded the Swiss ambassador: Porter, "Burnt Offering."
127   Özal named airline chief: Author's interview with Cem Kozlu, 2009.
128   Aftermath of 1980 coup: Feroz Ahmad, *The Making of Modern Turkey* (London: Routledge, 1993), pp. 181–88; Sina Akşin, *Turkey from Empire to Revolutionary Republic: The Emergence of the Turkish Nation from 1789 to Present* (New York: New York University Press, 2007), pp. 280–84; Andrew Mango, *The Turks Today* (Woodstock, N.Y.: Overlook Press, 2006), pp. 81–83; Hugh Pope and Nicole Pope, *Turkey Unveiled: Atatürk and After* (London: John Murray, 1997), pp. 141–57.
129   Özal: Pope and Pope, *Turkey Unveiled*, pp. 158–79; Erik J. Zürcher, *Turkey: A Modern History* (London: I.B.Tauris, 1993), pp. 305–19.
131   Bush publicly thanked him: American Presidency Project, "The President's News Conference with President Turgut Ozal of Turkey, March 23, 1991," accessible at http://www.presidency.ucsb.edu/ws/index.php?pid=19419#.
131   "For all his many flaws": *The Independent*, May 19, 1993.
138   "The Turkish case": M. Hakan Yavuz, ed., *The Emergence of a New Turkey: Democracy and the AK Party* (Salt Lake City: University of Utah Press, 2006), pp. 7, 3, 17.
138   "Our party is the product of continuity": Ibid., p. 118.

6. YOU WIN, YOU BALD-HEADED SON OF A BITCH

145 Roosevelt meets Ibn Saud: William A. Eddy, *FDR Meets Ibn Saud* (New York: American Friends of the Middle East, 1954); James Wynbrandt, *A Brief History of Saudi Arabia* (New York: Facts on File, 2004), pp. 197–98.

149 "You are very far away!": Parker T. Hart, *Saudi Arabia and the United States: Birth of a Security Partnership* (Bloomington: Indiana University Press, 1998), p. 38.

151 Truman & Jacobson: David McCullough, *Truman* (New York: Simon and Schuster, 1993), pp. 107–8, 145–50; Samuel A. Montague, "The Reform Jew Who Changed Truman's Mind," accessible at http://reformjudaismmag.net/998sam.html; Bernard Reich, *The United States and Israel: Influence in the Special Relationship* (New York: Praeger, 1984), p. 56.

152 "The future of one and one-half million Jews": Norman H. Finkelstein, *Friends Indeed: The Special Relationship of Israel and the United States* (Brookfield, Conn.: Millbrook Press, 1998), p. 39.

152 full power of the United States was applied: Michael B. Oren, *Power, Faith, and Fantasy: America in the Middle East, 1776 to the Present* (New York: W. W. Norton, 2007), p. 490.

152 "Mission accomplished": Michael J. Cohen, *Truman and Israel* (Berkeley: University of California Press, 1990), p. 168.

153 "I do not think I ever had so much pressure": Dan Raviv and Yossi Melman, *Friends in Deed: Inside the U.S.-Israel Alliance* (New York: Hyperion, 1994), p. 27.

153 "Jesus Christ couldn't please them": McCullough, *Truman*, p. 599.

153 "disrespectful and mean": Melvin Urofsky, *A Voice That Spoke for Justice: The Life and Times of Stephen S. Wise* (Albany: State University of New York Press, 1982), p. 25.

153 "neither Hitler nor Stalin": Oren, *Power, Faith, and Fantasy*, p. 492.

153 "all your life you had a hero": Finkelstein, *Friends Indeed*, pp. 41–42.

154 "You win": Oren, *Power, Faith, and Fantasy*, p. 495; Montague, "Reform Jew Who Changed Truman's Mind."

154 Jacobson's efforts were not all: Finkelstein, *Friends Indeed*, p. 36.

155 "I am Cyrus!": Oren, *Power, Faith, and Fantasy*, p. 501.

155 Bugsy Siegel: Raviv and Melman, *Friends in Deed*, p. 41.

155 Sinatra carries cash: Ibid., pp. 44–45.

156 more than $350 million: Tom Segev, *One Palestine, Complete: Jews and*

Arabs Under the British Mandate (New York: Metropolitan Books, 2000), p. 45.

157 Byroade speech: Reich, *United States and Israel*, p. 27.

157 "That's exactly what frightens me": Raviv and Melman, *Friends in Deed*, p. 72.

157 Dulles claims greatest triumph: Ibid., p. 66.

158 "The melodrama sweeps the reader up": Rachel Weissbrod, "Exodus as a Zionist Melodrama," *Israel Studies* 4, no. 1 (1999): 129–52.

159 *Ben-Hur*: Oren, *Power, Faith, and Fantasy*, p. 518.

159 Johnson's view of Israel: Ibid., pp. 522–23.

159 destruction of Egyptian air force: Ibid., p. 523; Martin Gilbert, *Israel: A History* (London: Black Swan, 1999), p. 385.

160 "the millstone around our necks": Oren, *Power, Faith, and Fantasy*, p. 513.

160 "Israel at war destroys the stereotype": Gershom Gorenberg, *The Accidental Empire: Israel and the Birth of the Settlements, 1967–1977* (New York: Times Books, 2006), p. 48.

160 resupply airlift: Rachel Bronson, *Thicker Than Oil: America's Uneasy Partnership with Saudi Arabia* (New York: Oxford University Press, 2006), p. 117.

162 arms supply to Guatemala: Bishara Bahbah, *Israel and Latin America: The Military Connection* (New York: Palgrave Macmillan, 1986), p. 147; Benjamin Beit-Hallahmi, *The Israeli Connection: Who Israel Arms and Why* (New York: Pantheon Books, 1987), p. 80; Andrew Cockburn and Leslie Cockburn, *Dangerous Liaison: The Inside Story of the U.S.-Israeli Covert Relationship* (Toronto: Stoddart, 1991), pp. 218–19.

162 "We've indicated we're not unhappy": Bahbah, *Israel and Latin America*, p. 167.

162 "The Uzi submachine gun is the preferred weapon": *Ha'aretz*, November 25, 1985.

162 advisers trained the Salvadoran secret police: Cockburn and Cockburn, *Dangerous Liaison*, pp. 238–39; Jane Hunter, *Israeli Foreign Policy: South Africa and Central America* (Boston: South End Press, 1987), pp. 99–100.

162 high school students sign petition: Cockburn and Cockburn, *Dangerous Liaison*, p. 240.

162 The third conflict: Ibid., pp. 228–29, 257; Jack Colhoun, "Israel and the Contras," *Race & Class* 28, no. 3 (1987): 61–66; Hunter, *Israeli Foreign Policy*, pp. 145–66.

163	Battalion 316: Cockburn and Cockburn, *Dangerous Liaison*, pp. 224–25.
163	Sharon visited Honduras: *New York Times*, December 6, 1982.
163	"We had Israeli advisors": Jon Lee Anderson, "Loose Cannons: On the Trail of Israel's Gunrunners in Central America," *New Outlook*, February 1989, p. 26.
164	Mike Harari: Cockburn and Cockburn, *Dangerous Liaison*, pp. 244–61.
164	"Israel is the 'dirty work' contractor": Beit-Hallahmi, *Israeli Connection*, p. 78.
164	Dictators around the world: Noam Chomsky, *Fateful Triangle: The United States, Israel and the Palestinians* (New Delhi: India Research, 2004), pp. 21–26; Cockburn and Cockburn, *Dangerous Liaison*, p. 161.
164	Israeli ties to South Africa: Cockburn and Cockburn, *Dangerous Liaison*, pp. 283–87; Beit-Hallahmi, *Israeli Connection*, pp. 108–74; Hunter, *Israeli Foreign Policy*, pp. 19–91.
164	Israelis trained more than a dozen: Cockburn and Cockburn, *Dangerous Liaison*, pp. 121, 214–15, 232.
165	"Israel's main role": Matti Golan, *The Road to Peace: A Biography of Shimon Peres* (New York: Warner Books, 1989), p. 119.
165	"*very* intimate dialogue": Cockburn and Cockburn, *Dangerous Liaison*, p. 12.
166	Saudi Arabia aids contras: Patrick Tyler, *A World of Trouble: The White House and the Middle East—From the Cold War to the War on Terror* (New York: Farrar, Straus and Giroux, 2009), pp. 312–15; Tim Weiner, *Legacy of Ashes: The History of the CIA* (New York: Doubleday, 2007), p. 399.
166	princes give Casey a villa: George Crile, *Charlie Wilson's War: The Extraordinary Story of the Largest Covert Operation in History* (New York: Atlantic Monthly Press, 2003), p. 340.
166	"Do what you can": Ibid., p. 238.
166	Saudi intelligence officer flew to Pakistan: Steve Coll, *Ghost Wars: The Secret History of the CIA, Afghanistan and Bin Laden, From the Soviet Invasion to September 10, 2001* (New York: Penguin Press, 2004), pp. 71–72.
167	more than $6 billion: Robert Baer, *See No Evil: The True Story of a Ground Soldier in the CIA's War on Terrorism* (New York: Three Rivers Press, 2002), p. 100; Bronson, *Thicker Than Oil*, p. 173; Coll, *Ghost Wars*, p. 151.
167	"We don't do operations": Coll, *Ghost Wars*, p. 72.

167 Saudis sent hundreds of millions: Ibid., pp. 73–81.
167 Sadat got an annual subsidy: Henry Kissinger, *Years of Upheaval* (Boston: Little, Brown, 1982), p. 661.
167 Saudi operations in Africa: Bronson, *Thicker Than Oil*, pp. 177–80; Robert Lacey, *Inside the Kingdom: Kings, Clerics, Modernists, Terrorists, and the Struggle for Saudi Arabia* (New York: Viking, 2009), pp. 64–74; *New York Times*, June 21, 1987, July 2, 1987.
167 Anytime a president . . . wanted money: Lacey, *Inside the Kingdom*, pp. 214–15.
167 diamonds for Nancy Reagan: Tyler, *World of Trouble*, p. 319.
168 job for Deaver: Ibid., p. 320.
168 "We don't put conditions on friends": Bob Woodward, *Veil: The Secret Wars of the CIA, 1981–1987* (New York: Simon and Schuster, 1987), p. 349.
168 Saudi Arabia bought more weaponry: Bronson, *Thicker Than Oil*, p. 127.
168 Congress approves AWACS sale: Raviv and Melman, *Friends in Deed*, pp. 190–95.
168 "If you knew": William Simpson, *The Prince: The Secret Story of the World's Most Intriguing Royal: Prince Bandar bin Sultan* (New York: Regan Books, 2006), p. 112.
168 *New York Times* headlines: November 13, 1990, and July 29, 2007.
170 Woolsey on essence of this deal: "The Global Spread of Wahhabi Islam: How Great a Threat?" accessible at http://pewforum.org/events/?EventID=77.
171 "Not a single rebel surrendered": Lacey, *Inside the Kingdom*, p. 34.
171 deaths inside the Grand Mosque: Lawrence Wright, *The Looming Tower: Al-Qaeda and the Road to 9/11* (New York: Knopf, 2006), p. 94.
172 "You know what they have done!": Lacey, *Inside the Kingdom*, p. 36.
172 "We killed the extremists": Public Broadcasting System, "The Arming of Saudi Arabia," *Frontline* 1112, February 16, 1993.
173 "Don't lie to me!": Tyler, *World of Trouble*, pp. 283–84.
174 "a deliberately disproportionate attack": *New York Times*, September 16, 2009.

7. SO DEEPLY ENTWINED

178 "at least $1.476 billion": Craig Unger, *House of Bush, House of Saud: The Secret Relationship Between the World's Two Most Powerful Dynasties* (New York: Scribner, 2004), p. 200.

NOTES

178 "By failing to help foster": Richard Haass, "Towards Greater Democracy in the Muslim World," speech to the Council on Foreign Relations, December 4, 2002.

179 Members of Congress: Rachel Bronson, *Thicker Than Oil: America's Uneasy Partnership with Saudi Arabia* (New York: Oxford University Press, 2006), p. 256.

180 oil protest in 1956: James Wynbrandt, *A Brief History of Saudi Arabia* (New York: Facts on File, 2004), p. 213.

180 accept a constitution: Ibid., pp. 219–20; Bronson, *Thicker Than Oil*, p. 83.

180 "revolutionary movement": *New York Times*, September 10, 1969; Alexei Vassiliev, *The History of Saudi Arabia* (New York: New York University Press, 2000), p. 371.

180 women driving: Robert Lacey, *Inside the Kingdom: Kings, Clerics, Modernists, Terrorists, and the Struggle for Saudi Arabia* (New York: Viking, 2009), pp. 134–40.

180 "letter of demands": Bronson, *Thicker Than Oil*, p. 213; Wynbrandt, *Brief History of Saudi Arabia*, pp. 259–60.

180 challenges since 2000: Sherifa Zuhur, "Saudi Arabia: Islamic Threat, Political Reform, and the Global War on Terror," Strategic Studies Institute, March 2005, accessible at http://www.strategicstudiesinstitute.army.mil/pdffiles/PUB598.pdf.

182 congressional report: Alfred B. Prados, "Saudi Arabia: Current Issues and U.S. Relations" (Washington, D.C.: Congressional Research Service, 2003).

183 "nightmare scenario": *Wall Street Journal*, February 11, 2009.

185 Peres and Olmert on Arab peace plan: *Washington Post*, April 2, 2007.

8. WHERE THEY COME TOGETHER

195 "Communication and dialogue is the path": M. Hakan Yavuz, ed., *The Emergence of a New Turkey: Democracy and the AK Party* (Salt Lake City: University of Utah Press, 2006), p. 337.

196 "historical lobotomy": Ian O. Lesser, *Beyond Suspicion: Rethinking U.S.-Turkish Relations* (Washington, D.C.: Woodrow Wilson Center, 2007), p. 27.

197 The Lebanese scholar: Meliha Benli Altunişik, "The Possibilities and Limits of Turkey's Soft Power in the Middle East," *Insight Turkey* 10, no. 2 (2008): 48.

197 Abbas admires Turkey: Sedat Laçiner et al., *European Union with Turkey: The Possible Impact of Turkey's Membership on the European Union* (Ankara, Turkey: ISRO, 2005), p. 61.

198 "Turkey's new search for independence": Graham E. Fuller, *The New Turkish Republic: Turkey as a Pivotal State in the Muslim World* (Washington, D.C.: United States Institute of Peace, 2008), pp. 5, 23, 180.

199 "When we look at the wreckage": George Friedman, *The Next 100 Years: A Forecast for the 21st Century* (New York: Doubleday, 2009), pp. 81–82.

202 "Should Turkey join the EU": Hakan Altinay et al., eds., *Reflections of EU-Turkey Relations in the Muslim World* (Istanbul: Open Society Foundation, 2009), p. 17.

203 Obama speech: http://www.whitehouse.gov/the_press_office/Remarks-By-President-Obama-To-The-Turkish-Parliament/.

205 "A government that is in danger": *Time*, May 8, 2006.

206 "They want to humiliate us": Bob Woodward, *State of Denial: Bush at War*, part 3 (New York: Simon and Schuster, 2007), p. 408.

207 "To us, it seemed out of the world": Suzanne Maloney, *Iran's Long Reach: Iran as a Pivotal State in the Muslim World* (Washington, D.C.: United States Institute of Peace, 2008), pp. 46–47.

207 "for thirty years": Bruce Riedel, "America and Iran: Flawed Analysis, Missed Opportunities, and Looming Dangers," *Brown Journal of World Affairs* 15, no. 1 (Fall–Winter 2008): 101.

207 "I was the point person": Ali Gharib, "Iran: Misreading the Protests in Tehran," IPS, June 25, 2009, accessible at http://ipsnews.net/news.asp?idnews=47375.

207 "We don't really have people": *Wall Street Journal*, June 8, 2007.

211 "It's probably better": *New York Times*, October 31, 1971.

211 Iran gave plenty: Flynt Leverett and Hillary Mann Leverett, "Obama's Iranian Lifeline," *Politico*, October 6, 2009; Riedel, "America and Iran," p. 107.

214 someone trained in psychology and philosophy: Nasser Ghaemi, "The Psychology of Iranian-American Relations: Delving into the Psyches of Iran and America," *Psychology Today*, February 2, 2009, accessible at http://www.psychologytoday.com/blog/mood-swings/200902/the-psychology-iranian-american-relations.

217 "I do not know why yet I live": William Shakespeare, *Hamlet* 4.4., 48–51.

218 "Why do you stay in prison": Coleman Barks, trans., *The Essential Rumi* (New York: Harper One, 1997), p. 3.

BIBLIOGRAPHY

Aarts, Paul, and Gerd Nonneman, eds. *Saudi Arabia in the Balance. Political Economy, Society, Foreign Affairs.* London: Hurst, 2005.
Abdo, Geneive, and Jonathan Lyons. *Answering Only to God: Faith and Freedom in Twenty-First-Century Iran.* New York: Henry Holt, 2003.
Abrahamian, Ervand. *A History of Modern Iran.* New York: Cambridge University Press, 2008.
———. *Iran Between Two Revolutions.* Princeton, N.J.: Princeton University Press, 1982.
Abramowitz, Morton, ed. *Turkey's Transformation and American Policy.* New York: Century Foundation, 2000.
Abukhalil, As'ad. *The Battle for Saudi Arabia: Royalty, Fundamentalism, and Global Power.* New York: Seven Stories Press, 2004.
Aburish, Said K. *The Rise, Corruption and Coming Fall of the House of Saud.* New York: St. Martin's Press, 1995.
Afary, Janet. *The Iranian Constitutional Revolution, 1906–1911: Grassroots Democracy, Social Democracy and the Origins of Feminism.* New York: Columbia University Press, 1996.
———. *Sexual Politics in Modern Iran.* New York: Cambridge University Press, 2009.
Ahmad, Feroz. *The Making of Modern Turkey.* London: Routledge, 1993.
———. *The Turkish Experiment in Democracy, 1950–1975.* Boulder, Colo.: Westview Press, 1977.

———. *The Young Turks: The Committee of Union and Progress in Turkish Politics, 1908–1914*. Oxford: Clarendon Press, 1969.

Akçan, Taner. *A Shameful Act: The Armenian Genocide and the Question of Turkish Responsibility*. New York: Holt Paperbacks, 2007.

Akşin, Sina. *Turkey from Empire to Revolutionary Republic: The Emergence of the Turkish Nation from 1789 to Present*. New York: New York University Press, 2007.

Alexander, Yonah, and Alan Nanes, eds. *The United States and Iran: A Documentary History*. Frederick, Md.: University Publications of America, 1980.

Allen, Harry S., and Ivan Volgyes, eds. *Israel, the Middle East, and U.S. Interests*. New York: Praeger, 1983.

Al-Rasheed, Madawi. *A History of Saudi Arabia*. Cambridge: Cambridge University Press, 2002.

Al-Saltana, Taj. *Crowning Anguish: Memoirs of a Persian Princess from the Harem to Modernity*. Washington, D.C.: Mage, 2003.

Alteras, Isaac. *Eisenhower and Israel: U.S.-Israeli Relations, 1953–1960*. Gainesville: University Press of Florida, 1993.

Altinay, Hakan, et al., eds. *Reflections of EU-Turkey Relations in the Muslim World*. Istanbul: Open Society Foundation, 2009.

Altunişik, Meliha Benli. "The Possibilities and Limits of Turkey's Soft Power in the Middle East," *Insight Turkey* 10, no. 2 (2008): 41–54.

Altunişik, Meliha Benli, and Özlem Tür Kavli. *Turkey: Challenges of Continuity and Change*. New York: RoutledgeCurzon, 2005.

Anderson, Irvine H. *Aramco, the United States, and Saudi Arabia: A Study of the Dynamics of Foreign Oil Policy, 1933–1950*. Princeton, N.J.: Princeton University Press, 1981.

Anderson, Jon Lee. "Loose Cannons: On the Trail of Israel's Gunrunners in Central America," *New Outlook*, February 1989.

Anderson, Perry. "After Kemal," *London Review of Books*, September 25, 2008.

Ansari, Ali M. *Confronting Iran: The Failure of American Foreign Policy and the Next Great Crisis in the Middle East*. London: Hurst, 2006.

———. *Modern Iran Since 1921: The Pahlavis and After*. London: Pearson, 2003.

Arakie, Margaret. *The Broken Sword of Justice: America, Israel and the Palestine Tragedy*. London: Quartet Books, 1973.

Aras, Bülent. "Turkey and the Russian Federation: An Emerging Multidimensional Partnership," *SETA Policy Brief* no. 35, August 2009.

Arfa, Hassan. *Under Five Shahs*. London: John Murray, 1964.

Arjomand, Said Amir. *The Shadow of God and the Hidden Imam*. Chicago: University of Chicago Press, 1984.

———. *The Turban for the Crown: The Islamic Revolution in Iran*. New York: Oxford University Press, 1988.

Armstrong, H. C. *Grey Wolf: An Intimate Study of a Dictator*. London: Arthur Barker, 1932.

———. *Lord of Arabia: Ibn Saud, An Intimate Story of a King*. Beirut: Khayats, 1966.

Atabaki, Touraj, and Erik J. Zürcher, eds. *Men of Order: Authoritarian Modernization Under Atatürk and Reza Shah*. London: I.B.Tauris, 2004.

Avery, Peter. *Modern Iran*. New York: Praeger, 1965.

Axworthy, Michael. *A History of Iran: Empire of the Mind*. New York: Basic Books, 2008.

Ayoob, Mohammed, and Hasan Kosebalaban, eds. *Religion and Politics in Saudi Arabia: Wahhabism and the State*. London: Lynne Rienner, 2009.

Azimi, Fakhreddin. *Iran: The Crisis of Democracy*. London: I.B.Tauris, 1989.

———. *The Quest for Democracy in Iran: A Century of Struggle Against Authoritarian Rule*. Cambridge, Mass.: Harvard University Press, 2008.

Badeau, John S. *The American Approach to the Arab World*. New York: Harper & Row, 1968.

Baer, Robert. *See No Evil: The True Story of a Ground Soldier in the CIA's War on Terrorism*. New York: Three Rivers Press, 2002.

———. *Sleeping with the Devil: How Washington Sold Our Soul for Saudi Crude*. New York: Three Rivers Press, 2003.

Bahbah, Bishara. *Israel and Latin America: The Military Connection*. New York: Palgrave Macmillan, 1986.

Bain, Kenneth R. *The March to Zion: American Policy and the Founding of Israel*. College Station: Texas A&M University Press, 1979.

Bakhash, Shaul. *The Reign of the Ayatollahs: Iran and the Islamic Revolution*. London: I.B.Tauris, 1985.

Ball, George W. *Error and Betrayal in Lebanon: An Analysis of Israel's Invasion of Lebanon and the Implications for U.S.-Israeli Relations*. Washington, D.C.: Foundation for Middle East Peace, 1984.

Banani, Amin. *The Modernization of Iran, 1921–1941*. Stanford, Calif.: Stanford University Press, 1961.

Bani-Sadr, A. H. *My Turn to Speak: Iran, the Revolution & Secret Deals with the U.S.* London: Brasseys, 1991.

Bard, Mitchell Geoffrey. *The Water's Edge and Beyond: Defining the Limits to Domestic Influence on United States Middle Eastern Policy*. New Brunswick, N.J.: Transaction, 1991.

Barks, Coleman, trans. *The Essential Rumi*. New York: Harper One, 1997.

Barrett, David M. *The CIA and Congress: The Untold Story from Truman to Kennedy.* Lawrence: University Press of Kansas, 2005.

Barsamian, David. *Targeting Iran.* San Francisco: City Lights Books, 2007.

Bass, Warren. *Support Any Friend: Kennedy's Middle East and the Making of the U.S.-Israel Alliance.* New York: Oxford University Press, 2003.

Beeman, William. *The "Great Satan" vs. the "Mad Mullahs": How the United States and Iran Demonize Each Other.* Chicago: University of Chicago Press, 2008.

Beilin, Yossi. *Israel: A Concise Political History.* New York: St. Martin's Press, 1992.

Beit-Hallahmi, Benjamin. *The Israeli Connection: Who Israel Arms and Why.* New York: Pantheon Books, 1987.

Beling, Willard A., ed. *King Faisal and the Modernisation of Saudi Arabia.* London: Croom Helm, 1980.

———. *The Middle East: Quest for an American Policy.* Albany: State University of New York Press, 1973.

Ben-Ami, Shlomo. "A War to Start All Wars: Will Israel Ever Seal the Victory of 1948?" *Foreign Affairs* 87, no. 5 (September–October 2008): 148–56.

Ben-Zvi, Abraham. *Alliance Politics and the Limits of Influence: The Case of the U.S. and Israel, 1975–1983.* Tel Aviv: Jaffee Center for Strategic Studies, 1984.

Bergen, Peter L. *Holy War, Inc.: Inside the Secret World of Osama bin Laden.* New York: Free Press, 2001.

Bernstein, Mark F. "An American Hero in Iran," *Princeton Alumni Weekly*, May 9, 2007.

Bialer, Uri. *Between East and West: Israel's Foreign Policy Orientation, 1948–1956.* Cambridge: Cambridge University Press, 1990.

Bill, James A. *The Eagle and the Lion: The Tragedy of American-Iranian Relations.* New Haven, Conn.: Yale University Press, 1988.

Bill, James A., and Carl Leiden. *Politics in the Middle East.* Boston: Little, Brown, 1979.

Bill, James A., and William Roger Louis, eds. *Mussadiq, Iranian Nationalism and Oil.* London: I.B.Tauris, 1988.

Birand, Mehmet Ali. *Shirts of Steel: An Anatomy of the Turkish Armed Forces.* London: I.B.Tauris, 1991.

Birger, D. M. "The Psychoanalytic Study of Society: 'Immortal' Atatürk—Narcissism and Creativity in a Revolutionary Leader," *Psychoanalytic Quarterly* no. 53 (1984): 221–55.

Bligh, Alexander. *From Prince to King: Royal Succession in the House of Saud in the 20th Century.* New York: New York University Press, 1984.

Bodurgil, Abraham. *Kemal Atatürk: A Centennial Biography*. Washington, D.C.: Library of Congress, 1984.

Bradley, John R. *Saudi Arabia Exposed: Inside a Kingdom in Crisis*. New York: Palgrave Macmillan, 2005.

Brock, Ray. *Ghost on Horseback: The Incredible Atatürk*. New York: Duell, Sloan and Pearce, 1954.

Bronson, Rachel. *Thicker Than Oil: America's Uneasy Partnership with Saudi Arabia*. New York: Oxford University Press, 2006.

Brown, Anthony Cave. *Oil, God and Gold: The Story of Aramco and Saudi Kings*. Boston: Houghton Mifflin, 1999.

Brysac, Shareen Blair. "A Very British Coup: How Reza Shah Won and Lost His Throne," *World Policy Journal* 24, no. 2 (Summer 2007): 90–103.

Brzezinski, Zbigniew. *The Grand Chessboard: American Primacy and Its Geostrategic Imperatives*. New York: Basic Books, 1997.

Brzezinski, Zbigniew, et al. *Iran: Time for a New Approach*. New York: Council on Foreign Relations, 2004.

Bulloch, John. *The Making of a War: The Middle East from 1967 to 1973*. London: Longman, 1974.

Bumiller, Elisabeth. *Condoleezza Rice: An American Life*. New York: Random House, 2009.

Burgener, Robert D. "Iran's American Martyr," *The Iranian*, August 31, 1998.

Çağaptay, Soner. "The Turkish Prime Minister Visits Israel: Whither Turkish-Israeli Relations?" Policywatch 987. Washington, D.C.: Washington Institute for Near East Policy, April 27, 2005.

Carpenter, Ted Galen, and Malou Innocent. "The Iraq War and Iranian Power," *Survival* 49, no. 4 (Winter 2007–8): 67–82.

Çetinsaya, Gökhan. "Essential Friends and Natural Enemies: The Historic Roots of Turkish-Iranian Relations," *Middle East Review of International Affairs* 7, no. 3 (September 2003): 116–32.

———. "The New Iraq, the Middle East and Turkey: A Turkish View," *SETA Report*, April 2006, www.setav.org/lang_en/?option=com_content&task=view&id=15&Itemid=6.

———. "Rethinking Nationalism and Islam: Some Preliminary Notes on the Roots of 'Turkish-Islamic Synthesis' in Modern Turkish Political Thought." *The Muslim World* 89, no. 3–4 (July–October 1999): 350–76.

Champion, Daryl. *The Paradoxical Kingdom: Saudi Arabia and the Momentum of Reform*. New York: Columbia University Press, 2003.

Chomsky, Noam. *Fateful Triangle: The United States, Israel and the Palestinians*. New Delhi: India Research, 2004.

Churchill, Winston S. *The World Crisis*. New York: Scribner, 1928.

———. *The World Crisis: The Aftermath*. London: Library of Imperial History, 1974.

Citino, Nathan J. *From Arab Nationalism to OPEC: Eisenhower, King Sa'ud, and the Making of U.S.-Saudi Relations*. Bloomington: Indiana University Press, 2002.

Clarke, Richard A. *Against All Enemies: Inside America's War on Terror*. New York: Free Press, 2004.

Cockburn, Andrew, and Leslie Cockburn. *Dangerous Liaison: The Inside Story of the U.S.-Israeli Covert Relationship*. Toronto: Stoddart, 1991.

Cohen, Michael J. *Truman and Israel*. Berkeley: University of California Press, 1990.

Cohen, Naomi W. *American Jews and the Zionist Idea*. New York: Ktav, 1975.

Cohen, Stephen P. *Beyond America's Grasp: A Century of Failed Diplomacy in the Middle East*. New York: Farrar, Straus and Giroux, 2009.

Colhoun, Jack. "Israel and the Contras," *Race & Class* 28, no. 3 (1987): 61–66.

Coll, Steve. *Ghost Wars: The Secret History of the CIA, Afghanistan and Bin Laden, from the Soviet Invasion to September 10, 2001*. New York: Penguin Press, 2004.

Commins, David. *The Wahhabi Mission and Saudi Arabia*. London: I.B.Tauris, 2006.

Committee on Foreign Affairs, Subcommittee on Europe, U.S. House of Representatives. *The United States and Turkey: A Model Partnership*. Washington, D.C.: U.S. Government Printing Office, 2009.

Conant, Melvin. *The Oil Factor in U.S. Foreign Policy, 1980–1990*. Lexington, Mass.: Lexington Books, 1982.

Cordesman, Anthony H. *Saudi Arabia: Guarding the Desert Kingdom*. Boulder, Colo.: Westview Press, 1997.

Cornell, Erik. *Turkey in the 21st Century: Opportunities, Challenges, Threats*. Richmond, Surrey: Curzon, 2001.

Cottam, Richard W. *Iran and the United States: A Cold War Case Study*. Pittsburgh, Pa.: University of Pittsburgh Press, 1988.

———. *Nationalism in Iran*. Pittsburgh, Pa.: University of Pittsburgh Press, 1979.

Crile, George. *Charlie Wilson's War: The Extraordinary Story of the Largest Covert Operation in History*. New York: Atlantic Monthly Press, 2003.

Cronin, Stephanie, ed. *The Making of Modern Iran: State and Society Under Riza Shah 1921–1941*. London: RoutledgeCurzon, 2003.

Curzon, Lord G. N. *Persia and the Persian Question*. London: Frank Cass, 1966.

BIBLIOGRAPHY

Dabashi, Hamid. *Iran: A People Interrupted.* New York: New Press, 2007.
Davison, Roderick H. *Turkey: A Short History.* Beverly, England: Eothen Press, 1981.
De Gaury, Gerald. *Faisal: King of Saudi Arabia.* London: Arthur Barker, 1966.
DeLong-Bas, Natana J. *Wahhabi Islam: From Revival and Reform to Global Jihad.* New York: Oxford University Press, 2004.
Deringil, Selim. *Turkish Foreign Policy During the Second World War: An Active Neutrality.* Cambridge: Cambridge University Press, 1989.
Diba, Farhad. *Mohammad Mossadegh: A Political Biography.* London: Croon Helm, 1986.
Dismorr, Ann. *Turkey Decoded.* London: Saqi, 2008.
Donovan, Robert. *Conflict and Crisis: The Presidency of Harry S. Truman, 1945–1948.* Columbia: University of Missouri Press, 1996.
Dorril, Stephen. *MI6: Inside the Covert World of Her Majesty's Secret Intelligence Service.* New York: Free Press, 2000.
Douglas, William O. *Strange Lands and Friendly People.* New York: Harper & Brothers, 1951.
Dowty, Alan. *Middle East Crisis: U.S. Decision-Making in 1958, 1970 and 1973.* Berkeley: University of California Press, 1984.
Draper, Theodore. *A Very Thin Line: The Iran-Contra Affairs.* New York: Hill and Wang, 1991.
Eban, Abba. *An Autobiography.* New York: Random House, 1977.
Eddy, William A. *FDR Meets Ibn Saud.* New York: American Friends of the Middle East, 1954.
Edib, Halide. *House with Wisteria: Memoirs of Turkey Old and New.* New York: Century, 1926.
Elm, Mostafa. *Oil, Power, and Principle: Iran's Oil Nationalization and Its Aftermath.* Syracuse, N.Y.: Syracuse University Press, 1992.
Eren, Nuri. *Turkey Today and Tomorrow: An Experiment in Modernization.* New York: Praeger, 1963.
Erlich, Reese. *The Iran Agenda: The Real Story of U.S. Policy and the Middle East Crisis.* Sausalito, Calif.: PoliPointPress, 2007.
Eveland, Wilbur Crane. *Ropes of Sand: America's Failure in the Middle East.* New York: W. W. Norton, 1980.
Ezrahi, Yaron. *Rubber Bullets: Power and Conscience in Modern Israel.* New York: Farrar, Straus and Giroux, 1977.
Fallaci, Oriana. *Interview with History.* Boston: Houghton Mifflin, 1976.
Fandy, Mamoun. *Saudi Arabia and the Politics of Dissent.* New York: St. Martin's Press, 1999.

Farman Farmaian, Sattareh, and Dona Munker. *Daughter of Persia: A Woman's Journey from Her Father's Harem Through the Islamic Revolution.* New York: Crown, 1992.

Fatany, Samar. *Saudi Perceptions and Western Misconceptions.* Riyadh: Ghainaa, 2005.

Fayazmanesh, Sasan. *The United States and Iran: Sanctions, Wars and the Policy of Dual Containment.* London: Routledge, 2008.

Feuerwerger, Marvin C. *Congress and Israel: Foreign Aid Decision-Making in the House of Representatives, 1969–1976.* Westport, Conn.: Greenwood Press, 1970.

Finkel, Caroline. *Osman's Dream: The History of the Ottoman Empire.* New York: Basic Books, 2007.

Finkelstein, Norman H. *Friends Indeed: The Special Relationship of Israel and the United States.* Brookfield, Conn.: Millbrook Press, 1998.

Forbes-Leith, F. A. C. *Checkmate: Fighting Tradition in Central Asia.* London: G. G. Harrap, 1927.

Forbis, William H. *Fall of the Peacock Throne: The Story of Iran.* New York: McGraw-Hill, 1981.

Foreign and Commonwealth Office. *Documents on British Foreign Policy 1919–1939.* First Series, vol. 4. London: Government Printing Press, 1971.

Fregosi, Paul. *Jihad in the West: Muslim Conquests from the 7th to the 21st Centuries.* Amherst, N.Y.: Prometheus Books, 1998.

Friedman, George. *America's Secret War: Inside the Worldwide Struggle Between America and Its Enemies.* New York: Doubleday, 2004.

———. *The Next 100 Years: A Forecast for the 21st Century.* New York: Doubleday, 2009.

Fromkin, David. *A Peace to End All Peace: The Fall of the Ottoman Empire and the Creation of the Modern Middle East, 1914–22.* New York: Henry Holt, 1989.

Frye, Richard N., and Lewis V. Thomas. *The United States and Turkey and Iran.* Cambridge, Mass.: Harvard University Press, 1951.

Fuller, Graham E. *The New Turkish Republic: Turkey as a Pivotal State in the Muslim World.* Washington, D.C.: United States Institute of Peace, 2008.

Fuller, Graham E., et al. *Turkey's New Geopolitics: From the Balkans to Western China.* Boulder, Colo.: Westview Press, 1993.

Gabor, Zsa Zsa, with Gerold Frank. *Zsa Zsa Gabor: My Story.* Cleveland, Ohio: World, 1960.

Gabriel, Richard A. *Operation Peace for Galilee: The Israeli-PLO War in Lebanon.* New York: Hill and Wang, 1984.

Ganji, Akbar. *The Road to Democracy in Iran.* Cambridge, Mass.: MIT Press, 2008.

Gardner, David. *Last Chance: The Middle East in the Balance.* London: I.B.Tauris, 2009.

Gardner, Lloyd C. *The Long Road to Baghdad: A History of U.S. Foreign Policy from the 1970s to the Present.* New York: The New Press, 2008.

Gasiorowski, Mark J. *Mohammad Mossadeq and the 1953 Coup in Iran.* Syracuse, N.Y.: Syracuse University Press, 2004.

———. *U.S. Foreign Policy and the Shah: Building a Client State in Iran.* Ithaca, N.Y.: Cornell University Press, 1991.

Geller, Doron. "The Lavon Affair," Jewish Virtual Library, http://www.jewish virtuallibrary.org/jsource/History/lavon.html.

Ghaemi, Nassir. "The Psychology of Iranian-American Relations: Delving into the Psyches of Iran and America," *Psychology Today*, February 2, 2009, accessible at http://www.psychologytoday.com/blog/mood-swings/200902/the-psychology-iranian-american-relations.

Ghani, Cyrus. *Iran and the Rise of Reza Shah: From Qajar Collapse to Pahlavi Power.* London: I.B.Tauris, 1998.

Gilbert, Martin. *Israel: A History.* London: Black Swan, 1999.

Gilboa, Eytan. *American Public Opinion Toward Israel and the Arab-Israeli Conflict.* Lexington, Mass.: D. C. Heath, 1987.

Gilboa, Eytan, and Efraim Inbar, eds. *US-Israeli Relations in a New Era: Issues and Challenges After 9/11.* London: Routledge, 2009.

Giragosian, Richard. "Redefining Turkey's Strategic Orientation," *Turkish Policy Quarterly* 6, no. 4 (Winter 2008): 33–40.

Golan, Matti. *The Road to Peace: A Biography of Shimon Peres.* New York: Warner Books, 1989.

Goode, James. *The United States and Iran: In the Shadow of Mussadiq.* London: Macmillan, 1997.

Gorenberg, Gershom. *The Accidental Empire: Israel and the Birth of the Settlements, 1967–1977.* New York: Times Books, 2006.

Graham, Robert. *Iran: The Illusion of Power.* London: Croom Helm, 1978.

Grose, Peter. *Israel in the Mind of America.* New York: Knopf, 1983.

Güney, Nurşin Ateşoğlu. *Contentious Issues of Security and the Future of Turkey.* Burlington, Vt.: Ashgate, 2007.

Gunther, John. "King of Kings: The Shah of Iran—Which Used to Be Persia," *Harper's*, December 1938, pp. 60–69.

Hale, William. *Turkish Politics and the Military.* London: Routledge, 1994.

Hanioğlu, M. Sükrü. *Young Turks in Opposition.* New York: Oxford University Press, 1995.

Hart, Parker T. *Saudi Arabia and the United States: Birth of a Security Partnership.* Bloomington: Indiana University Press, 1998.

———. *Two NATO Allies at the Threshold of War: Cyprus: A Firsthand Account of Crisis Management, 1965–1968.* Durham, N.C.: Duke University Press, 1990.

Hedayat, Sadeq. *The Blind Owl.* New York: Grove Press, 1994.

Hegghammer, Thomas. *Jihad in Saudi Arabia: Violence and Pan-Islamism Since 1979.* Cambridge: Cambridge University Press, 2009.

Heiss, Mary Ann. *Empire and Nationhood: The United States, Great Britain, and Iranian Oil, 1950–1954.* New York: Columbia University Press, 1997.

Heller, Deane Fons. *Ataturk: Hero of Modern Turkey.* New York: Julian Messner, 1972.

Heller, Joseph. *The Stern Gang: Ideology, Politics, and Terror, 1940–1949.* London: Frank Cass, 1995.

Helms, Christine Moss. *The Cohesion of Saudi Arabia: Evolution of Political Identity.* London: Croon Helm, 1981.

Heper, Metin. *The State Tradition in Turkey.* Beverley, North Humberside, England: Eothen Press, 1985.

Hersh, Seymour M. *The Samson Option: Israel's Nuclear Arsenal and American Foreign Policy.* New York: Random House, 1991.

Hertzberg, Arthur. *The Zionist Idea: A Historical Analysis and Reader.* New York: Atheneum, 1973.

Holden, David, and Richard Johns. *The House of Saud: The Rise and Rule of the Most Powerful Dynasty in the Arab World.* London: Holt, Rinehart and Winston, 1981.

Housepian, Marjorie. *Smyrna 1922: The Destruction of a City.* London: Faber and Faber, 1972.

Howard, Harry N. *The Partition of Turkey: A Diplomatic History, 1913–1923.* Norman: University of Oklahoma Press, 1931.

Howarth, David. *The Desert King: A Life of Ibn Saud.* Beirut: Librairie du Liban, 1964.

Hunter, Jane. *Israeli Foreign Policy: South Africa and Central America.* Boston: South End Press, 1987.

Ide, Arthur Frederick. *Jihad, Mujahideen, Taliban, George W. Bush & Oil: A Study in the Evolution of Terrorism and Islam.* Garland, Tex.: Tanglewild Press, 2002.

Ikbal, Sirdar Ali Shah. *The Controlling Minds of Asia.* London: H. Jenkins, 1937.

International Crisis Group. "Saudi Arabia Backgrounder: Who Are the Islamists?" *ICG Middle East Report,* no. 31, September 21, 2004.

Ironside, Edmund. *High Road to Command: The Diaries of Sir Edmund Ironside, 1920–1922.* London: Leo Cooper, 1972.
Janin, Hunt. *The Pursuit of Learning in the Islamic World, 610–2003.* Jefferson, N.C.: McFarland, 2005.
Jung, Dietrich. "The Sèvres Syndrome: Turkish Foreign Policy and Its Historical Legacies," www.unc.edu/depts/diplomat/archives_roll/2003_07-09/jung_sevres/jung_sevres.html, January 5, 2009.
Katouzian, Homa. *Iranian History and Politics: The Dialectic of State and Society.* London: Routledge, 2007.
———. *Mussadiq and the Struggle for Power in Iran.* London: I.B.Tauris, 1990.
———. *Sadeq Hedayat: The Life and Literature of an Iranian Writer.* London: I.B.Tauris, 1991.
Kazemzadeh, Firuz. *Russia and Britain in Persia, 1864–1914: A Study in Imperialism.* New Haven, Conn.: Yale University Press, 1968.
Keddie, Nikki R. *Modern Iran: Roots and Results of Revolution.* New Haven, Conn.: Yale University Press, 2006.
———. *Qajar Iran: The Rise of Reza Khan, 1796–1925.* London: I.B.Tauris, 1999.
———. *Roots of Revolution: An Interpretive History of Modern Iran.* New Haven, Conn.: Yale University Press, 1981.
Kedourie, Sylvia, ed. *Seventy-Five Years of the Turkish Republic.* London: Frank Cass, 2000.
Kenen, L. L. *Israel's Defense Line: Her Friends and Foes in Washington.* Buffalo, N.Y.: Prometheus Books, 1981.
Khalidi, Rashid. *Sowing Crisis: The Cold War and the American Search for Dominance in the Middle East.* Boston: Beacon Press, 2009.
Khouri, Fred J. *The Arab-Israeli Dilemma.* Syracuse, N.Y.: Syracuse University Press, 1968.
Kinross, Lord. *Atatürk: The Rebirth of a Nation.* New York: William Morrow, 1965.
Kinzer, Stephen. *All the Shah's Men: An American Coup and the Roots of Middle East Terror.* New York: Wiley, 2003.
———. "Inside Iran's Fury," *Smithsonian*, October 2008.
Kissinger, Henry. *The White House Years.* Boston: Little, Brown, 1979.
———. *Years of Upheaval.* Boston: Little, Brown, 1982.
Kramer, Gudrun. *A History of Palestine: From the Ottoman Conquest to the Founding of the State of Israel.* Princeton, N.J.: Princeton University Press, 2008.
Kramer, Heinz. *A Changing Turkey: Challenges to Europe and the United States.* Washington, D.C.: Brookings Institution Press, 2000.

Kuniholm, Bruce. *The Origins of the Cold War in the Near East: Great Power Conflict and Diplomacy in Iran, Turkey and Greece.* Princeton, N.J.: Princeton University Press, 1980.

Lacey, Robert. *Inside the Kingdom: Kings, Clerics, Modernists, Terrorists, and the Struggle for Saudi Arabia.* New York: Viking, 2009.

Laçiner, Sedat, et al. *European Union with Turkey: The Possible Impact of Turkey's Membership on the European Union.* Ankara, Turkey: ISRO, 2005.

Landau, Jacob M., ed. *Atatürk and the Modernization of Turkey.* Boulder, Colo.: Westview Press, 1984.

Lengyel, Emil. *They Called Him Atatürk: The Life Story of the Hero of the Middle East.* New York: John Day, 1962.

Lesch, David W., ed. *The Middle East and the United States: A Historical and Political Reassessment.* Boulder, Colo.: Westview Press, 2003.

Lesser, Ian O. *Beyond Suspicion: Rethinking U.S.-Turkish Relations.* Washington, D.C.: Woodrow Wilson Center, 2007.

Lewis, Bernard. *The Emergence of Modern Turkey.* London: Oxford University Press, 1961.

———. *The Jews of Islam.* Princeton, N.J.: Princeton University Press, 1987.

Limbert, John W. *Iran: At War with History.* Boulder, Colo.: Westview Press, 1987.

———. *Negotiating with Iran: Wrestling the Ghosts of History.* Washington, D.C.: United States Institute of Peace, 2009.

Lippman, Thomas W. *Inside the Mirage: America's Fragile Partnership with Saudi Arabia.* Boulder, Colo.: Westview Press, 2004.

Long, David E. *The United States in Saudi Arabia: Ambivalent Allies.* Boulder, Colo.: Westview Press, 1985.

———. "US-Saudi Relations: Evolution, Current Conditions, and Future Prospects," *Mediterranean Quarterly* 15, no. 3 (Summer 2004): 24–37.

Lorentz, John H. *Historical Dictionary of Iran.* Lanham, Md.: Scarecrow Press, 2007.

Lytle, Mark. *The Origins of the Iranian-American Alliance, 1941–1953.* New York: Holmes & Meier, 1987.

MacFarquhar, Neil. *The Media Relations Department of Hizbollah Wishes You a Happy Birthday: Unexpected Encounters in the Changing Middle East.* New York: PublicAffairs, 2009.

Mackey, Sandra. *The Iranians: Persia, Islam, and the Soul of a Nation.* New York: Dutton, 1996.

———. *The Saudis: Inside the Desert Kingdom.* Boston: Houghton Mifflin, 1987.

Majd, Mohammad Gholi. *Great Britain and Reza Shah: The Plunder of Iran, 1921-1941.* Gainesville: University Press of Florida, 2001.

———. *The Great Famine and Genocide in Persia, 1917-1919.* Lanham, Md.: University Press of America, 2003.

Maloney, Suzanne. *Iran's Long Reach: Iran as a Pivotal State in the Muslim World.* Washington, D.C.: United States Institute of Peace, 2008.

Mango, Andrew. *Atatürk: The Biography of the Founder of Modern Turkey.* London: John Murray, 1999.

———. *Turkey: The Challenge of a New Role.* New York: Praeger, 1994.

———. *The Turks Today.* Woodstock, N.Y.: Overlook Press, 2006.

Mangold, Peter. *Superpower Intervention in the Middle East.* New York: St. Martin's Press, 1978.

Mansel, Philip. *Constantinople: City of the World's Desire 1453-1925.* London: John Murray, 1995.

Mansfield, Peter. *A History of the Middle East.* London: Penguin, 1991.

Marlowe, Christopher. *Tamburlaine.* London: Ernest Benn, 1971.

McAlister, Melani. *Epic Encounters: Culture, Media, and U.S. Interests in the Middle East, 1945-2000.* Berkeley: University of California Press, 2001.

McCullough, David. *Truman.* New York: Simon and Schuster, 1992.

McDowall, David. *A Modern History of the Kurds.* London: I.B.Tauris, 1996.

Ménoret, Pascal. *The Saudi Enigma: A History.* London: Zed Books, 2005.

Meyer, Karl E., and Shareen Blair Brysac. *Kingmakers: The Invention of the Modern Middle East.* New York: W. W. Norton, 2009.

Middle East Institute. *The Iranian Revolution at 30.* Washington, D.C.: Middle East Institute, 2009.

———. *The Seizure of the Grand Mosque.* Washington, D.C.: Middle East Institute, 2009.

Milani, Abbas. *The Persian Sphinx: Amir Abbas Hoveyda and the Riddle of the Iranian Revolution.* Washington, D.C.: Mage, 2001.

Millspaugh, Arthur C. *American in Persia.* Washington, D.C.: Brookings Institution Press, 1946.

Montagu, Mary Wortley. *The Turkish Embassy Letters.* London: Virago Press, 1994.

Morison, Samuel Loring, and Norman Polmar. *The American Battleship.* Osceola, Wis.: Zenith Press, 2003.

Morris, Chris. *The New Turkey: The Quiet Revolution on the Edge of Europe.* London: Granta, 2005.

Mottahedeh, Roy. *The Mantle of the Prophet: Religion and Politics in Iran.* New York: Pantheon Books, 1985.

Neff, Donald. *Warriors at Suez: Eisenhower Takes America into the Middle East*. New York: Linden Press, 1981.

———. *Warriors for Jerusalem: The Six Days That Changed the Middle East*. New York: Simon and Schuster, 1984.

New York University Center for Dialogues. "Iran-U.S. Relations: Imagining a New Paradigm," March 2009, accessible at http://islamuswest.org/events_Islam_and_the_West/Iran-US-relations/IranUSRelations.pdf.

Niblock, Tim. *Saudi Arabia: Power, Legitimacy, and Survival*. London: Routledge, 2006.

Ojanen, Hanna, and Igor Torbakov. "Turkey: Looking for a New Strategic Identity," *Europe's World*, May 12, 2009, accessible at http://www.europesworld.org/NewEnglish/Home_old/CommunityPosts/tabid/809PostID/396/Default.aspx.

Olson, Robert W., and William F. Tucker. "The Sheik Sait Rebellion in Turkey (1925): A Study of the Consolidation of a Developed Uninstitutionalized Nationalism and the Rise of Incipient (Kurdish) Nationalism," *Die Welt des Islams* 18, no. 3–4 (1978): 195–211.

Öniş, Ziya. "Between Europeanization and Euro-Asianism: Foreign Policy Activism in Turkey During the AKP Era," *Turkish Studies* 10, no. 1 (2009): 7–24.

———. "Conservative Globalism at the Crossroads: The Justice and Development Party and the Thorny Path to Democratic Consolidation in Turkey," *Mediterranean Politics* 14, no. 1 (March 2009): 21–40.

Oren, Michael B. *Power, Faith, and Fantasy: America in the Middle East, 1776 to the Present*. New York: W. W. Norton, 2007.

Ottaway, David. *The King's Messenger: Prince Bandar bin Sultan and America's Tangled Relationship with Saudi Arabia*. New York: Walker, 2008.

Özel, Soli. "The Back and Forth of Turkey's 'Westernness,'" *On Turkey*, January 29, 2009, accessible at http://www.gmfus.org//doc/Soli_Analysis_Turkey_0209_Final.pdf.

———. "Committed to Change, or Changing Commitments? Turkish-American Relations Under a New U.S. President," *On Turkey*, November 17, 2008, accessible at http://www.gmfus.org/template/bio_pubs.cfm?id=5009.

———. "Divining Davutoğlu: Turkey's Foreign Policy Under New Leadership," *On Turkey*, June 4, 2009, accessible at http://www.gmfus.org//doc/Soli_Analysis_Turkey_0609_Final_new.pdf.

Özel, Soli, and Şuhnaz Yilmaz. *Rebuilding a Partnership: Turkish-American Relations for a New Era: A Turkish Perspective*. Istanbul: Tusiad, 2009.

Pahlavi, Mohammad Reza. *Answer to History.* New York: Stein and Day, 1980.
———. *Mission for My Country.* London: Hutchinson, 1961.
Palmer, Alan. *Kemal Atatürk.* London: Sphere, 1991.
Parsi, Trita. *Treacherous Alliance: The Secret Dealings of Israel, Iran, and the U.S.* New Haven, Conn.: Yale University Press, 2007.
Parsons, Anthony. *The Pride and the Fall: Iran, 1974–1979.* London: J. Cape, 1984.
Perlmutter, Amos. *Politics and the Military in Israel.* London: Frank Cass, 1978.
Peters, Joan. *From Time Immemorial: The Origins of the Arab-Jewish Conflict over Palestine.* New York: Harper & Row, 1984.
Petras, James. *The Power of Israel in the United States.* Atlanta, Ga.: Clarity Press, 2006.
Philby, St. John. *Arabia of the Wahhabis.* London: Constable, 1928.
———. *Saudi Arabia.* New York: Praeger, 1955.
Polk, William R. *The Elusive Peace: The Middle East in the Twentieth Century.* London: Croom and Helm, 1979.
———, *Understanding Iran: Everything You Need to Know, from Persia to the Islamic Republic, from Cyrus to Ahmadinejad.* New York: Palgrave Macmillan, 2009.
Pollack, Kenneth M. *The Persian Puzzle: The Conflict Between Iran and America.* New York: Random House, 2004.
Pollock, David. *The Politics of Pressure: American Arms and Israeli Policy Since the Six Day War.* Westport, Conn.: Greenwood Press, 1982.
Pollock, David, et al. *Which Path to Persia? Options for a New American Strategy Toward Iran.* Washington, D.C.: Brookings Institution Press, 2009.
Pope, Hugh. *Sons of the Conquerors: The Rise of the Turkic World.* New York: Overlook Duckworth, 2005.
Pope, Hugh, and Nicole Pope. *Turkey Unveiled: Atatürk and After.* London: John Murray, 1997.
Porter, Gareth, "Burnt Offering," *The American Prospect,* May 21, 2006.
Posner, Gerald. *Secrets of the Kingdom: The Inside Story of the Saudi-U.S. Connection.* New York: Random House, 2005.
Pouton, Hugh. *Top Hat, Grey Wolf and Crescent: Turkish Nationalism and the Turkish Republic.* New York: New York University Press, 1997.
Prados, Alfred B. "Saudi Arabia: Current Issues and U.S. Relations." Washington, D.C.: Congressional Research Service, 2003.
Public Broadcasting System. "The Arming of Saudi Arabia." *Frontline* 1112, February 16, 1993.

Pushel, Karen L. *US-Israeli Strategic Cooperation in the Post–Cold War Era: An American Perspective.* Boulder, Colo.: Westview Press, 1993.

Quandt, William B. *Decade of Decisions: American Policy Toward the Arab-Israeli Conflict, 1967–1976.* Berkeley: University of California Press, 1977.

Rabin, Yitzhak. *The Rabin Memoirs.* Berkeley: University of California Press, 1996.

Radosh, Allis, and Ronald Radosh. *A Safe Haven: Harry S. Truman and the Foundation of Israel.* New York: HarperCollins, 2009.

Randal, Jonathan C. *After Such Knowledge, What Forgiveness?: My Encounters with Kurdistan.* Boulder, Colo.: Westview Press, 1998.

Rashid, Nasser Ibrahim. *Saudi Arabia and the Gulf War.* Joplin, Mo.: International Institute of Technology, 1992.

Raviv, Dan, and Yossi Melman. *Friends in Deed: Inside the U.S.-Israel Alliance.* New York: Hyperion, 1994.

Ray, James Lee. *The Future of American-Israeli Relations: A Parting of the Ways?* Lexington: University of Kentucky Press, 1985.

Reich, Bernard. *Quest for Peace: United States–Israel Relations and the Arab-Israeli Conflict.* New Brunswick, N.J.: Transaction, 1977.

———. *Securing the Covenant: United States–Israel Relations After the Cold War.* Westport, Conn.: Praeger, 1995.

———. *The United States and Israel: Influence in the Special Relationship.* New York: Praeger, 1984.

Reisman, Arnold. *Turkey's Modernization: Refugees from Nazism and Ataturk's Vision.* Washington, D.C.: New Academia, 2006.

Rentz, George S. *The Birth of the Islamic Reform Movement in Saudi Arabia: Muhammad Ibn Abd al-Wahhab (1703/4–1792) and the Beginnings of Unitarian Empire in Arabia.* London: Arabian, 2004.

Rezun, Miron. *The Soviet Union and Iran.* Boulder, Colo.: Westview Press, 1988.

Riedel, Bruce. "America and Iran: Flawed Analysis, Missed Opportunities, and Looming Dangers," *Brown Journal of World Affairs* 15, no. 1 (Fall–Winter 2008): 101–11.

Roberts, Samuel J. *Survival or Hegemony? The Foundation of Israeli Foreign Policy.* Baltimore: Johns Hopkins University Press, 1973.

Robins, Philip J. *Suits and Uniforms: Turkish Foreign Policy Since the Cold War.* Seattle: University of Washington Press, 2003.

Roosevelt, Kermit. *Arabs, Oil and History.* New York: Harper & Brothers, 1949.

———. *Countercoup: The Struggle for the Control of Iran.* New York: McGraw-Hill, 1979.
Rubenberg, Cheryl. *Israel and the American National Interest: A Critical Examination.* Urbana: University of Illinois Press, 1986.
Rubin, Barry. *The Arab States and the Palestinian Conflict.* Syracuse, N.Y.: Syracuse University Press, 1981.
———. *Paved with Good Intentions: The American Experience and Iran.* New York: Oxford University Press, 1980.
Sachar, Howard M. *A History of Israel: From the Rise of Zionism to Our Time.* New York: Knopf, 1976.
Safran, Nadav. *Israel, the Embattled Ally.* Cambridge, Mass.: Belknap Press, 1978.
———. *Saudi Arabia: The Ceaseless Search for Security.* Cambridge, Mass.: Belknap Press, 1985.
Sandler, Stanley. *The Korean War: No Victors, No Vanquished.* Lexington: University Press of Kentucky, 1999.
Schoenbaum, David. *The United States and the State of Israel.* New York: Oxford University Press, 1983.
Schwartz, Stephen. *The Two Faces of Islam: The House of Sa'ud from Tradition to Terror.* New York: Anchor, 2003.
Sciolino, Elaine. *Persian Mirrors: The Elusive Face of Iran.* New York: Free Press, 2000.
Segev, Tom. *One Palestine, Complete: Jews and Arabs Under the British Mandate.* New York: Metropolitan Books, 2000.
Shadid, Mohammad K. *The United States and the Palestinians.* London: Croom and Helm, 1981.
Shafagh, S. R. *Howard Baskerville 1885–1909, Fiftieth Anniversary: The Story of an American Who Died in the Cause of Iranian Freedom and Independence.* Tabriz, Iran: Keyhan, 1959.
Shaw, Stanford J., and Ezel Kural Shaw. *History of the Ottoman Empire and Modern Turkey.* Vol. 2: *Reform, Revolution, and Republic: The Rise of Modern Turkey, 1808–1975.* Cambridge: Cambridge University Press, 1977.
Shawcross, William. *The Shah's Last Ride: The Fate of an Ally.* New York: Simon and Schuster, 1988.
Shlaim, Avi. *The Iron Wall: Israel and the Arab World.* New York: W. W. Norton, 2001.
Shulman, David. *Dark Hope: Working for Peace in Israel and Palestine.* Chicago: University of Chicago Press, 2007.
Shultz, George. *Turmoil and Triumph: Diplomacy, Power, and the Victory of the American Ideal.* New York: Scribner, 1995.

Shuster, Morgan. *The Strangling of Persia: A Record of European Diplomacy and Oriental Intrigue.* London: T. Fisher Unwin, 1912.

Sicherman, Harvey. *Broker or Advocate? The U.S. Role in the Arab-Israeli Dispute, 1973–1978.* Philadelphia: Foreign Policy Research Institute, 1978.

Sick, Gary. *All Fall Down: America's Tragic Encounter with Iran.* New York: Random House, 1985.

———. "The Republic and the Rahbar," *The National Interest Online,* www.nationalinterest.org/PrinterFriendly.aspx?id=20482, January 6, 2009.

Sicker, Martin. *The Bear and the Lion: Soviet Imperialism and Iran.* New York: Praeger, 1988.

Simpson, William. *The Prince: The Secret Story of the World's Most Intriguing Royal, Prince Bandar bin Sultan.* New York: Regan Books, 2006.

Slavin, Barbara. *Bitter Friends, Bosom Enemies: Iran, the U.S., and the Twisted Path to Confrontation.* New York: St. Martin's Press, 2007.

Smith, Dan. *The State of the Middle East: An Atlas of Conflict Resolution.* Berkeley: University of California Press, 2008.

Snetsinger, John. *Truman, the Jewish Vote, and the Creation of Israel.* Stanford, Calif.: Hoover Institution Press, 1974.

Spiegel, Steven L. *The Other Arab-Israeli Conflict: Making America's Middle East Policy from Truman to Reagan.* Chicago: University of Chicago Press, 1985.

Stookey, Robert W. *America and the Arab States: An Uneasy Encounter.* New York: Wiley, 1975.

Taheri, Amir. *Nest of Spies: America's Journey to Disaster in Iran.* New York: Pantheon Books, 1988.

Takeyh, Ray. *Hidden Iran: Paradox and Power in the Islamic Republic.* New York: Times Books, 2006.

Taylor, Gordon. *The Pasha and the Gypsy: Writings on Turkey, Kurdistan, and the Eastern Mediterranean,* part 4, April 6, 2008, accessible at http://pashagypsy.blogspot.com/2008/04/pasha-and-gypsy-part-iv.html.

Teicher, Howard, and Gayle Radley Teicher. *Twin Pillars to Desert Storm: America's Flawed Vision in the Middle East from Nixon to Bush.* New York: William Morrow, 1993.

Telhami, Shibley. *The Stakes: America in the Middle East: The Consequences of Power and the Choice for Peace.* Boulder, Colo.: Westview Press, 2002.

Temperley, H. W. V., ed. *A History of the Peace Conference of Paris,* vol. 4. New York: Oxford University Press, 1969.

Tezel, Yahya Sezai. *Transformation of State and Society in Turkey: From the Ottoman Empire to the Turkish Republic.* Ankara, Turkey: Roma, 2005.

Tillman, Seth P. *The United States in the Middle East: Interests and Obstacles.* Bloomington: Indiana University Press, 1982.

Tirnan, John. *A New Approach to Iran: A Need for Transformative Diplomacy.* Cambridge, Mass.: MIT Center for International Studies, 2009.

Toktaş, Şule, and Ümit Kurt. "The Impact of EU Reform Process on Civil-Military Relations in Turkey," *SETA Policy Brief,* www.setav.org/document/Policy_Brief_No_26_Sule_Toktas_Umit_Kurt.pdf, no. 26, November 2008.

Touval, Saadia. *The Peace Brokers: Mediators in the Arab-Israeli Conflict.* Princeton, N.J.: Princeton University Press, 1982.

Troeller, Gary. *The Birth of Saudi Arabia: Britain and the Rise of the House of Sa'ud.* London: Frank Cass, 1976.

Turkish Ministry of Press Broadcasting and Tourism. *The Life of Atatürk.* Istanbul: Dizerkonca Matbaazi, 1961.

Tyler, Patrick. *A World of Trouble: The White House and the Middle East—From the Cold War to the War on Terror.* New York: Farrar, Straus and Giroux, 2009.

Ullman, Richard. *The Anglo-Soviet Accord,* vol. 3 of *Anglo-Soviet Relations 1917–1921.* Princeton, N.J.: Princeton University Press, 1973.

Unger, Craig. *House of Bush, House of Saud: The Secret Relationship Between the World's Two Most Powerful Dynasties.* New York: Scribner, 2004.

Urofsky, Melvin. *A Voice That Spoke for Justice: The Life and Times of Stephen S. Wise.* Albany: State University of New York Press, 1982.

Vassiliev, Alexei. *The History of Saudi Arabia.* New York: New York University Press, 2000.

Vitalis, Robert. *America's Kingdom: Mythmaking on the Saudi Oil Frontier.* Stanford, Calif.: Stanford University Press, 2007.

Volkan, Vamik D., and Norman Itzkowitz. *The Immortal Atatürk: A Psychobiography.* Chicago: University of Chicago Press, 1984.

Walker, Barbara K., et al. *To Set Them Free: The Early Years of Mustafa Kemal Atatürk.* Grantham, N.H.: Tompson & Rutter, 1981.

Washington Institute for Near East Policy. *Enduring Partnership: Report of the Commission on U.S.-Israel Relations.* Washington, D.C.: Washington Institute for Near East Policy, 1993.

Wehrey, Frederic, et al. *Dangerous But Not Omnipotent: Exploring the Reach and Limitations of Iranian Power in the Middle East.* Santa Monica, Calif.: Rand, 2009.

Weiker, Walter F. *The Modernization of Turkey: From Atatürk to the Present Day.* New York: Holmes & Meier, 1981.

Weiner, Tim. *Legacy of Ashes: The History of the CIA.* New York: Doubleday, 2007.

Weissbrod, Rachel. "Exodus as a Zionist Melodrama," *Israel Studies* 4, no. 1 (1999): 129–52.

White, Jenny. *Islamic Mobilization in Turkey: A Study in Vernacular Politics.* Seattle: University of Washington Press, 2002.

———. "State Feminism, Modernization and the Turkish Republican Woman," *NWSA Journal* 15, no. 3 (2003): 149–59.

Wilber, Donald N. *Iran Past and Present.* Princeton, N.J.: Princeton University Press, 1975.

———. *Reza Shah Pahlavi: The Resurrection and Reconstruction of Iran.* Hicksville, N.Y.: Exposition Press, 1975

Wilson, Evan M. *Decision on Palestine: How the U.S. Came to Recognize Israel.* Stanford, Calif.: Hoover Institution Press, 1979.

Woodard, Kathryn. "Music Mediating Politics in Turkey: The Case of Ahmed Adnan Saygun," *Comparative Studies of South Asia, Africa and the Middle East* 27, no. 3 (2007): 552–62.

Woodhouse, C. M. *Something Ventured.* London: Granada, 1982.

Woodward, Bob. *Bush at War.* New York: Simon and Schuster, 2002.

———. *The Commanders.* New York: Simon and Schuster, 1991.

———. *State of Denial: Bush at War,* part 3. New York: Simon and Schuster, 2007.

———. *Veil: The Secret Wars of the CIA, 1981–1987.* New York: Simon and Schuster, 1987.

Wortham, H. E. *Mustafa Kemal of Turkey.* Boston: Little, Brown, 1931.

Wright, Lawrence. *The Looming Tower: Al-Qaeda and the Road to 9/11.* New York: Knopf, 2006.

Wynbrandt, James. *A Brief History of Saudi Arabia.* New York: Facts on File, 2004.

Yavuz, M. Hakan, ed. *The Emergence of a New Turkey: Democracy and the AK Party.* Salt Lake City: University of Utah Press, 2006.

Yergin, Daniel. *The Prize: The Epic Quest for Oil, Money, and Power.* New York: Simon and Schuster, 1991.

Zaman, Amberin. "Turkey and Obama: A Golden Age in Turkey-U.S. Ties?" *On Turkey,* March 20, 2009, accessible at http://www.gmfus.org//doc/Amberin_Analysis_Turkey031909.pdf.

———. "Turkey and the United States Under Barack Obama: Yes They Can," *On Turkey,* November 13, 2008, accessible at http://www.gmfus.org//doc/Amberin_Analysis_Turkey_US1108_FINAL.pdf.

Zonis, Marvin. *Majestic Failure: The Fall of the Shah*. Chicago: University of Chicago Press, 1991.

Zuhur, Sherifa. "Saudi Arabia: Islamic Threat, Political Reform, and the Global War on Terror," Strategic Studies Institute, March 2005, accessible at http://www.strategicstudiesinstitute.army.mil/pdffiles/PUB598.pdf.

Zürcher, Erik J. *Turkey: A Modern History*. London: I.B.Tauris, 1993.

ACKNOWLEDGMENTS

A host of people opened their hearts and minds to me as I traveled through the Middle East conducting research for this book. After reflection and consultation with several of them, though, I have decided not to thank them by name. Some of the ideas and conclusions I present in this book may be unwelcome in certain quarters. Naming those who helped me might imply that they endorse what I have written. Rather than place them in that awkward position, I prefer to thank them collectively. To my Iranian, Saudi Arabian, and Israeli friends: You know who you are. Thank you, no matter what you think of what I've written.

The one country where my conclusions might not place my interlocutors in uncomfortable situations is Turkey. That leaves me free to thank three insightful scholars who generously gave me hours of their time: Gökhan Çetinsaya, Ziya Öniş, and Ergun Özbudun. One of the wisest modern commentators on Turkish affairs, my dear friend Şahin Alpay, was especially helpful.

Other friends showed me the warm hospitality for which their part of the world is rightly famous: Anne and Cem Kozlu in Istanbul, and Husam Al-Ghailani in Riyadh. I am deeply in their debt.

James Stone, David Shuman, Fariba Amini, and James Linkin offered pithy and uncensored comments as my chapters emerged. So did the multitalented *editrice* Elmira Bayrasli. Once the manuscript was complete, it was further sharpened by the pen of Paul Golob, editorial director of Times Books.

The most unexpected of my private critics was my sister Jane, who surprised me as I set off on this project by telling me that her true and undiscovered talent was editing manuscripts. She turned out to be right. After making trenchant, highly detailed, and unforgiving comments on my writing, she suggested that I be promoted this way: "A master storyteller, especially when his sister's keen eye for a good story goads him into making the sometimes boring come to vivid life on the page."

One of my most outstanding students at Northwestern University, Benjamin Armstrong, served as my research assistant and proved invaluable. His mastery of data bases was surpassed only by his enthusiasm for this project and his interest in the themes on which it focuses. Jason Joven helped Ben locate photos and worked painstakingly to draw illuminating maps.

My faithful literary agent, Nancy Love, proved her professionalism once again by helping to steer this book from conception to birth. Librarians in Oak Park, Illinois, and Truro, Massachusetts, were unfailingly helpful and resourceful.

I received generous help from the Keyman Family Fund, administered by the Buffett Center for International and Comparative Studies at Northwestern University. My gratitude extends to the Keyman family as well as to those who have made the Buffett Center a vibrant hub of discourse about world affairs: Andrew Wachtel, Hendrik Spruyt, Brian Hanson, and Rita Koryan.

Faculty colleagues at Northwestern and Boston University gave me every consideration as I worked on this book. So did close relatives and far-flung friends. Thank you all.

INDEX

Entries in *italics* refer to maps.

Abadan refinery, 93, 120, 122
Abbas, Mahmoud, 197
Abdul Hamid, Sultan of Ottoman Empire, 6, 9–11, 44, 60, 72
Abdullah, King of Saudi Arabia, 178, 180–81, 185
Abdul Mecit, Sultan of Ottoman Empire, 6, 57
Abrahamian, Ervand, 113
Afghanistan, 12, 14, 125, 169, 196–98, 206, 208, 211
  Soviet War of 1979–88, 114, 166–67, 168, 169
  War of 2002–10, 125–26, 201, 206
Agamemnon, HMS (British ship), 37–38
Agnew, Spiro, 104
Ahmadinejad, Mahmoud, 207, 216
Ahmad Qajar, Shah of Persia, 24, 30
AKP (Justice and Development Party, Turkey), 133–34, 137–38
Alawite Muslims, 135
Albania, 33
Albright, Madeleine, 123–24
Alexander the Great, 104
Ali Fuat (Cebesoy), 44, 68

Ali (Shiite holy figure), 174
Allies
  WW I, 35–51, 58
  WW II, 89
Alphabet Reform, 67
al-Qaeda, 12, 125, 173, 206
alternative energy, 182–83
Amasya Circular, 44–45, 68
American Iranian Council, 123
American Israel Public Affairs Committee (*formerly* American Zionist Council, AIPAC), 124, 156
Amir Mansur, Prince of Saudi Arabia, 147–48
Amir Mohammed, Prince of Saudi Arabia, 147
Amnesty International, 110
Anatolia, partition of, and Turkish War of Independence, 40–41, 43–45, 48–51, 58, 79, 82, 101
Anglo-Iranian Oil Company (*formerly* Anglo-Persian Company), 26, 92–94
Anglo-Persian Agreement (1918), 26, 29
Anglo-Russian Convention (1907), 4, 19, *20*

Angola, 14, 165, 167
Annapolis Peace Conference, 174
anti-Communism, 14, 130, 150, 161,
    165–67
antiwar protests, 163
Arabia, Allies gain, post–WW I, 38
Arabic script, 67, 81
Arab-Israeli conflict, 156, 159–61, 174,
    184–92, 206
Arab League, 185
Arafat, Yasser, 174
Aramco, 92–93
Arava planes, 161–62
Argentine Jewish community center
    bombing, 215
Armenia, 197–98, 200
Armenians, 48, 51, 74, 131
    genocide, 37, 69, 140
arms sales and military aid
    to Central American and other
        dictatorships, 161–65
    to Iran, 107–10, 122
    to Iraq, 1980, 121–22
    to Israel, 155–56
    to Saudi Arabia, 14, 147, 168, 182
Armstrong, H. C., 81
Atatürk, Mustafa Kemal, 7–9, 136
    dissident and ethnic groups suppressed
        by, 68–71
    early life of, 31–34, 65
    elected first president of Turkey,
        59–60
    illness and death of, 79–80
    legacy of, 81–83, 138–40
    marriage and divorce of, 57–58, 74
    modernization and reforms of, 61–62,
        66–68, 71, 73–75, 90, 140, 197
    name Atatürk taken by, 67
    name "Gazi Pasha" bestowed on, 52
    one vs. two-party system and,
        100–101
    personality of, 64–65, 82

revolt vs. Allies and Turkish
    Independence War led by, 38–58
Reza Shah and, 64–65, 76–78, 83–84
Turkish sultanate and caliphate
    abolished by, 56–57, 82
WW I and, 34–37
AWACS surveillance planes, 110, 168
Azerbaijan, 89, 197, 200, 210

Baghdad Pact, 105
Bahamas, 118
Balkans, 88, 196
    War of 1912, 33
Baluchistan, 27
Bandar bin Sultan, Prince of Saudi Arabia,
    165, 168
Bandirma (Ottoman freighter), 43
Baskerville, Howard, 1–2, 4–6, 11, 21, 97,
    212
Batarfi, Khaled, 176, 184
Battalion 316, 163
Bechtel company, 121
Begin, Menachem, 173–74
Beirut bombings, 173–74
Bele, Refet, 44, 55, 57, 68
Bell Helicopter, 108
Ben-Gurion, David, 156, 189
Ben-Hur (film), 159
Berlin, 96
Bill, James, 99, 112
Bismarck, Otto von, 61
Boer War, 3
Bolivia, 164
Boone, Pat, 159
Bosnia, 169
Bosnia-Herzegovina, 9
Braizat, Fares, 197
Brazil, 179
Brezhnev, Leonid, 105
British oil companies, 107
British Royal Navy, 75
British Secret Intelligence Service, 95

INDEX

British War Council, 35
Buckley, William, 215
Bulgaria, 9, 33–34, 88
Burma, 164
Burns, Nicholas, 207
Bush, George H. W., 130–31, 172
Bush, George W., 126–27, 170, 178, 206–7, 211
Byroade, Henry, 156

Caesar, Julius, 44
Camp David Accords, 174
Carmen (opera), 33
Carter, Jimmy, 110–12, 117–19, 162, 167, 170
Caruso, Enrico, 24
Casey, William, 166
Caucasus, 88, 131, 196, 198
Cavad Pasha, 42
Cavour, Camillo Benso, Count of, 61
censorship, 110, 122
Central America, 162–64
Central Asia, 114, 131
Central Intelligence Agency (CIA), 95–99, 105, 111, 113, 118, 125–26, 157, 163–64, 166–67, 215
Central Treaty Organization, 105
Chechnya, 169, 198
chemical weapons, 121–23
Chile, 164
China, 96, 200, 206, 208, 216–17
Christians and Christianity, 40–41, 65, 159, 169
Churchill, Winston, 25–26, 29, 35–36, 49–50, 88, 93, 95, 145
Clinton, Bill, 123–25
Cohen, Mickey, 155
cold war, 13–14, 87–89, 96–97, 100, 158, 161, 174–75, 178–79, 182–84, 196
Cole, USS (destroyer), 173
colleges and universities, 102, 128
Colombia, 165

Committee of Union and Progress (CUP), 8–9. *See also* Young Turks
Communism, 96, 106. *See also* anti-Communism; cold war; Soviet Union
Constantine, King of Greece, 51
Contras, 163, 166
Coolidge, Calvin, 63
Crete, 9
Cuba, 20–21, 97
Curzon, Lord, 26–27, 58, 76
Cyprus, 103, 198
Cyrus, King of Persia, 3, 72
Czechoslovakia, 163

Dalitz, Moe, 155
D'Arcy, William Knox, 24–25
Dardanelles, 35
Darius I, King of Persia, 3, 104–5
Davutoğlu, Ahmet, 197
Deaver, Michael, 168
Defense Intelligence Agency, 112
democracy and democratization, 64–65, 138, 178–79
   Iran and, 1–6, 21, 23–24, 61, 65, 82, 90–99, 113–14, 118–20, 140–41, 212–13
   Saudi Arabia and, 180–81
   Turkey and, 6–11, 61, 65, 76–77, 82, 90, 101–2, 128–29, 133–35, 137–38, 140, 196–200, 204
"democratic exception," 179
Democrat Party (Turkey), 101
Denmark, 104
Dervish sects, 65
Dhahran air base, 180
Dominican Republic, 164
Doty, Edward, 4
Douglas, William O., 98
dress codes, 66–67, 77–78
drug trafficking, 164–65
"dual containment" policy, 122
Dubai, 210

Dulles, Allen, 96, 157
Dulles, John Foster, 96–97, 156, 158, 160
Dumlupinar, Battle of, 53

Ebadi, Shirin, 205
Eban, Abba, 156–57
Ebert, Carl, 71
Eddy, William, 146–48, 150
Edib, Halide, 10, 50, 52–53, 68
education
    Iran and, 21, 73, 106
    Turkey and, 65, 71, 73–74, 140, 200
    women and, 73–74
Edward VIII, King of England, 84
Egypt, 102, 118, 156–61, 167, 174, 181, 199, 209, 212
    Suez crisis and, 157–58
Eisenhower, Dwight, 96–97, 105, 123, 156–58
El Salvador, 162–63
Enver Pasha, 33–35, 37
Erbakan, Necmettin, 132
Erdoğan, Recep Tayyip, 132–38, 195, 199
Ertegun, Munir, 87–88
Erzurum Congress, 45
ethnic cleansing, 69
Europe, 9, 161
    Arab nations created by, 186–87
European Convention on Human Rights, 134
European Union (EU), 135–36, 201–4
Exodus (Uris), 158–59, 174

Fahd, King of Saudi Arabia, 166, 172
Fallaci, Oriana, 105
Federal Bureau of Investigation (FBI), 155, 211
Ferdinand, King of Bulgaria, 33
Ferdinand and Isabella, King and Queen of Spain, 72
Fethi Bey, 33

Fighting Lady, The (film), 147
Forrestal, James, 154
Forrestal, USS (aircraft carrier), 103
France, 40, 42, 49, 51, 96, 107, 157
Francis, Connie, 159
Franco, Francisco, 64
Franz Ferdinand, Archduke of Austria, 34
freedom of speech, 3, 100, 176, 199
freedom of the press, 3, 176
free market ideology, 129–30
Friedman, George, 199
Fuller, Graham, 199

Gabor, Zsa Zsa, 64
Gallipoli campaign, 35–36, 41, 77, 81
Gates, Robert, 209
Gaza, 174, 186, 198, 200
General Electric, 108
Georgia, 200
Gerges, Fawaz, 122
Germany, 35, 37, 61, 205
    Nazi, 71–72, 149, 159, 164
Ghaemi, Nassir, 214
Goiran, Roger, 96–97
Goldman, Frank, 153–54
Grace, Princess of Monaco, 104
Great Britain
    Boer War and, 3
    Cold War and, 88
    Iran and, 3, 19–22, 25–30, 65, 72, 75–76, 79–81, 89–99, 117
    Palestine and, 152, 154
    Saudi Arabia and, 169
    Suez crisis and, 157
    Turkey and, 35–52, 54–55, 58
    WW I and, 35–38
Greece, 33, 51–54, 81, 88, 103–4, 117
Greeks, forced out of Turkey, 69, 74, 131
Grey, Sir Edward, 4
Grumman Aerospace, 108
Guatemala, 161, 163
"guest workers," 102, 132

Gül, Abdullah, 137
Gulf War (1990), 130-31, 172-73
Gunther, John, 83

Ha'aretz, 162
Haass, Richard, 179
Habib, Philip, 173
Haile Selassie, Emperor of Ethiopia, 104
Hamas, 126, 186, 197, 208
Harari, Mike, 164
Harbord, Gen. J. G., 46
Harper's, 83
Hat Reform (Turkey, 1925), 67, 78
Heiss, Mary Ann, 97
Helskinki Accords (1975), 217
Hezbollah, 126, 197, 208
Hikmet, Nazim, 40
Hitler, Adolf, 64, 71, 72
Holocaust, 151, 154, 216
Honduras, 163
Hoover, J. Edgar, 211
House of Bush, House of Saud (Unger), 178
human rights
 Iran and, 109-10, 215-16
 Saudi Arabia and, 180-81
 Turkey and, 139
Hussein, King of Jordan, 104
Hussein, Saddam, 120-22, 124, 172, 206-7, 211

Ibn Saud, Abdul-Aziz ibn Abd al-Rahman, King of Saudi Arabia, 145-50, 170, 177-78, 183
Imperial Bank of Persia, 75
import-substitution model, 130
Incirlik air base, 130
Independent, 131
India, 27, 75, 93, 206
Indonesia, 164, 199
Inönü, Ismet (Ismet Pasha), 41, 52, 58, 79, 88-89, 101

intifadas, 174
Iranian Parliament, 3, 6, 19-24, 27, 61-62, 81, 90, 92, 98, 105
 Oil Committee, 92-93
Iran-Iraq War (1980-88), 120-22, 124
Iran (Persia), 200
 abolition of caliphate and, 62
 Afghanistan and, 125
 American hostage crisis and, 116-20, 122, 205, 215
 Anglo-Russian Convention and spheres of influence in, 3, 19, *20*
 anti-Americanism in, 108-9
 Atatürk and, 80
 British influence and oil in, 24-27, 65, 74-76, 80-81, 90-94
 Constitutional Revolution of 1906, 1-3, 5-6, 11, 21, 83, 91, 98, 212
 contemporary isolation of, 126-27
 coup of 1953 and, 98-99, 113, 116-19, 123
 democracy and, 1-3, 6, 11-12, 19-23, 139-40
 early history of, 19-20
 education and, 73-74
 election protests of 2009, 12, 211, 216
 Iran-Iraq War and, 122-23
 Islamic Revolution of 1979 and religious dictatorship in, 104-20, 140-41, 150
 Jews and, 72-73
 map of, *viii*
 modernization and reforms in, 21, 61, 65, 70, 73, 76-78, 83, 90, 106, 109, 140
 Mohammad Reza Shah rule in, 90-91, 94, 98-99, 106, 107-10
 Mossadegh presidency and fledgling democracy in, 91-99
 9/11 attacks and, 125-27
 nuclear weapons and, 209
 oil and, 12, 24-27, 75, 92-93, 107-8
 potential partnership with, 12-13, 123-27, 141, 206-17

Iran (Persia) (*cont'd*)
   Reza Shah rule in, 29–30, 61–70, 73–76, 79, 82–84, 139–40
   Shiite authority in, 66–68
   Soviets and, 75, 89–90
   Truman and, 89–90, 94–95
   Turkey and, 139–41, 197–98
   women's rights in, 73–74, 78
Iraq, 12, 58, 102, 126, 156, 186, 196–98, 206–7, 215
   Gulf War and, 130–31, 172–73
   Iran-Iraq War and, 120–22
   War of 2003 and, 181, 184, 198–99, 201, 207, 211
Ironside, Edmund, 28–30
Islam. *See also* specific branches
   caliphate abolished, 61–62, 65, 81–82
   democracy and, 70, 137–38, 141
   Iran and, 67–68, 78–79, 110, 114, 141
   religious orthodoxy and reforms and, 64–68, 73, 78, 114, 119–20, 122
   Saudi Arabia and, 147–48, 169, 180
   Turkey and, 11–12, 31, 45, 47, 59–60, 65–67, 69–70, 77, 133, 137–38, 141, 196–98
Islamic fundamentalists, 14, 170, 172–73, 190, 198, 206
Islamic Jihad, 126
Ismet Pasha. *See* Inönü, Ismet
Israel, 12–13, 123–24, 156–65, 168, 174–75, 195–97, 200, 208–10
   creation of, 149, 151–56, 158–59, 186–87
   occupied territories and, 160, 174
   Lebanon and, 173–74
   need to reshape relationship with, 13–15, 177, 184–92
   Six-Day War and, 159–60
   Suez crisis and, 157–58
   Yom Kippur War and, 160–61
Israel Defense Forces (IDF), 158, 162
Israeli Knesset, 164
Israeli-Palestinian conflict, 184–92, 206

Istanbul, 9–10, 31–33, 35, 38–39, 48
Istanbul University, 71, 73
Italy, 49, 51, 61, 96
Izmir (Smyrna), 42–43, 48, 53–55, 81

Jacobson, Eddie, 151–55
Japan, 3, 61, 87, 206
Jeddah
   arrests of 2007, 180
   consulate attack, 183
Jerusalem, 72, 160, 186
Jerusalem Post, 124
Jewish fundamentalists, 190
Jewish Theological Seminary, 154–55
Jews and Judaism, 71–72, 131, 149–50, 152–54, 159, 200, 216
John, King of England, 3
John F. Kennedy Center for the Performing Arts, 167
Johnson, Lyndon B., 103, 105–6, 159–60, 211
Jordan, 156, 181, 186
"Just Say No" campaign, 167

Karabakh, 198
Karabekir, Kazim, 41, 44, 51, 58, 68
Kars, Turkey, 40–41, 51, 88
Karzai, Hamid, 125
Kemal, Mustafa. *See* Atatürk, Mustafa Kemal
Kemalism, 100, 136–37
Kennan, George, 89
Kennedy, John F., 105, 159
Kenya, U.S. embassy bombing, 173
Khamenei, Ayatollah Ali, 124
Khan, Mirza Ali Kuli, 20
Khatami, Mohammad, 124–25
Khobar Towers bombing, 172, 215
Khomeini, Ayatollah Ruhollah, 106–7, 111, 113–14, 117, 119–22, 124
Khrushchev, Nikita, 157
Kimche, David, 165

INDEX

Kinross, Lord, 42, 44, 55
Kissinger, Henry, 108, 118, 122, 167, 206
Kollek, Teddy, 155
Korean War, 96, 99–100
Kurds, 48, 130, 135, 140, 199
   revolt of 1925, 68–70
Kuwait, 130, 172, 181, 186

labor unions, 102, 109–10, 163
Lacey, Robert, 171
Laçiner, Sedat, 198
Laden, Osama bin, 173
Laingen, Bruce, 116–17, 119
land-for-peace, 188
land reform, 106
Lansky, Meyer, 155
Lausanne Treaty (1923), 58
Lebanon, 156, 173–74, 181, 186, 196–97, 206, 208
Lenin, V. I., 64
Leverett, Flynt, 125–26
Libya, 33, 102, 165
Lloyd George, David, 40, 55
Lockheed, 108
London *Daily Mail*, 55
López, Walter, 163
Loraine, Lady, 62
Loraine, Sir Percy, 63–64, 75
Ludwig X, King of Bavaria, 72
Lütfü, Corinne, 31–32, 34, 55

MacArthur, Douglas, 87, 100
Macedonia, 33
MacFarlane, Robert, 165–66
Madrid Conference, 174
Magna Carta, 3
Malaya, HMS (battleship), 57
Marcos, Ferdinand, 104, 165
Marcos, Imelda, 104
Marlowe, Christopher, 39
Marshall, George, 154

Mashad protest of 1935, 78
Masjid-i-Suleiman oil find, 25–26
McCarthy, Joseph, 96
McDonnell Douglas, 108
McPherson, Harry, 160
Mehmet VI Vahdeddin, Sultan of Ottoman Empire, 37, 39, 55–57
Mein Kampf (Hitler), 71
Menderes, Adnan, 101–2, 130, 139
Mexico, 118
Missouri, USS (battleship), 87–89, 103
Mobutu Sese Seko, 167
modernization and reform
   Iran and, 21, 61, 65, 70, 73, 76–78, 83, 90, 106, 109, 140
   Turkey and, 56–57, 61–62, 65–68, 70–71, 73–78, 81–82, 90, 100, 133, 137, 140, 204
Mohammad Ali Qajar, Shah of Persia, 3, 6
Mohammad Reza Pahlavi, Shah of Iran, 82, 91, 98, 104–11, 123, 209
   exile of, 111–13, 117–19, 150
Mongols, 117
Morocco, 118, 167
Mossadegh, Mohammad, 62, 91–99, 113, 116–17, 123–24, 139–40, 212
Mossad (Israeli intelligence agency), 105, 164
Motherland Party (Turkey), 129
Mudros armistice (1918), 37–38
Muhammad, Prophet, 169
Munich Olympics of 1972, 164
Murphy, USS (destroyer), 146–48
Mussolini, Benito, 64
Muzaffer (Mozaffer) al-Din Qajar, Shah of Persia, 3, 25

Nasr al-Din Qajar, Shah of Persia, 28
Nasser, Gamal Abdel, 157–59
National Bank of Iran, 75
nationalism, 75–76, 82, 96, 100, 108

Netanyahu, Benjamin, 186
Newman, Paul, 159
Newsweek, 92
New York Times, 167, 168, 180
Next 100 Years, The (Friedman), 199
Nicaragua, 14, 163, 165–66
Nicholas II, Czar of Russia, 3, 21–22
Nicolson, Sir Harold, 62
Nightline (TV program), 117
Nixon, Richard, 107, 161, 216–17
nomadic tribes, 69–70
Noriega, Manuel Antonio, 163–64
North, Oliver, 163
North Africa, 196, 199
North Atlantic Treaty Organization (NATO), 12, 100, 103, 133
Northern Alliance, 125
North Korea, 126
Northrop, 108
North Vietnam, 216
Norway, 104
nuclear weapons, 126, 207, 208–10, 213, 215–16

Obama, Barack, 203–4
oil
   Iran and, 12, 24–27, 75, 79, 89–90, 92–96, 98, 107–8, 120–21, 123, 208
   pipelines, 130, 198
   Saudi Arabia and, 14, 149–50, 168, 170, 177, 180, 182–83
   shock of 1973–74, 108
Olmert, Ehud, 186
Operation Ajax, 96–97
Operation Tipped Kettle, 163
Orbay, Rauf, 44, 68
Oren, Michael, 159
Oslo Process, 174
al-Otaybi, Juhayman, 170–72
Ottoman Army, 41
Ottoman Constitution of 1876, 6, 9
   amendment of 1909, 11

Ottoman Empire, 3, 6–9, 74, 82, 131, 196–97, 199. *See also* Turkey
   abolition of sultanate and demise of, 56–57, 59–61
   "Action Army" of, 10–11
   Allied occupation and partition of, post-WW I, 38–43
   Atatürk (Kemal) and transformation of, to Republic of Turkey, 7–10, 31–33, 39–48, 56–61
   Balkan War of 1912 and, 33–34
   elections of 1908, 10
   Jews and, 72
   Young Turks and, 9–11, 33–34
Ottoman Parliament, 6, 9–11, 47
   Tanzimat reforms and, 6, 136
   WW I and, 34–37
Özal, Turgut, 127–32, 136
Özsoy (Pure Lineage) (opera), 76–77

Pahlavi dynasty, 82, 113
Pakistan, 12, 166–67, 196, 198–99, 203
Palestine, 198
   partition of, 149–50, 152–56
Palestinian Authority, 174, 185, 192
Palestinians, 13, 164, 184–92
Panama, 163–64
Papoulas, Anastasios, 52
Paul, Saint, 8
Peace Corps, 110
Peled, Mitityahu, 164
Peres, Shimon, 165, 185–86, 195
Persepolis, 104, 107, 122
Persian Cossack Brigade, 28–30
Persian Empire, 3, 63, 72–73.
   See also Iran
Philippines, 20, 21, 97, 164, 165
"Point Four" program, 156
Poland, 163, 179
political parties, Turkey and, 128–19, 200
Precht, Henry, 108
Preminger, Orro, 159

INDEX

protectionism, 127
Psycholanalytic Quarterly, 82
Puerto Rico, 97
Punishment Committee (Iran), 27

Qadaffi, Muammar, 165
Qajar dynasty, 1, 3, 91, 62, 73
Qavam, Ahmad, 89–90
Qazvini, Aref, 22
Qibya massacre, 156
Qom, 68, 106
Quincy, USS (cruiser), 148, 170, 177

Rabin, Yitzhak, 164, 174
Rafsanjani, Ali Akbar Hashemi, 124
Rainier, Prince of Monaco, 104
Rais, Rasul Bakhsh, 203
Raytheon, 108
Reagan, Nancy, 167–68
Reagan, Ronald, 121–22, 162–65, 168, 173–74
Red Army, 88–89, 114, 166
religious freedom, 132, 135–36, 199
Republican Party (U.S.), 95–96, 101
Republican People's Party (Turkey), 60, 100
Reuter, Ernst, 71
Reza Pahlavi, Shah of Iran, 64
    Atatürk and, 64–65, 76–78, 83–84
    exile and death of, 79–81, 90–92
    legacy of, 82–83, 138–40
    modernization and reforms of, 61–62, 66, 73–75, 78, 90, 140
    Nazi Germany and, 72–73
    personality of, 64–65
    repression by, 69–70
    rise to power of, 27–30, 61–64
    surname "Pahlavi" taken by, 63
Rice, Condoleezza, 207
Riedel, Bruce, 207
Riyadh women's car caravan, 180
Rockefeller, David, 118

Roosevelt, Franklin D., 145–50, 170, 177–78
Roosevelt, Kermit, 95–97
Roosevelt, Theodore, 97
Rumbold, Sir Horace, 57
Rumi, 218
Rumsfeld, Donald, 121
Russia. *See also* Soviet Union
    czarist, 3, 6, 19–24, 26–28, 35, 37, 75, 89, 99, 117
    post-Soviet, 12, 200, 206, 208
Russo-Japanese War, 3

Sabra and Shatila refugee camps, 174
Sackville-West, Vita, 62–63
Sadat, Anwar, 167, 174
Said, Sheik, 69
Saint, Eva Marie, 159
Sakarya, Battle of, 51–52
Salazar, António de Oliveira, 64
Salonika rebellion, 8–9
Samsun uprising, 41–44
Sandinistas, 163
Sarafatti, Rabbi Isaac, 72
Saud al-Faisal, Prince of Saudi Arabia, 207
al-Saud family, 169–72, 177, 180–81, 183–84
Saudi Arabia, 212, 215
    cold war partnership with, 12–13, 145–50, 165–69, 174–75
    early history of, 14, 169–70
    Gulf War and, 172
    Iran and, 207, 209–10
    Iraq and, 207
    Islamic fundamentalists and, 169–72
    need to reshape relations with, 13–15, 176–84
    9/11 attacks and, 173
    oil and, 93, 168
    protests for reforms in, 180–81
SAVAK (Iranian security agency), 105, 110, 112

Scott, Sir Walter, 2
September 11, 2001, 14, 125–26, 173, 179, 201, 211
Serbs, 33
Sèvres, Treaty of, 48–49, 58
Shanghai Communiqué, 216–17
Sharifzadeh, Hussein, 4
Sharon, Ariel, 163
Shatt al-Arab waterway, 120
Sheyhulislam fatwa, 47
Shiite Islam, 66, 94, 120, 125, 169, 207
Shultz, George, 121
Shuster, Morgan, 19–24, 97
Siegel, Bugsy, 155
Sinai Peninsula, 160, 174, 188–89
Sinatra, Frank, 155
Sivas Congress, 45–46
Six-Day War, 159–60, 185
Society for the Elevation of Women, 10
Somalia, 167
South Africa, 3, 81, 119, 164
southeastern Europe, 199
South Korea, 179
Soviet Union, 103, 114, 157–58, 178–79, 167. *See also* Russia
   Afghanistan War of 1979–88 and, 168
   breakup of, 131
   Helsinki Accords and, 217
   Iran and, 26, 72, 75, 80–81, 89–90, 96, 105, 108, 114
   Turkey and, 37, 40–41, 51, 88–89, 104, 131
Spain, 72
Stalin, Joseph, 64, 88–90, 145, 157
State Department, 108, 119, 126, 162, 179
"status of forces" agreements, 106
Stinger antiaircraft missiles, 168
Strangling of Persia, The (Shuster), 23–24
"strategic depth" concept, 197
Suez crisis, 157–58
Sufi Islam, 130, 169
Sunni Islam, 12, 66, 135, 196

Sweden, 104
Syria, 102, 156, 160, 181, 186, 196–97

Taba peace conference (2000), 185
Tabatabai, Sayyed Zia, 29–30
Tabriz, siege of, 1–6
Taft, William Howard, 20
Taliban, 12, 125–26, 197, 206
Tanzania, U.S. embassy bombings, 173
Taqizadeh, Sayyed Hasan, 5
Tatars, 117
Tehran University, 73, 112
terrorism, 14, 124–25, 179, 182–83, 190, 198, 215
Teymurtash, Abdol-Hussein, 62–63, 79
Thatcher, Margaret, 129
Time, 94, 103
Tito, Marshall, 104
Tolstoy, Leo, 7
Transjordan, 156
Truman, Harry S., 87–89, 94–96, 151–55
Turkey. *See also* Ottoman Empire
   Atatürk reign and legacy in, 65–75, 79–84, 140
   breakup of Soviet Union and, 131
   cold war relations with, 87–90, 150
   constitution of 1982–83, 128–29
   crisis of 1979–80 and, 114–15
   Cyrpus and, 103
   democracy and, 11–12, 100–103, 138–41, 212
   elections of 1950 end one-party rule in, 101
   elections of 1983, 129
   elections of 2002–4, 134, 136–37
   Erdoğan reshapes, 127, 132–38
   ethnic cleansing and, 69, 140
   EU membership and, 135–36, 202–4
   formation of and revolt vs. Allied attempt to partition Anatolia, 47–51, 70–71, 101
   Gulf War and, 130–31

INDEX

Gül presidency and, 137
Independence War in, 51–58, 82
Iran and, 209
Iraq and, 130–31
Israel and, 200
Jews and, 71–72
Korean War and, 99–100
Kurds and, 68–69
map of, *viii*, 49
military coups and political violence in, 102–4, 114–15, 128–29, 133
modernization and reforms in, 56–57, 61–62, 65–68, 70–71, 73–78, 81, 90, 140
NATO and, 12, 100
neutrality of, under Atatürk, 88
new partnership and strategic potential of, 12–13, 195–204
Özal reshapes, 127–33
Republic established, 59–61
Turki al-Faisal, Prince of Saudi Arabia, 167
Turkish Airlines, 127
Turkish Cypriots, 103
Turkish Grand National Assembly, 47–48, 52, 56–57, 59–60, 62, 68, 70, 74, 80, 134, 137, 195, 199, 203–4
suspended by 1980 coup, 128
Turkish language, 79
transliterated, 67, 81
Turkish National Security Council, 128, 134
Turkmani, Abdullah, 202

Ülkur company, 132
Unger, Craig, 178
United Nations, 90, 94, 121, 152–53, 155–56, 158, 161, 174, 186, 188–89
United States
Afghanistan War of 2002 and, 125
cold war and Middle East, 178–79
Gulf War and, 130–31
Iran and, during fight vs. British and Russians, 19–20

Iran and, potential partnership, 12–13, 141, 205–17
Iran and, under Mohammad Reza Shah, 105–11
Iranian coup of 1953 and, 92, 94–99, 116–18, 123–24
Iranian overtures to, after 9/11, 125–27
Iranian Revolution and hostage crisis and, 98, 112–14, 116–22, 205
Israel and, during cold war, 156–65, 174–75
Israel and, during early statehood, 151–56
Israel and, need to reshape relationship, 12–15, 150–51, 173–75, 184–92
Israeli-Palestinian peace process and, 160, 186–92
Kenya and Tanzania embassy bombings and, 173
"power triangle" of, with Turkey and Iran, 12–13
Saudi Arabia and, during cold war, 145–50, 165–71
Saudi Arabia and, need to reshape relationship, 12–15, 150–51, 174–84
Turkey and, during cold war, 87–88, 90, 99–100, 103–4
Turkey and, potential partnership with, 12–13, 141, 195–204
Turkey and, under Özal, 130–31
Turkish revolt vs. British-led Allies and 46–49
UN Security Council, 94, 160
Resolution 242, 160, 185
U.S. Army, 6
U.S. Congress, 109, 156, 161–63, 165, 168, 179
Uris, Leon, 158
Uşşaki, Latife, 54–55, 57–58, 74

Vahdeddin, Sultan. *See* Mehmet VI Vahdeddin

Vatan (secret society), 8
Vietnam War, 103, 117, 216
Voltaire, 7
Vorster, John, 164

Wahhabi Islam, 14, 146, 169–70, 173, 176–77, 179–80
Weigert, Edith, 71
Weinberger, Caspar, 121
Weissbrod, Rachel, 158
Weizmann, Chaim, 153–54
West Bank, 174, 186
Westinghouse, 108
Williams, Andy, 159
Wilson, Annie, 5
Wilson, Rev. Samuel, 5
Wilson, Woodrow, 2
Winston, Harry, 167
women's rights, 10, 81
   Iran and, 21, 73, 83, 106, 122
   Saudi Arabia and, 14, 176, 180–81, 183
   Turkey and, 34, 73–74, 78, 82, 136

Woolsey, James, 170
World Bank, 127, 128
World Court, 94
World Trade Organization (WTO), 179
World War I, 26, 34–36, 64, 152
World War II, 80–81, 87, 89, 145, 149, 164
Wye River Memorandum, 174

Xerxes, King of Persia, 3, 104–5

Yalta conference, 145
Yavuz, Hakan, 138
Yemen, 167, 173
Yom Kippur War, 160–61, 185
Young Turks, 9–11, 33–34, 37, 73, 136, 140

Zaire, 167
Zia al-Haq, Muhammad, 166–67
Zionists, 152–56, 158
Zoroaster, 2